Yale Studies in Political Science, 29

WORKERS' CONTROL
UNDER PLAN AND MARKET

Implications of Yugoslav Self-Management

Ellen Turkish Comisso

New Haven and London, Yale University Press, 1979

Published with assistance from the foundation
established in memory of Calvin Chapin of the
Class of 1788, Yale College.

Set in Press Roman type.
Printed in the United States of America by
The Murray Printing Co., Inc., Westford, Mass.

Published in Great Britain, Europe, Africa, and
Asia (except Japan) by Yale University Press,
Ltd., London. Distributed in Australia and
New Zealand by Book & Film Services, Artarmon,
N.S.W., Australia; and in Japan by Harper & Row,
Publishers, Tokyo Office.

Library of Congress Cataloging in Publication Data

Comisso, Ellen Turkish.
  Workers' control under plan and market:
implications of Yugoslav self-management.

  (Yale studies in political science ; 29)
  Includes bibliographical references and index.
  1. Works councils—Yugoslavia. 2. Industrial
management—Yugoslavia. 3. Industry and state—Yugo-
slavia. 4. Socialism in Yugoslavia. I. Title.
II. Series.
HD5660.Y8C56   338.6   79-64227
ISBN 0-300-02334-0

Contents

List of Figures and Tables

Preface

The notion that our actions often have unintended consequences and that chosen ends do not invariably follow from the means rationally calculated to attain them is fundamental to an understanding of any political action and crucial in an attempt to come to terms with the politics of workers' control. The paradoxes involved in political action are graphically demonstrated in the experience of Yugoslav self-management, confounding attempts to draw neat implications from it and dramatically reminding us of the highly conditional nature of any political judgments we might make.

This book explores the paradoxes of workers' control in theory and practice. Its central argument grew out of my frustration with much of the current discussion of Yugoslav self-management, a discussion that all too often appears more intent on evaluating than on understanding, more anxious to package the Yugoslav experience with a seal of approval or disapproval than to explain and analyze its operation. I myself may not have entirely avoided the temptation to pass judgments, but I have tried to make my evaluations as limited and conditional as possible—especially as I myself have not come to any firm conclusions on the practical desirability of workers' control or adapting the Yugoslav model elsewhere.

I would like at this time to extend my appreciation for the assistance given me by students, colleagues, and friends too numerous to be mentioned individually. In particular, Robert Dahl, my adviser, and C. E. Lindblom both exerted a profound influence on my thinking long before I stumbled onto workers' control and into Yugoslavia; they continued to do so throughout the ups and downs of the project. Along with Deborah Milenkovitch, Susan Woodward, and Sidney Tarrow, they gave needed moral support and perceptive criticisms, comments, and suggestions at various stages of my research and writing; their encouragement was a major factor in the completion of the book.

Nancy Schwartz, Ed Harris, Jane Flax, Susan Bridge, and Steve Backman all made contributions to the design of the project and later to formulation of the argument. Mladen Šoić, formerly of the Yugoslav Information Service, took the time to warn me "not to evaluate, just understand us." Bogdan Denitch was kind enough to counsel me in the early stages of the project and helped me acquire preliminary language training. The Fulbright program and Yale

University generously contributed support for the time I spent in Yugoslavia.

During my stay in Zagreb, Tom Oleszczuk, Jo Sothern, Starr and Rudy Gordh, Zoran Munjin, Zlatko Uzelac, Smilja Blažević, Mario Braun, and Sonja Humel provided their companionship as well as their insights into the nature of Yugoslav politics in general and self-management in particular. I am also indebted to my husband, Vittorio, for introducing me to Yugoslavia as well as showing me that workers and intellectuals can engage in a meaningful dialogue.

Special thanks must go to Dr. Josip Obradović of the University of Zagreb. Without his valiant efforts on my behalf, this entire work would not have been possible. Zlatko Jeličić of the Zagreb Confederation of Trade Unions was also kind enough to introduce me to the firm where I eventually did the case study. Antun Suknaić, my host in Zagreb, was an adviser, counselor, and friend; his witty discussions of self-management and bureaucracy helped me to understand the events I was observing daily in the factory, while his personal accounts of the prewar Yugoslav Communist party and the National Liberation War supplied me with a historical perspective few others could have provided. I greatly regret that he did not live to see the work to which he contributed so much.

Finally, I must express my deep appreciation and great affection for the entire work collective of the firm I call "Klek." Although I came to them anxious to learn about self-management, that was only the least of what they taught and shared with me. Contrary to their teachings, however, I accept sole responsibility for whatever mistakes the book contains.

Introduction

Interest in Yugoslav self-management extends far beyond the borders of Yugoslavia. In particular, the successes and failures the Yugoslavs have encountered in elaborating an institutionalized system of workers' control over economic and political decision making are highly relevant to the labor movements of other countries, where various methods of guaranteeing workers greater influence in industrial and governmental policy making are being actively debated.

A critical issue in this debate is whether workers' councils would best serve the ends of workers' control by operating within a competitive market or in a planned economy. Yugoslavia's experience is frequently invoked by partisans on both sides of the debate, both in the Western labor movement and in Yugoslavia itself. Many who see planning as essential to workers' control are highly critical of Yugoslav practice, attributing its problems to the "inevitable" irrationalities of the market.[1] In contrast, others argue that workers' control can be achieved only in a competitive market and interpret inadequacies in the Yugoslav system as the product of a continuing concentration of economic and political power in the hands of political authorities.[2] The discussion is further complicated by those who maintain that whatever problems Yugoslavia has experienced with self-management are traceable to national peculiarities of Yugoslavia itself rather than to any defects in the methods of resource allocation.[3]

Like all great debates, this one starts with certain shared assumptions and values; without them, there would be no argument. All agree that workers' control on a microeconomic level would consist of some system of councils, elected by the labor force of a firm, that would make decisions in areas traditionally under the sole jurisdiction of management. Further, all agree that such a system—as opposed to "administrative" socialism or modern-day capitalism—should ideally include a guarantee to workers of power in industry and government, more political participation and awareness among workers, abolition of class differences, greater equality among different kinds of labor, greater solidarity among workers, less alienation and more efficiency at work, and an increased possibility for individuals and groups to control their lives both on the job and outside. Finally, all share the assumption that regardless of who makes decisions inside the individual enterprise, each of the two mechanisms of resource allocation, planning and the market, in principle represent stable organizational alternatives to one another.

It is one aspect of the logical and empirical consistency of these assumptions that I question. My argument is that, given enterprise-level workers' councils with economic power and political influence, planned and market economies are no longer stable alternatives to one another; that is, regardless of whether a politicoeconomic system relies primarily on planning or on the market for resource allocation at the outset, the presence of workers' councils and a government responsive to their claims creates pressures and tensions that cause the system to move in the opposite direction. Stated as a set of propositions, my argument can be summarized as follows:

1. If enterprise-level workers' councils operate within a planned economy, they will become a primary source of pressures for enlarging the sphere of enterprise autonomy. If the government proves responsive to these pressures, there will be a movement toward replacing the decisions of political planning bodies with the cues provided by a market system.

2. If enterprise-level workers' councils operate within a market economy, they will become a primary source of pressures to restrict the scope of the market through political means. If the government proves responsive to these pressures, there will be a movement toward replacing the allocation of resources according to the market with the allocation of resources according to the decisions of political bodies.

In a sense, these propositions can be read as an adaptation of a very familiar theme in political science and economics: the use of the market leads to the growth of private and public hierarchies in the economy and the polity, while reliance on hierarchy—and especially on large, highly centralized hierarchies—leads to pressures for decentralization and, if allocation is at issue, for the wider application of competitive prices. Read in the light of this literature, the argument I propose suggests that the presence of both workers' councils and a responsive government not only does little to prevent the same kinds of strains and pressures from arising in planned and market economies, but may actually exacerbate their effects.

The argument, then, is not entirely new to studies of the dynamics of planned and market mechanisms of resource allocation; rather, it is an application of the lessons of some of this literature to a new context: the labor-managed economy. At the same time, however, the argument is a substantial departure from what is frequently hypothesized about workers' control.

Indeed, insofar as its advocates see workers' control in both planned and market economies as an institutional mechanism capable of providing equity, participation, and efficiency, they imply that the establishment of workers' control would blunt the economic and political strains encountered in non-worker-controlled planned and market economies. My analysis shows that quite the contrary is the case.

In sum, although the operation of workers' councils within either a planned or market economy may bring about some progress toward the goals of workers' control, it is precisely the attempt to realize these goals within one type of politicoeconomic system that produces strains leading it to introduce elements of its opposite. The "choice" between plan and market in the context of workers' control may, then, be much less significant than the operation of plan or market in the context of workers' control. It is the latter which this work seeks to analyze in some detail, illustrating how both hypothetical and empirical systems of workers' control in planned and market economies generate changes in the system of workers' control itself.

I shall try to demonstrate the validity of these propositions theoretically and empirically by interpreting Yugoslav self-management as a synthesis of two complementary yet contradictory schemas of workers' control. The first, articulated by Antonio Gramsci, envisions workers' councils functioning within a planned economy. The second takes its philosophical bases and politicoeconomic outlines from P. J. Proudhon and deals with workers' councils operating in a competitive market system.

I have chosen the works of Gramsci and Proudhon for a theoretical analysis of workers' control for several reasons. Historically, both have had a major impact on the Western labor movement, and their arguments tend to reappear in various forms in the current plan-market debate in Western Europe and Yugoslavia. Hence, the parallels between the operation of their versions of workers' control and the Yugoslav experience with self-management allow me to put the empirical analysis of Yugoslavia in a broader perspective as well as to separate those features of self-management relevant to the general discussion of workers' control from those that appear to be the product of Yugoslavia's particular circumstances.

Second, the schemas of workers' control put forward by Gramsci and Proudhon embody the assumptions of the debate I am seeking to examine and represent theoretical attempts to prescribe an ideal institutional setting appropriate to them. Certainly the institutional outlines Gramsci and Proudhon supply are not "realistic," and it would be difficult, to put it mildly, to approximate such pure cases of workers' control in a planned or market economy in the real world. That they are unrealistic is not critical for my purposes, however, for what I wish to demonstrate theoretically is that even if one could imagine a utopian model of workers' control in a planned or market economy, one would still find strains and tensions pushing it away from wherever it is at any given time.

Part I is devoted to an exposition of Gramsci and Proudhon's contrasting views of workers' control. Each exposition is followed by an analysis in which I will examine the structural characteristics of each model which lead to pressures for the introduction of elements of its alternative. I will show that if we grant the assumption of responsive government, an assumption both Gramsci and Proudhon make, these pressures will result in a major economic and political restructuring, moving workers' control away from one model of allocation with workers' control towards its opposite. In this way, Part I constitutes a theoretical demonstration of the propositions stated above.

Part II deals with the overall political and economic evolution of Yugoslav self-management and constitutes an empirical demonstration of the propositions. Yugoslav self-management has never been a "pure" model of workers' control with a planned or market economy as described respectively by Gramsci and Proudhon. Nevertheless, the relative predominance of political and market influences in the Yugoslav economy have varied in a way consistent with the propositions stated above. There are many parallels between the economic and political institutions and values of Yugoslav self-management at different times and the Gramsci and Proudhon models as well; as we shall see, the reasons underlying the various reforms that Yugoslavia has enacted over a thirty-year period are quite similar to those causing the alterations in workers' control in the theoretical designs.

How the plan-market dynamic postulated in the propositions looks on the level of the individual firm is a question this book cannot directly answer, for the field research it is based on took place over a seven-month period, and even the archives of the enterprise observed only went back to 1966. Hence, there was no reliable information on the firm's behavior and reactions prior to the reforms of 1965.

The propositions can, however, be indirectly demonstrated at the microeconomic level by examining the enterprise and work collective's reaction to market controls and entrepreneurial decisions on the one hand and to hierarchical and political decisions on the other over a short time period. In addition, by looking at the firm's relations with political authorities, it is possible to get a clearer idea of what mechanisms are available in Yugoslavia

to worker-controlled firms for making their grievances heard and how effective these mechanisms can be in producing the desired political responses.
Part III, then, represents an additional, supportive empirical proof of the
propositions stated above, this time on a microeconomic level.

The conclusion is devoted to summarizing and making explicit the parallels
of these three demonstrations of the central propositions. It goes on to raise
some general questions about workers' control and the plan-market debate
in countries other than Yugoslavia.[4]

PART I

Alternative Theoretical Outlines of Workers' Control

1

Gramsci: The Worker as Producer

Antonio Gramsci, the Italian Marxist, was one of the earliest theorists of workers' control in a planned economy. Although Gramsci never laid out a detailed blueprint of worker-controlled socialism, the key elements of what he termed "workers' democracy"can be extrapolated from his comments on the activities of the soviets in the early years of the Russian Revolution and from his analysis of the post-World War I labor movement in Turin, Italy.

Gramsci's outline of workers' democracy foresees the plant-level factory council as both the lowest unit in and the "model" for a new, specifically proletarian state in which citizenship is a function of one's status as a "producer" and all are members of a productive community. The state itself is a centralized, hierarchical, but elected pyramid of producers' councils, organized on production lines and designed to perform economic (planning) as well as political (law-making) functions.

Ideologically, Gramsci retains the traditional Marxist emphases on the centrality of production in human history, the ultimate desirability of producing goods for their social "usefulness" rather than their profitability, and the primacy of the producers and "productive" labor in social, economic, and political life. According to Gramsci, it is their activity as producers that form ties binding individuals together; socialism is classless because it is first and foremost a society of producers.

THE FACTORY AS A PRODUCTIVE COMMUNITY

"In the factory," Gramsci writes, "the working class becomes a definite 'instrument of production' in a definite, organic constitution: every worker represents a definite necessity of the labor process and of production."[1] To Gramsci, the modern factory, with its precise division of labor and its orderly, hierarchical system of authority, represents a paradigm of social organization adapted to expanding human productive powers.

Far from abolishing the industrial division of labor, Gramsci would actually reinforce it:

> In a factory, the workers are producers insofar as they collaborate,
> ordered in a way determined precisely by industrial technology. . . .[2]
> The worker can conceive of himself as a producer only if he lives in the
> unity of the industrial process, which requires the collaboration of the
> manual laborer, the skilled worker, the administrative clerk, the engineer,
> the technical director.[3]

Nor does Gramsci perceive the division of labor as a cause of alienation. On
the contrary, he sees it as a source of equality and solidarity: equality, in that
it defines everyone, regardless of specific task or function, as equally "necessary" to production;[4] and solidarity, in that a narrow division of labor literally
compels individuals to cooperate if anything is to be produced. Thus, he
writes:

> The more the proletariat specializes in a professional task, the more he
> feels the indispensability of his fellows, the more he feels he is a cell in
> an organized body, a cohesive and intimately unified body. . .[5]

Gramsci would not only retain the division of labor as the heart of the production process; he would reinforce it by making it the basis for political
representation in factory councils, the lowest unit of the state:

> Every worker represents a definite necessity of the labor process and of
> production. . . . If the worker acquires a clear consciousness of this
> "definite necessity" and poses it at the base of a representative apparatus
> of a state-type . . . the working class initiates the era of the workers' state.[6]

Representation in factory councils would be based on the shop, the boundaries of which would be determined functionally by the product it supplies.
Significantly, modern shop organization often includes workers of different
trades and skills; in this respect, Gramsci's model of factory councils differs
sharply from syndicalism, which posits the trade as the basic unit of representation. This is consistent with Gramsci's view that the labor process is only
instrumental to the larger goal of production for use, and he criticizes syndicalism for reversing these priorities by subordinating production to pre-
serving the integrity of the trade.[7] As Gramsci's factory councils would not
run up against an institutionalized barrier of entrenched trades committed to
traditional modes of work, they are also well designed to facilitate the technological and organizational innovation he expects from them.

Gramsci does not eliminate authority and hierarchy in plant-level industrial
relations either; authority is generalized, politicized, and made responsive to

the labor force, but it is by no means eliminated: the decisions of the factory council are clearly viewed by Gramsci as authoritative decisions, even though executed in a decentralized manner.

It is the authority of the capitalist which is eliminated by the abolition of private property in workers' democracy. In its place, Gramsci puts the factory council, which would assume the internal functions of planning, coordinating, and disciplining previously performed by the capitalist factory hierarchy.[8] The factory council now allocates resources within the productive community, sets production schedules, estimates labor needs, organizes the work process, "spontaneously creates new modes of production and work, new forms of discipline."[9]

As for management, the "nonessential . . . prevalently nonproductive, policing functions" of the "petit bourgeoisie" in the plant[10] would no longer be performed. To the extent that "the entire mass participates in the life of the councils,"[11] responsibility for executing decisions devolves upon the individual members of the productive community. Theoretically, labor time would thereby be freed for genuinely "productive" activity, reducing "the multiplicity of bureaucratic and disciplinary functions inherent in private property relations . . . to pure industrial necessity."[12] Nevertheless, to the degree that managerial functions are part of the division of labor, in other words, to the extent that the professional skills of individual supervisors are needed to coordinate the activities of others, management would remain.

However, whereas in Gramsci's view, industrial authority in capitalism was exercised solely to increase private profits, in workers' democracy it would be exercised for "producing social wealth disinterestedly." According to Gramsci's analysis, private property and the control of nonproducers over production pit worker against foreman, manual against mental labor. With the ascendancy of production for social use over labor for private profits, Gramsci foresees all kinds of labor working together to solve common problems posed by a production process in which all collaborate. Accordingly, he suggests, the class antagonisms of previous plant authority relations would disappear along with the arbitrary and oppressive aspects of the division of labor. Despite the diversity of activities going on within it, the productive community of workers' democracy is envisioned as "an organic whole, a homogeneous and compact system."[13] Moreover, because of its diverse activities, the basic unit of production is the most fundamental unit of social solidarity in workers' democracy and, as such, is the paradigm for society and the state as a whole:

The factory council is the model of the proletarian state. In one and
the other, the concept of the citizen declines, replaced by the concept
of comradeship: collaboration to produce usefully and well develops
solidarity and multiplies the ties of affection and brotherhood. Everyone
is indispensable, everyone is at his place, and everyone has a function and
a place. Even the most ignorant and backward worker, even the vainest
and most "civil" engineer ends by being convinced of this truth in the
experience of factory organization.[14]

THE WORKERS' STATE

The vision of an egalitarian, solidaristic community functionally ordered
to produce useful goods through collaboration in the labor process not only
describes Gramsci's view of the factory, but also his hopes for socialist
society as a whole. Accordingly, the factory council, the authoritative organ
of the productive community, represents both the lowest unit of government
and the prototype of the proletarian state.

Unlike a political party or trade union, participation in the activity of the
factory council is not voluntary. One does not "join" Gramsci's system of
workers' councils the way one decides to become a member of a secondary
association. One is automatically ("necessarily") an element of the system by
virtue of one's status as a producer. Further, as socialism requires everyone to
be a producer,[15] all members of society are included in the council system
"in the same way that the citizen enters to take part in the democratic-
parliamentary state."[16] Hence Gramsci's contention that the council system
is the new state.

Whereas representation in the liberal-democratic parliament is based on the
formal, legal equality of residency in a geographically circumscribed territory,
representation in a workers' state according to Gramsci, must be based on the
"real activity" of its members as producers.[17] Thus, the principle of political
units corresponding to units of production, already elaborated at the plant
level in the factory council, also characterizes workers' democracy as a whole:
individual factory councils are linked together through their election of
district councils, municipal councils, regional councils, and so on.[18] In such
a way, individuals vote and interests are aggregated on production, rather
than strict territorial, lines.

Furthermore, just as specialization and the division of labor are the bases
of representation within productive communities, they are also the bases of
representation of entire productive communities. The functional and product
specialization characterizing shops and departments in the plant, expressed

politically in the factory council, is to be replicated on wider and higher
levels, as the delegates from districts, cities, regions, and the nation are indirectly elected through their respective factory councils on the basis of the
goods and services each produces. Turin, for example,

> is the city of the automobile. As in a factory the workers assume a shape,
> ordering themselves for the production of a definite object . . . so in the
> city the proletarian class assumes the shape of the prevalent industry,
> which orders and governs the whole urban complex. So, on a national
> scale, a people assumes the shape of its exportations, from its real contri-
> bution to the economic life of the world.[19]

Organized on production lines and encouraging regional specialization, the
"state is [not only] the apparatus of political power, but it is also an apparatus
of production writ large."[20]

Just as hierarchy would coordinate the various activities undertaken in the
industrial plant, so too would it coordinate the diversity of productive activities undertaken in society as a whole. If the political authority of the factory
council replaces the economic power of the private capitalist in the firm, the
decisions of higher-level producer councils serve to eliminate the competitive
market.[21] Thus, what is produced, scheduled for consumption, and put aside
for investment is not determined by a competitive price mechanism, but by
a centralized, hierarchic, but elected and presumably responsive system of
producers' councils. Economic decisions, therefore, are not controlled by a
market but through a political process and reflect producers' rather than consumers' preferences as to what constitutes, in Gramsci's terms, "socially
useful" production.

Gramsci himself never specifies exactly what "socially useful" production
entails; presumably it is concretely determined through an ongoing political
process among the different kinds of producers represented on the councils.
However, insofar as he regards the industrial proletariat as the "hegemonic"
group in workers' democracy,[22] the group that "tends to impose . . . [and]
propagate itself throughout the whole social sphere"[23] by diffusing its values
and ideology among all other groups, it stands to reason that industrial development and expansion will be a key priority of workers' democracy.

In another definition of "productive labor" in socialism, Branko Horvat—
himself an advocate of market socialism—gives a more specific description of
"socially useful" production which is at least consistent with Gramsci's use
of the term:

> Under socialism, the criteria of productivity consist in the satisfaction of

needs. . . . But in that context, one kind of labor contributes to increasing well-being, while another kind does not change well-being but only
creates the conditions for its realization and in a way represents an
expenditure from production. The first kind of labor is productive, the
second is non-productive. In the first kind . . . may be included labor
that produces commodities, educational and scientific labor, medical and
cultural labor; in the second kind: government administration, police,
the armed forces, the work of politicians. It is a characteristic of socialism . . . that it stimulates labor of the first kind and limits labor of the
second kind.[24]

   Political life in workers' democracy, then, lies essentially in making and
taking the decisions that increase social wealth, stimulating "productive"
work, and limiting "nonproductive" labor. Information on plant capacity,
labor needs, input requirements, and so forth are presumably supplied in plan
proposals formulated by lower units of production and presented for approval
to higher-level producers' councils by the delegates that units themselves
elect.
   Yet although authoritative decisions are made within a centralized hierarchy
of producers' councils, Gramsci would have them executed in a decentralized
fashion on a functional basis.[25] In other words, once basic quotas and allocations have been agreed upon by all producing groups, the division of labor
sets in, and each sector, industry, and plant administers itself. Again, although
the council system is clearly a representative, not a direct, democracy, "everyone participates in the life of the councils" through their collaboration in
the production process.
   As described by Gramsci, a key instrument in this creation of the "hegemony"
of the producers is a political party. Its role is not to take part directly in
"state life" but to create the conditions for others to do so.[26] As an organized
group, the party thus has no representation on producers' councils, according
to Gramsci. Its individual members, however, insofar as they are simultaneously members of producer groups and elected by them to the councils,
may articulate the party's stands inside of state organs, the councils.[27] Consequently, although the party itself has no formal authority in Gramsci's
state, it may influence both the evolving structure of the state as well as its
actions and decisions by the force of its prestige and its ability to articulate
the underlying political will of the class it represents, the producers.
   According to Gramsci, the party in workers' democracy effectively operates
outside the political process: it is a "collective intellectual," so to speak. Its
prestige, in fact, derives precisely from its ability to stand outside and above

the routine entanglements of daily political life. Because its task is to speak for the proletariat as a producer in the "universal" sense, it must not as a body end up representing a particular corporate segment of it, such as steel workers or automobile workers; in this way, the party can remain "disinterested" in the specific outcomes of day-to-day political decisions.[28]

As a consequence, when and if the party should take a position, its recommendations would be made solely from the overall historical perspective of advancing the interests of the producers as a collective whole. The party's role, then, is viewed by Gramsci as one of analysis more than ruling, of persuasion and leadership rather than coercion. It "organizes and connects" demands from below, allowing "a continuous intrusion of elements that emerge from the depths of the masses into the solid frame of the apparatus of rule . . . ; and, at the same time, it takes account of what is relatively stable and permanent."[29]

On the one hand, the party is seen by Gramsci as an essential intellectual agent in creating a political culture and consciousness appropriate to workers' democracy. On the other, its powers of analysis, political persuasion and leadership theoretically ensure that the state evolves in a way congruent with and supportive of that political culture. In effect, Gramsci's political party acts both to shape the political demands and activity of the producers in their factory councils and to organize and articulate them in the workers' state.

The centerpiece of workers' democracy is, then, the factory council, designed to exercise political as well as economic power. Above it stands the rest of the state: a hierarchical system of producers' councils, elected by and responsive to the factory councils at the base, replacing the competitive market as well as the liberal democratic state. And at its side is a political party, committed to the hegemony of the producers and to the further evolution of workers' control over political and economic life. In this way, Gramsci's worker-controlled socialism attempts to substitute private ownership with state ownership, competition with "collaboration"; it seeks to eliminate not only what Gramsci views as the agents of capitalism, the private entrepreneur and the bourgeois state, but also what he considers the capitalist system itself, namely, the competitive market.

SOLIDARITY IN WORKERS' DEMOCRACY

Looked at statically, Gramsci's workers' democracy contains several features that interact to make the individual productive community its fundamental unit of social solidarity. This is where the individual "collaborates in produc-

tion" on a day-to-day basis, where he forms his first and strongest links to
the wider community, where he initially comes in contact with political
authority in the guise of his own factory council. As political identities are
formed on the basis of the various products individuals supply, political
loyalties will also be most strongly conditioned by the immediate work
community. The improved climate of labor relations which theoretically
accompanies the establishment of workers' control, the lack of institutionalized antagonism between mental and manual labor, the consciousness of
the need to cooperate and that each is "indispensable" also serve to cement
loyalties to the individual unit of production.

Operating within a planned economy of the type Gramsci describes should
further strengthen ties to the basic productive community. Since everyone,
regardless of function or location, is theoretically "equally necessary" to the
particular production process in which he is engaged, wage differentials can
be held to a minimum, reflecting neither the scarcity of particular skills nor
the profitability of specific firms or industries but only individual differences
in physical productivity and/or the time and resources used to train specialized personnel. Moreover, as planning would, in theory, minimize the layoffs
and production curtailments characteristic of market economies, the threat
of unemployment and dismissal would be substantially lessened.

The cumulative impact of greater income equality within and between
firms, increased job security, and reduced labor mobility and turnover should
be to encourage stability of employment, thus again enhancing solidarity
among immediate work colleagues.

Ideology, placing a premium on "productive" labor and encouraging identification with the product of one's labor further solidifies the ties that bind a
productive community together. The individual and his work unit take pride
in what they "contribute" to society and in their ability to cooperate in the
basic unit of production. Also, their productive activity and contributions
justify the political and economic claims they make on society.

The solidarity and cohesion of the basic unit of production are not only
present as subjective feelings. The factory council also gives these sentiments
an institutional form so that they are expressed, appealed to, and reinforced
on a daily basis and are manifested in action as well as thought. Further
strengthening the ties of the productive community to its factory council is
the indirect electoral system, which makes the plant councils into the main
body articulating the various individual and collective interests of the basic
work community before higher-level political authorities.

Finally, according to Gramsci, solidarity in the basic productive community
is both the result of a highly specialized and rationalized work process and an

independent factor leading to increased quantitative and qualitative efficiency in production. Efficient individual (each works as hard as he can) and collective (all are organized to provide maximum output with highest quality at lowest social cost) production of a useful object is thus both a condition and a result of plant-level solidarity and the proper operation of factory councils.

Nevertheless, the more cohesion created in the individual unit of production, the more pressures it will generate to enlarge its authority over its own activities. Further, if the state is responsive to such pressures, there may well be movement towards granting individual productive communities greater independence—but only at the expense of the very conditions generating workplace solidarity in the first place. To trace the dynamic behind this paradox, let us analyze workers' democracy as it hypothetically would operate.

THE DYNAMICS OF WORKERS' DEMOCRACY

A number of factors will create major tensions between the workers' state and its basic units. The first is that planning decisions are made democratically.

Planning, whether democratic or not, involves setting priorities between investment and consumption, between sectors, industries, and firms to be invested in, between geographical areas making claims for the use of funds, between alternative uses for different types of labor and raw materials, etc. In Gramsci's design, these priorities are a function of some larger agreed-upon goals that set criteria for judging what constitutes "socially useful" production. Yet such goals and criteria are necessarily general and would have to be interpreted and applied in order to set priorities. If this is accomplished through a democratic political process of the kind Gramsci describes, specific priorities will be arrived at through bargaining among the various representatives of economic sectors and industries.

Not only is it difficult to imagine an economically rational or socially optimal solution arising out of such a politicized allocation process, but it may prove impossible to reach any agreement at all on priorities among agents with competing claims, equal rights, and equally intensely felt needs and with no objective way of measuring costs and benefits. The problem of arriving at a consensus on priorities—let alone an economically and socially optimal one—is exacerbated by the fact that the agents setting the priorities are accountable to those directly affected by them; the representatives are elected not only to make allocation decisions, but also to advocate the proposals and protect the interests of the producers they represent. Thus, the delegates are closely identified with their respective constituencies at the same time that each industry and productive community is highly committed to and identified with the products it supplies and/or plans to produce. In other words, not only do all producer preferences have an equal right to expression, but because of its emphasis on solidarity and identification with the product of one's labor, the entire system is biased towards maximizing the intensity of the preferences expressed.

In addition, to the degree that Gramsci's worker-controlled socialism is initially successful and expansion of production for use does occur, an even greater element of choice, and hence of conflict, is introduced into the planning process. It is far less difficult to agree on building railroads if a country has no railroads at all than it is to choose between constructing an additional railroad station and reasphalting two hundred miles of highway. Thus, the more successful the democratic planning system is in stimulating production and enhancing plant-level solidarity, the more difficult it will become to arrive at the overall political consensus needed to continue it.

A second, related factor leading to conflict between planning bodies and production units derives from certain difficulties inherent in the planned economy regardless of whether elected producers' councils of appointed administrators make the main decisions. Here we need only mention a few of these difficulties,[30] starting with the inadequacy of cost information.

Since there is no price system in Gramsci's worker-controlled socialism, there is no objective way to measure either the "usefulness" of an item or the "productivity" of a given amount or type of labor. If all judgments on such questions are necessarily subjective, it stands to reason that an individual plant's estimate of its optimal level of efficiency need not coincide with the estimates or requirements, made from a different vantage point, of higher-level producers' councils, which make most of the decisions determining whether an individual plant will be able to achieve what it regards as optimal efficiency.

For example, an electronics plant may correctly judge that it could double its output by modernizing its equipment, submit a request to the planning authorities to this effect, and have its request quite democratically turned down over the protests of its elected representative. Alternatively, it may be told to cut back its production of transistors, either forcing a transfer of part of its work force to some other activity—after these same workers have spent months preparing a proposal to justify the object's social utility—or maintaining the same labor force to keep everyone employed. In the latter case, it would be rather difficult for the members of the production unit to be conscious of themselves as "indispensable."

An analogous situation would occur in the case of product innovation: a firm has designed an improved product that would require additional raw materials but would represent a substantial advance over the older version. How is the planning council to estimate the cost to society of the added materials compared to the cost of continuing to produce an inferior product? More to the point, without an objective measure of "usefulness," how is the planning council to justify a negative decision to a work community already convinced of the innovation's validity?

Another common difficulty in planned economies—democratic or not—lies in the bottlenecks created by a confusion of "fact and goal" in setting production targets. For example, say a power plant has agreed to generate a certain number of kilowatt hours a day over the amount generated the previous year; it is unable to do so not because of any dysfunctional organization of its own, but because the targets set for the coal industry have been overoptimistic. Meanwhile, the plant has already—and rationally—hired extra workers to meet its higher projected annual quotas. In such a situation, what began as a highly functional division of labor ends with one in which each was hardly "in his place."

The point is not simply that planning, by elected councils or a nonrepresentative elite, makes for certain difficulties in the allocation of resources; so does a market, although the distortions it introduces into economizing are of a different nature. But to the degree that the decisions of planning bodies in workers' democracy conflict with what individual production units see as their optimally efficient mode of operation and insofar as both evaluations are subjective yet based on an application of the same principle (how the basic production unit can best contribute to society), the workers' state and its "first cell" are headed for a major political conflict.

That planning allows individual productive communities to identify specific, human agencies as the source of their difficulties brings us to the third factor exacerbating relations between planning councils and producer units: the ideology of productive labor and the assumption that every member of society is a producer.

Setting economic priorities is as difficult as it is time consuming, and time spent in political decision making is all time taken out of the production process itself. As Horvat noted, "government administration" and the "work of politicians . . . does not increase well-being but . . . represents an expenditure from production." This observation is not only consistent with Gramsci's remarks on the evils of government bureaucracy, but it would also be perfectly evident to the producer in workers' democracy who watches his comrade take more and more time off from work in the plant in order to attend planning council meetings.

Furthermore, the higher the level of the planning body, the more discretion it has in allocating resources; as the stakes are raised, the potential for conflict and the time taken to make any individual decision also increase. So too does the number of decisions a planning body must make, again enlarging the total time going into "non-productive" activities. One arrives, then, at the paradox that the most important desicions affecting productive priorities are made by those who spend the least time producing. While this need not mean that the interests of the productive communities are not adequately represented, it does suggest that dissatisfactions at the plant level with planning priorities can now be expressed in the same "universal" principles the workers' state is founded upon: "power to the producers" is a double-edged sword.

Moreover, in addition to the time lost from production in political decision making, additional time will be lost in information gathering and control functions. Even if we grant Gramsci's assumption that bureaucracy will be minimized in the workers' state because these functions will be decentralized and delegated out to the productive communities themselves, the production time lost in bookkeeping and control is still time lost, no matter who loses it. Bureaucratic functions are not eliminated simply by making everyone a part-time bureaucrat.

If it is found, however, that less total time would be lost from production by delegating information and control functions to specialists or if specialists could perform these tasks better, the seeds of formal bureaucracy are already planted. The probability of such a development is enhanced by the ideological and practical stress on production as a goal and the division of labor and specialization as a means. The "psychology of the producer" itself suggests that the worker will want to spend his time producing, not taking care of paperwork and checking up on his comrades' production quotas.

Thus, the "multiplicity of bureaucratic and disciplinary functions" Gramsci criticized in capitalism may well be reduced to "industrial necessity" and still remain quite substantial. Combined with an ideology stressing productive labor and the hegemony of the producers, the development of a planning bureaucracy may well become a major source of frustration for many individual work communities, especially those whose requests for investment funds are cut or denied while huge sums of money are allocated to administrative expenses.

The final factor leading to tension between the workers' state and its basic unit is the inevitable comparisons that will be made between the relatively smooth functioning of the factory council and the lengthy, tormented conflicts in higher-level bodies. If discretion—and hence conflict—is greatest at the top of the council pyramid, it is smallest at the bottom. As the plant-level factory council's alternatives are greatly limited by the fact that its resources are given and its product prescribed from the outset, it engages more in resolving technical problems than in adjudicating conflicting claims. Moreover, as factory council composition is based on the division of labor in the plant, it stands to reason that the recommendations of whomever is considered most competent to solve a particular problem will normally be adopted without a great deal of conflict or loss of time. The factory council would thus appear as a rational, functional body that would operate even more effectively if it were not for the restrictive conditions imposed on it by outside, "nonproductive" agencies.

In sum, the very factors in workers' democracy that operate to create workplace solidarity also act to put the productive community on a collision course with workers' democracy itself. Two possibilities for the productive community present themselves: solidarity as a result of optimal plant efficiency and producers' control will decline and give way to apathy, lowering productive output and threatening the economic rationale of workers' democracy; or solidarity as a factor leading to increased rationality in production will assert itself as a demand for more direct control over productive activities at the grass roots, a demand for enlarging the autonomy of the basic productive community. Which possibility will materialize is a product of many complex factors, the most important being the presence of factory councils and the nature of the state to which demands can be addressed.

As we have seen, solidarity in the plant is not just a subjective feeling of the individuals working there. It grows out of and is manifested socially in cooperation to produce a given object, economically in a desire to increasingly rationalize and improve the labor process, and politically in the decisions made by the factory council. Thus, when the bases of solidarity in production are threatened by forces outside the immediate productive community, it is not just an atomized agglomeration of individuals whose personal welfare is threatened, but an already tightly and effectively organized group, united and conscious of their interests and possessing an articulate, specifically political means of expressing those interests: the factory council. Ironically, Gramsci's observation that "at every moment, the factory council seeks to depart from legality" and "to universalize every rebellion" is as valid in worker-controlled socialism as in "plutocratic" capitalism.[31]

Moreover, the factory council is a highly effective agent for articulating demands for political change because of the nature of the socialist state Gramsci designs: its legitimacy is unquestionable; the goal it is promoting— less wasteful, more efficient production—is among those goals the government itself is formed to achieve; and it clearly speaks on behalf of the producers.

In addition, the organs of the state are elected by the factory councils themselves, so decision makers are quite likely to be responsive to any broad
alliance of productive communities which cuts across narrow industrial lines.

Finally, the natural ally of factory councils seeking greater autonomy will
be the party. If functioning according to Gramsci's notion of democratic
centralism, the party itself will "organize and connect closely together what
is alike," crystallizing into concrete proposals and reform initiatives the
dissatisfaction felt at the base and expressed by the separate factory councils.
The paradoxical result of this alliance's success, however, will be a movement
to substitute price mechanisms for the coordination supplied by the political
commands of producers' councils and in the direction of a much more decentralized system of workers' councils. To such a system we now turn.

2

Proudhon: The Worker as Entrepreneur

In contrast to Gramsci, Pierre Joseph Proudhon proposed a system of workers' control in a market economy as an alternative to capitalism. Where Gramsci felt that social equality, freedom, and collaboration were based on and manifested themselves in the production of useful goods, Proudhon finds equality, liberty, and cooperation a condition and outcome of proper distribution and fair exchange. And where Gramsci argued that the fundamental form of social organization in a worker-controlled system should be the factory, the institution Proudhon finds central to social life is the market.

Proudhon's "mutualism" represents an attempt to embody what he calls "the principle of justice" in human relations. To Proudhon, justice is a relation, a "balance," between persons and forces, both of which are equal and free in the sense that neither can be subordinated to the will or force of the other or of some third party.[1] In practice, justice means guaranteeing each member of society an equal share of wealth and equal conditions for producing it so that there can be free contract between equal parties for the reciprocal exchange of equivalents.[2]

It was precisely to the infrigement of the principle of free exchange of equivalents caused by the growth of class inequalities to which Proudhon ascribes the evils of nineteenth-century capitalism.[3] The solution he advocated was a radical redistribution of property so that each member of society would possess both his own labor and his own property in equivalent amounts.[4] This was not to be accomplished through the abolition of private property, expropriation of large capitalists, progressive taxation, or even militant trade unionism. Rather, the "windfall" profits (*aubaines*) of capitalist "feudalism" were to be eliminated by increasing competition in the market so that the equilibrium state of perfect competition would be attained. And the mechanism for doing so was the formation of "mutualist" associations: egalitarian, worker-controlled enterprises and credit associations that, by increasing competition on labor and product markets, would simultaneously raise and equalize the price of labor while eliminating profits over and above the entrepreneur's opportunity cost.[5]

23

THE MUTUALIST ECONOMY

According to Proudhon, mutualist associations are formed when a group of workers joins together, pooling equal amounts of labor and property, dividing work so that each works for all, and through reciprocal guarantees, sharing equally in profits and losses (conceived of as the returns to labor).[6] Where capitalism had reduced workers to propertylessness, Proudhon would initially provide highly advantageous credit terms made available by other mutualist associations or, if necessary, by the state.[7]

Associated according to the principle of justice, each member of a mutualist association is "free" and "equal."[8] He is free insofar as the association is purely voluntary; should a member feel he is not receiving a "just" return on his labor and capital inputs compared with what he might receive from a different association, he can withdraw at any time, taking his share of property with him. Such a condition not only satisfies the moral requirements of justice, but also helps maintain the labor mobility necessary to minimize "inequality of fortunes and conditions."

Each member of the association is also equal, both as an entrepreneur and a laborer. As entrepreneurs, each contributes an equal amount of property and each has an equal voice in decision making within the association. Ideally, once mutualist society was established on a firm basis, the equality association members enjoy as entrepreneurs would be complemented by their equality qua exchangeability as workers. Although the division of labor, "[multiplying] the power of labor above what it would be if left to individual liberty" would remain, it would no longer be "stultifying . . . immobilizing the worker within one infinitely small area of production."[9] Instead, Proudhon suggests, education under mutualism would stress diversification;[10] rotation of labor by common agreement would be the norm. Furthermore, given equal inputs of labor and capital, each member of a mutualist association is entitled to an equal share of the returns: wealth is to be divided equally among all the worker-entrepreneurs in the association.[11]

Decisions in mutualist associations accordingly would be made by a council on which each member possessed one vote. Its primary tasks would be to respond to market cues so as to satisfy the interests for which the association was formed (to maximize the return to worker-entrepreneur inputs, in monetary or nonmonetary terms)[12] while maintaining a "just" distribution of income. In contrast to workers' democracy, solidarity in mutualism does not stem from being "equally necessary" or from "collaboration to produce useful goods" but rather from a quantitatively equal distribution of income and the fact that the interests of the members of a mutualist association happen to coincide. Hence, council decisions are neither authoritative nor enforced through hierarchy. They are followed because it is in the members' interests; otherwise, they would simply leave the association.[13]

Reciprocal exchange of equivalents not only characterizes relationships within mutualist associations, but also among them. Put into the framework of a coherent economic theory, the justice, liberty, and equality of mutualist society translates into the ideal of a perfectly competitive market in equilibrium.[14]

The economic actors in mutualist society are accordingly individual worker-entrepreneurs, acting either individually or in mutualist associations, seeking to maximize the return to their labor by engaging in "friendly rivalry" according to the laws of supply and demand.[15] Perfect competition—the "equilibrium of opposing forces" of which justice consists—theoretically ensures both a rational allocation of resources and the original equality of "conditions and fortunes" Proudhon demands. That is, in an economy of numerous and well-informed buyers and sellers,[16] free mobility of the factors of production, free entry and exit into and out of the market, and prices determined by aggregate supply and demand, both "pure profit"and large wage differentials should cease to exist for any substantial length of time.

Thus, the market mechanism is Proudhon's means of embodying justice in human relations and reconciling moral right with economic law.[17] "Equality of fortunes," Proudhon predicts, will both stimulate growth and guarantee full employment.[18] At the same time, he argues, the "opposing forces" of labor and capital will be held "in equilibrium" through the exchange relations of individual and groups of worker-entrepreneurs, thereby creating "a situation in which there will no longer be either bourgeois or proletarian; that is, they will absorb each other."[19]

THE FEDERALIST STATE

Just as economic justice involves balancing the opposing forces of labor and capital, political justice to Proudhon consists of finding the proper equilibrium between authority and liberty.[20] In Proudhon's federalist state, "the notion of government is succeeded by that of Contract";[21] political units are formed through "synallagmatic" and "commutative" agreements between free and equal individuals and/or associations. Such agreements are reached "spontaneously"; they are valid as long as each receives from the "federative" unit as much as he sacrifices and insofar as each retains all of his "liberty, sovereignty and initiative" other than what is necessary to fulfilling the obligation for which he voluntarily contracts. Each party to an agreement thus has equal rights and is free to break the contract and secede from the federative association formed by it should benefits received no longer equal sacrifices incurred.[22]

Any organized group has the right to join with another group to form a unit of the state. There is no hierarchical pyramid of units, no subordination of one unit to another, regardless of size, aggregate wealth, geographic boundaries, etc.[23] If municipalities contract to form a regional association and one local government refuses to sign, the regional association has no authority over it. Nor, in fact, does the regional "government" have any authority over its component units; the relation is the reverse.[24] Smaller units agree to cooperate to achieve some common goal; as long as they are in fact cooperating, the agreement is in force; should one or two of them balk, they merely cease to be parties to the contract. Similarly, a local government apparently would have no authority over a mutualist association located within its boundaries unless the association itself was a party to the agreement establishing the government or if it had contracted separately with the federative unit for specific purposes.

Thus, in Proudhon's federalist state, de facto and de jure authority and law are precisely the same. If units act according to contracts, then contracts exist; if they do not, the contracts are ipso facto abrogated.[25] There is no third force over and above the contracting parties to enforce agreements; the only force working to maintain such agreements is the benefits the contractors derive from them. Proudhon notes quite aptly, "Transported into the political system, what we have up to now been calling mutualism . . . takes the name of federalism";[26] political authority is, in effect, little more than an incentive system.

What distinguishes political from economic units is neither the former's legitimate monopoly of force nor any difference in the kinds of activities they respectively undertake. A local government formed by individual citizens and various economic groups may finance a public school system while one of its component mutualist associations manufactures textiles. Yet the reverse may also occur: a group of individual teachers may open a school while a local government supplies the initial investment for a textile plant.

Nevertheless, "the state is not an entrepreneur of public services. . . . The people do not ask . . . that the government take over commerce, industry and agriculture . . . and make the . . . nation into a nation of wage-earners."[27] On the contrary, the state is merely an initiator. Federative associations, as opposed to their mutualist counterparts, do not themselves accomplish the goal for which an agreement has been made but merely combine members' resources in order to set up or finance some new organization, which is then subject only to the authority of its own members and no longer has any particular obligation to the body that originally established it.[28] While members of mutualist associations pool equal amounts of labor and property and receive direct, individual benefits from doing so, members of federative associations only make equal (monetary) contributions to a common fund and receive indirect, collective benefits from the uses to which their savings qua taxes are put.

For example, a local union of citizens can finance the construction of a textile plant upon the request of a group of worker-entrepreneurs who will go on to work and manage it. Such an operation would involve (at least) two contracts: between the citizens, regulating contributions, and between the citizens and the mutualist association, regulating repayment terms on the credit. Meanwhile, once the plant is in operation, the citizen's union no longer has any claim on it as long as the loan is repaid; the mutualist association, the group that actually operates the factory, is its sole proprietor. In fact, strictly speaking, the citizen's association does not even have the power to force repayment of the loan; only the threat of future denials of credit would motivate the textile firm to repay the loan.

Similar relations would prevail in all other services normally regarded as "public": schools, police, sanitation, etc. The local "government" or citizen's union may organize the police force initially; once in operation, however, it is independent and self-governing. Presumably it continues to finance itself through "reciprocal exchange": the citizens it protects pay a user's fee for the service it supplies in accordance with the going market price for police protection or arrived at by "amicable discussion" between the parties concerned.

The main difference, then, between economic and political units in Proudhon's framework is that production of goods and services is performed by equal and autonomous mutualist associations, while the state is essentially a cooperative bank, insurance company, and stock exchange all rolled into one. As Proudhon puts it: "The government is the public economy, the supreme administration of the labors and goods of the entire nation. The nation is like a huge corporation in which every citizen is a stockholder."[29]

Meanwhile, authority, even if only an authority of incentives, cannot be the only "principle" embodied in the just state; the force of liberty must be present to balance it and ensure that social contracts establishing federative units are indeed voluntary and that individuals and/or associations can secede should benefits be reduced. The means by which Proudhon guarantees liberty, the possibility of choice, is none other than the institution of private property.[30]

To Proudhon, property is "absolute" and subject only to the control of its individual owner, who can use or abuse it as he sees fit.[31] The problem with capitalism, according to Proudhon, was that it encourages the "abuse" of property, leading to class divisions and in turn to the establishment of a state that stands as an authoritarian, coercive force vis-à-vis the propertyless worker. In mutualist society, however, where everyone has property and perfect competition prevails, each property owner "will soon learn to his cost that property cannot live by abuse and that it too must bow to common sense and morality."[32]

In other words, authority (economic incentives,) will act to restrain liberty, (abuse of property or refusal to exchange a "product for product"), while liberty (the citizen's ability to "dispose of his intelligence, his hands, his capital and his land as he sees fit")[33] balances state power. Using Proudhon's analogy, no one can be coerced to buy stock in the great national corporation, although an increase in its value will provide an incentive to do so; meanwhile, each stockholder can sell his share or cash it in at will. In very practical terms, what acts to prevent the establishment of the "bureaucratic arbitrariness" and the "dictatorship of industry . . . commerce . . . thought [and] social and private life"[34] that Proudhon finds so repellent in communism is the fact that individual small property owners acting to maximize their personal incomes will normally resist the taxes needed to pay the administrative expenses of a large governmental apparatus.

In this context, universal suffrage is both a political and economic characteristic of worker-controlled mutualism; in both political and economic units, one's vote is equivalent to the way in which one disposes of one's property, one's labor, and one's income. To Proudhon, market choice and political choice, like politics and economics, are simply "two different ways of conceptualizing the same thing."[35] As there is no enforcement mechanism beyond economic incentives, majority rule must give way to consensus as a decision-making formula.[36] Decisions will accordingly reflect the market situation of the groups and individuals making them.[37] In such a situation, it is hardly surprising that Proudhon never mentions political parties. It would seem that the only kind of secondary political associations that could arise in the federalist state would be pressure groups, temporary alliances among members of federative and mutualist associations which perform the role of interest brokers in shaping a consensus.

The federalist state, then, has no independent role in mutualist society except insofar as it is able to stimulate competition by establishing new, independent mutualist associations. Its equal and autonomous units thus act to facilitate entrance to the market, provide some insurance against risk, and keep buyers and sellers informed of prices, provided, of course, that its citizens and component associations consent to donate resources for these purposes. In short, the state merely reflects and stimulates the free market. In this way, according to Proudhon,

> the notions of power and authority are . . . replaced in people's minds . . . by the notions of labor and exchange. . . . Once industrial functions have taken over from political functions, then business transactions and exchange alone produce the social order. In these conditions, each man could call himself his own master.[38]

THE DYNAMICS OF MUTUALISM AND FEDERALISM

If the operation of Gramsci's worker-controlled socialism stood and fell with its focal point, the solidarity of the grass-roots productive community, so does the functioning of Proudhon's mutualism stand and fall on the basis of its central organizing tenet, free exchange of equivalents between equal and autonomous units. That is, on the macroeconomic level, the more unrestrained the competition between and among individual businesses and mutualist associations, the greater the pressures to create a political (hierarchical) mechanism to redress the imbalances created by the market. At the same time, on the microeconomic level, enterprise loyalties will increasingly be replaced by class and occupational loyalties in whose conflicts mutualist and federative associations will have to take sides. Either they will be co-opted by the top of the class structure or they will be "trade-unionized" and politicized by the bottom. In the latter case, workers' councils will constitute a political force implicitly and explicitly pushing toward planning and hierarchy in the allocation of resources. Finally, if a government is formed or given authority to remedy these grievances, there will be a movement toward replacing the allocation of resources according to the competitive market with the allocation of resources as shaped by the authoritative decisions of political bodies.

To see how this dynamic operates, let us assume that the transition has been made from centralized and planned worker-controlled socialism or from imperfectly competitive, oligopoly capitalism to Proudhon's decentralized worker-controlled mutualism operating under conditions of perfect competition and equal distribution of the factors of production. All economic units are now either mutualist associations or individual small entrepreneurs;[39] credit and banking functions are performed primarily by federative units and, to some degree, by mutualist associations. Business decisions are made by either the small entrepreneur himself or by councils composed of all the members of mutualist or federative associations, and all worker-entrepreneurs seek to maximize the return to their labor.

If the mutualist economy is to operate according to Proudhon's designs, there should be no "return" to any factor of production other than labor; while we clearly cannot grant him this assumption and still have a coherent, working model of mutualism, we can approach it by assuming a social norm that requires the reinvestment of all returns to capital and land. In this way, we can approximate his condition that all members of mutualist society must work for a living and derive their incomes from their labor; the incentive to invest comes not from direct benefits derived in the form of personal "dividends" but from the indirect benefits accruing to labor through increased productivity. This assumption also provides for the growth and innovation Proudhon promises will result from the joining of economic law to justice. Proudhon's requirement of no-interest loans must also be modified if a rational allocation of capital is to occur. Here, we can assume that since federative associations must compete with each other, interest rates will be as low as supply and demand permit; at the same time, the earnings the association acquires from interest are not distributed back to members directly in the form of income ("savings accounts" qua taxes do not carry "interest") but are either recirculated as credit or used as payment for services supplied by mutualist associations or by private entrepreneurs under contract with the membership. The initial incentives to set up federative associations are twofold: by helping new businesses get started and by aiding existing ones to expand, the community is able indirectly to raise the personal standard of living; by having more funds available to pay for the delivery of collective goods and services, the community can lift its social standard of living as well.

Finally, let us assume that even lacking a third force to enforce contract obligations, the members of mutualist society nonetheless respect them out of moral and ideological conviction and because respecting contract terms coincides with their long-term interests.

The first difficulties for the above-defined mutualist society arise from the vagaries of the business cycle. If there is full employment and the high rate of investment Proudhon assumes, the price system will be subject to severe inflationary strains. As demand peaks, production will fall back causing unemployment. Nor will these difficulties hit everyone equally: some industries and regions are going to suffer far more than others as demand rises and falls, destroying the initial equality of the system. Some mutualist associations and small entrepreneurs will simply go bankrupt, along with federative associations whose mutualist and individual debtors are unable to pay back the credit extended them when times were good. The absence of any centrally coordinated fiscal or monetary policy-setting bodies will further aggravate the crisis. While loans bailing out mutualist associations that experience temporary

difficulties adapting to market competition may be forthcoming in periods
of prosperity, when citizens can afford to put aside some of their income in
the form of savings, they will be few and far between once recession sets
in. For the same reason, "government" spending will not be available to stimulate the economy out of the doldrums. In short, Proudhon's vision of
perfect competition among mutualist firms will produce an economy that experiences drastic oscillations between periods of boom and bust, fluctuations
that will necessarily upset the "just" distribution with which the system
began.

Inequalities in income and property distribution will not only occur because
of the operation of the business cycle. Even in the normal course of market
competition, the need for labor and capital mobility to meet the exigencies
of demand implies not only easy market entry, but also easy market exit;
some mutualist associations are going to have to disband. If such a breakup
occurs voluntarily, each member may still salvage a portion of his original
property investment to contribute to the new, expanding mutualist association
he hopes to join. But the value of such property will probably be well below that of the original value invested, for we assume that mutualist associations break up because there is no demand for what they produce. Meanwhile,
the property shares of the members of the profitable mutualist association
will have increased: if a "product" is to be exchanged for a "product," the new
member's income will accordingly have to be lower than those of his co-
workers for some time, in order to make up for the initial disparity in capital
contributions. On the other hand, mutualist associations may disband in-
voluntarily, driven out of business because they are unable to compete. In this
case, members will simply lose their original property entirely. Theoretically,
they can reacquire it by the earnings they accumulate through their labor, but
even here, they are at a distinct disadvantage on the labor market, having no
capital to invest in a prospective employer. Nor will federative associations
rush to lend the now propertyless worker-entrepreneur venture capital to set
up his own business: the risk of extending credit to someone with a record of
business failure and no current assets to offer as collateral would be prohib-
itive, and as Proudhon himself says, "The working class wants justice, not
charity." The point is simply that "pure profit" may well cease to exist under
conditions of perfect competition, but these conditions themselves imply
that "normal profit" must, in some cases, also disappear.

Once initial inequalities are introduced through the normal operations of
competition and the fluctuations of the business cycle, continued operation
of the unregulated market will probably reinforce them. Associations entering
a new line of business may reap sufficient profits prior to the entry of new

firms to set reinvestment levels that easily outdistance those of even relatively
well financed competitors. Further, even assuming that the swings of the
business cycle leave a sufficient number of firms on a given product market
intact to maintain competitive conditions, there is no reason to suppose that
it will leave the capital-labor ratios of these firms at identical levels. Some
firms, because of greater previous savings, better access to credit, better
management, or whatever, will be able to weather the storm better than others.
Once demand revives, this initial advantage will grow cumulatively. In other
words, the "long run" over which profits tend to disappear under perfect
competition may simply be too long to permit the maintenance of the competitive conditions necessary to bring about the desired equilibrium.

    This brings us to the problem of monopoly in mutualist society. The first
monopolies will be natural; in these cases, the only countervailing forces
consumers can bring against monopoly pricing are substitution and boycotts,
for public regulation or operation has been excluded from the start. While
substitution and boycotts can mitigate somewhat the worst abuses of monopoly, they will tend to be ineffective in the long run, especially where there
is a real need for the product supplied by the monopoly. Note that the local
federative association would also be helpless against a local monopoly: the
bargaining power it derives from its lending facilities becomes irrelevant the
moment the monopoly can get credit from a competitor in another area of
the country. Other monopolies will arise because there is simply not enough
demand for a service or product to make competition practically feasible: a
small town's demand for railroad transport may warrant running one train
through it, but would hardly supply enough business to warrant investment in
a second line. A third source of monopolies may arise out of technical innovation: by developing a new production process or product and keeping it
secret, a firm might drive out all competitors. This leads us to the most ominous source of monopolies in mutualism, those growing out of capital and
labor concentrations. In periods of prosperity, expanding mutualist associations
may simply combine with each other, rather than engage in individual investment. While this clearly does not prohibit the entrance of new firms into
the market, if the combinations are large enough, the risks borne by the new
entrant become much greater. Because of this increased risk, federative credit
associations may find it far more attractive to extend credit to mutualist
combinations than to continue funding new firms. Labor resources will also
be more readily available to large established mutualist combinations than to
newcomers: the former presumably already have large accumulations of
capital for investment, while the latter must first begin to form these resources
by diverting funds from wages to investment. Meanwhile, the effects of the

business cycle, hitting some industries and firms harder than others, will enable mutualist associations in some industries to simply buy out firms in others, all the while rigorously respecting the norms of fair exchange. Vertical monopoly thus complements horizontal combination, for the mutualist association is "unlimited" in the scope of its "guarantees."

The third-party effects of Proudhon's "exchange of equivalents" will present another problem for mutualist society. If it is cheaper for factories to pollute the air than to install antipollution controls, there is no way for society to prevent this.

Finally, the inequalities that begin to develop among mutualist associations and small entrepreneurs will be parallelled by those sprouting up among federative associations. If an association invests largely in local industries and the area is hit badly by a downturn in the business cycle, its residents' savings as well as their property may be wiped out. Further, associations will have memberships of different sizes; the larger, with contributions made by more individuals, will also have more capital to lend; being larger to start with, they may well grow much faster than smaller associations, widening the disparity.

Without going into further detail, it should be clear that even were the conditions of perfect competition to be made operative and even with initially equal distribution of the factors of production, Proudhon's mutualism would lead to precisely the state of affairs it was intended to correct: increasing inequalities between mutualist associations, corresponding disparities between financial capabilities of federative units, formation of a growing group that possesses no property at all, the growth of monopolies and oligopolies, and weak or nonexistent remedies to inconveniences experienced by third parties to business transactions.

Far from correcting these imbalances, the continued operation of an unrestrained market will only aggravate them; the only solution lies in some adaptation of hierarchy and bargaining techniques. Thus, we would expect those groups and individuals put in a disadvantageous position by the unregulated operation of market forces to begin forming their own "natural" associations, not for the purposes of competing on the market but in order to blunt competition through political means. And the bodies they will have to ally with or capture will be none other than the workers' councils of the mutualist and federative associations.

The "solidarity" holding the mutualist associations together will hardly last very long under the pressures of the competitive market. Solidarity, in the context of Proudhon's mutualist association, is based first on the equality qua exchangeability of labor and capital inputs, manifested in the equal distribution of income among all members and in equal participation in decision making. Second, solidarity assumes that every member joins and remains in the association voluntarily., because he maximizes the return to his labor through such association. In short, solidarity is both cause and consequence of the mutualist association's simultaneously maximizing its revenue and dividing its revenue equally among all its members. When either of these conditions is not met, solidarity within the association will cease. Operation of the market, however, is precisely what will make it impossible to satisfy both these conditions.

In the first place, under conditions of market competition, each mutualist association will seek to cut costs. Eventually, one of them is going to discover increasing specialization as an effective means to raise and improve output at a lower cost: rather than the association's dissipating its resources in training all of its members to do everything, it will find it less expensive and more productive to train a few people to do a small number of specified tasks and to assign them these jobs permanently. Such a move would also permit the funds freed up from education to be put to other, more remunerative purposes, from lowering prices to capture a greater share of the market to raising investment to allow for higher future earnings. Additional savings can be made, for specialization somewhat cuts down on labor turnover: individuals will no longer be qualified for as many different jobs as they were before. Meanwhile, competitors at a disadvantage because they have continued to rotate labor also will be pushed toward specialization.

Second, the uncertainties produced by a competitive market will place quick decision making and execution at a premium. At a certain point, some of the more innovative mutualist associations are going to see that if they amend their social compacts to delegate some amount of decision making to individuals and small groups, allowing the membership as a whole to share only in broad, policy-making questions, they will be better able to take advantage of various short-term market opportunities that arise. Not only will this cause a certain inequality in day-to-day decision-making power, but informal influence on even the resolution of broader questions will tend to flow disproportionately to those who deal with these questions on a more limited, routine basis. Information, too will tend to concentrate in the hands of specialists who must constantly deal with it as part of their specific jobs and not merely in their occasional functions as members of a decision making council of equals. At the same time, the innovative association may also agree to establish some sort of managerial hierarchy to insure prompt compliance with decisions or at least to have some specific individuals responsible for the coordination of group tasks on an ongoing basis. While such individuals would not have authority to give orders, presumably their recommendations would be followed by subordinates, for all share a common interest in maximizing the association's revenue.

Note that Proudhon's notion of solidarity within the mutualist association theoretically can still continue to exist despite the introduction of specialization and (voluntary) hierarchy. Although the qualitative "exchangeability" of labor inputs is no longer possible once years of training separate the mechanical engineer from the unskilled laborer, quantitative exchangeability may still continue if equal distribution of income still prevails. Similarly, although inequality of influence and responsibility will develop with the onset of hierarchy, the formal equality of common entrepreneurial risk assumption still remains, for everyone has an equal vote on the association council by virtue of his possession of an equal share of property. Furthermore, the association remains, as it always has been, voluntary: hierarchy and specialization are quite freely accepted initially because they improve the firm's market position and everyone stands to gain equally from them. Indeed, associations that reject these innovations in their organizations will find their solidarity evaporates entirely once they are put at a competitive disadvantage. In other words, if Proudhon's contractual solidarity stands a chance of survival with specialization and hierarchy, it is doomed without them.

Nevertheless, the development of specialization and hierarchy carries ominous overtones for the future of the mutualist association. While specialization will increase the association's revenue by raising productivity, combined with a competitive labor market, it will increase income differentials within the association as well: at any given time, some skills are going to be scarcer relative to demand than others and will be able to command a higher price. At the same time, once individual earnings are as much, if not more, a result of the skills possessed rather than being a simple function of the association's net revenue, loyalities to the enterprise as a whole will tend to be replaced by loyalities to the occupational group within and outside of the association to which individuals belong. Such an identification is reinforced by the fact that even in the days of primitive equality and exchangeability of labor, loyalty to the association was always of a highly conditional nature; because of the requirement of labor and capital mobility, mutualist society has a built-in mechanism to discourage the formation of long-lasting ties to any one association.

Hierarchy, too, will initially serve to raise individual incomes by improving the association's market position through increased efficiency. At the same time, however, it will de facto destroy the de jure relationship of equal responsibility for the association's gains and losses essential to mutualist entrepreneurship. The havoc wrought by specialization and a competitive labor market on equality of labor inputs, hierarchy performs for the equality of capital inputs. The occupational groups on the low end of the income-influence scales may in fact be receiving more for their labor than they could in any alternative association and may voluntarily accept the recommendations made on the job or at council meetings by managerial personnel. Nevertheless, their ownership of a small piece of property in the firm from which they acquire no direct income will become increasingly irrelevant to their life situation. Especially if the viability of small, independent businesses becomes increasingly fragile as product markets become dominated by large-scale producers, individual shares of property will begin more and more to resemble a kind of mutualist unemployment compensation instead of the means for an alternative to joining mutualist associations.

The market will increase the momentum of the tendencies put into motion by hierarchy and specialization within the association. In years of prosperity, groups whose skills were scarce to begin with can use their added bargaining power to enlarge differentials further. In years of decline, either the entire collective will share equally in losses, for legally all are equally "responsible," in which case those at the bottom will still feel the pinch the most, for their income was lower to start with, or again, those with skills difficult to replace will use their bargaining power to shunt the burden of the losses off onto the less privileged members. And as the gap between high- and low-income groups is enlarged, lower-income groups will find it increasingly difficult to continue paying voluntary contributions to their federative associations. The financial projects of the "state" will therefore tend to reflect the needs of the wealthier, rather than the poorer, citizens; instead of being a mechanism for redistribution, the federalist state will only reinforce the inequalities arising in the economy.

Meanwhile, as loyalty to the mutualist association decreases, conflict within it increases. And the central issue in this conflict will be none other than the question the mutualist society had supposedly resolved: what constitutes a "just distribution" of wealth. On one side are arrayed the high-income groups, arguing for differentials on the basis of justice as an equilibrium between supply and demand for labor power, a balance of "free and competing forces"; on the other are the low-income groups, seeking equalization on the grounds that the "product" of labor is created through the common efforts of all engaged in production, and because "a service must be rendered for a service." Furthermore, although conflicts over distribution may remain latent in good years, they will tend to sharpen in bad ones, when total revenue has declined and the demands of underprivileged groups cannot even be partially satisfied. If occupational loyalties are crystallized in the form of cross-associational organizations (for instance, trade unions) from which smaller, intra-associational groups can derive strength, support, and leadership, fuel will be added to the fire.

Such conflicts are not going to be settled by the force of ideological and intellectual arguments alone. Decisions on distribution in mutualist society cannot simply be delegated out to a technical expert. Rather, they must be decided by the council of the association, either according to the requirements of a competitive labor and product market, in which case differentials will be maintained, or according to the amount of force the parties seeking to surmount the decrees of the market can bring to bear on the decision-making process. While under capitalism, the strike supplies the technique for raising the price of labor, in mutualism the situation is simplified: wage determination by the market is replaced by wage determination by the decisions of the mutualist association councils, dominated by lower-income members. Yet determining income levels according to the wishes of council members rather than according to market requirements can only be viable economically if members of the association with scarce skills in high demand can be made to remain in the association even if they are not maximizing the return to their labor, and the firm's position on the product market will not deteriorate despite the fact that labor is no longer allocated according to optimally efficient standards. In short, competitive mutualist associations will have to transform themselves into the Gramsci model of worker-controlled state monopolies.

Feeding into intra-associational pressures for replacing wage determination according to the impersonal forces of the market with wage determination according to consciously set, humanly determined standards will be the external pressures of other disadvantaged groups in mutualist society who are seeking some political means to redress the economic imbalances stemming from market competition. These pressures, too, will be strongest during the troughs of mutualism's business cycle and will manifest themselves in attempts to take over mutualist society's economic resources in order to allocate them to meet the needs that can no longer be expressed in the terms of the free market alone. Here the federative credit associations form the obvious targets, as "natural" groups petition them for funds to initiate projects providing employment, services that satisfy lower-income groups' needs, and so on. Joining—and possibly leading—these groups may well be the mutualist associations themselves, should they be dominated by the low-income groups within them.

None of these requests, however, may be economically viable in market terms, regardless of their social desirability; in a period of economic downturn, it may well be wiser for a federative association to turn a deaf ear to proposals for funding new and risky ventures. Again, demands to abandon the price system as a definitive guide for capital and resource allocation will be implicit and explicit as disadvantage groups press federative councils for relief. Should a political party link these groups together to organize and establish a government with real power to replace nonauthoritarian federalism, mutualist society and the federalist state will be pushed toward a form of workers' control that relies much more heavily on hierarchical methods of resource allocation and contrasts dramatically with Proudhon's original vision of a competitive economy composed of autonomous, labor-managed firms.

PART II

The Evolution of Yugoslav Self-Management

Both Gramsci and Proudhon present us with "pure" models of workers' control in planned and market economies. Reality, of course, is inevitably more complex, and the Yugoslav economy is no exception. Nevertheless, the overall historic evolution of Yugoslav self-management does suggest that the tension between the use of hierarchy and the use of the market with workers' control which appears in exaggerated form in a theoretical analysis of the Gramsci and Proudhon models, also tends to occur in empirical practice.

The development of Yugoslav self-management can roughly be divided into three periods. From 1950 to 1965, the system shared many of the characteristics of Gramsci's outline of workers' democracy; in the 1965-74 period, it was more closely analogous to Proudhon's mutualism. After 1974, attempts to construct a decentralized system of planning made Yugoslav self-management again begin to resemble Gramsci's model of worker-controlled socialism.

Like all classifications, this one is somewhat arbitrary, and both the transition to a market economy and the introduction of a revised form of planning in Yugoslavia were more gradual and less complete than such a categorization implies. Yet major reforms along these lines have clearly taken place; moreover, the tensions and pressures leading to them were quite analogous to the factors theoretically postulated as causing the internal contradictions in the Gramsci and Proudhon schemas.

Despite many similarities, however, Yugoslav practice frequently departs from the respective assumptions made by Gramsci and Proudhon. Accordingly, the shape of events behind the plan-market tension hypothesized earlier also looks somewhat different in the Yugoslav context. In what follows, I attempt to indicate what the broad parallels are and their results.

Nevertheless, in doing so, I have necessarily had to simplify Yugoslavia's remarkably complex system of economic and political policy making. In particular, I deal only summarily with the function and role of trade unions, the Socialist Alliance, economic chambers, professional associations, and the Councils of Producers. According to most accounts, these organizations have had only a peripheral influence on the actual shaping of policy. Less defensible perhaps is my decision not to dwell on the ramifications for the Yugoslav economy of foreign trade and balance-of-payments difficulties. These factors assumed increasing importance in the 1960s and 1970s, and I treat them

40

tangentially mainly because they fall outside the purview of my analysis, which concentrates on politicoeconomic relations in the domestic Yugoslav economy. Similarly, I do not deal at any length with the intricacies of Yugoslav foreign policy, largely because after the Cominform break, they do not seem to have affected the development of self-management in any consistent way. Indeed, one might even argue that the unifying thread in Yugoslav foreign policy has been the goal of creating a "space" in which self-management could develop in response to domestic, rather than external, pressures.

Finally, perhaps to the dismay of Balkan specialists, I have chosen to de-emphasize Yugoslavia's colorful ethnic conflicts in order to stress the economic factors that brought these to the surface in the 1960s and 1970s. This is because I wish to focus on the aspects of Yugoslav self-management that can be generalized. While the centrifugal forces to which the system gives political life do indeed appear to be structurally inseparable from it, Yugoslavia's particular national antagonisms fortunately are not.

3

Self-Management and Planning, 1950-65

Self-management was introduced to Yugoslavia in 1950, when the labor force of every Yugoslav enterprise was authorized to elect both a workers' council and a managing board. Together, these bodies were responsible for various aspects of enterprise decision making, and their powers were gradually enlarged over the ensuing decade. A combination of political, ideological, and economic motives underlay the establishment of what was soon to become a hallmark of Yugoslav socialism.

THE INTRODUCTION OF SELF-MANAGEMENT

The primary political factor leading to the introduction of self-management was Yugoslavia's expulsion from the Cominform in 1948. In its aftermath, it was necessary to rally all sources of domestic support to the regime; introducing workers' councils "offered a novel, non-coercive . . . method of mobilizing the worker to raise the output of his plant."[1]

The political reasoning behind the introduction of self-management from the top down was thus quite similar to Gramsci's line of thought in advocating the establishment of factory councils from the bottom up: institutionalizing solidarity and cooperation in the work place would, it was hoped, strengthen loyalty to the larger community for whom the units produced.

At the time workers' councils were first established in Yugoslavia, they did not represent an alternative to hierarchical methods of economizing outside the individual firm. For the first year or so of their operation, they functioned merely as elected bodies overseeing completion of the targets set down by the First Five Year Plan, complementing enterprise directors as the lowest unit of authority in the planning bureaucracy. Only with diastrous economic conditions, increasingly apparent from 1950 on, did the Yugoslav political leadership decide to abandon the Soviet–style command economy. Ideology provided the connecting link between what were actually separate, if parallel, reforms.

Ideologically, the move to transform workers' consultative organs in eco-

nomic enterprises into workers' councils grew out of increasingly strident
Yugoslav criticism of the Soviet internal order. Even the more conservative
analyses contended that "bureaucratism takes power from the hands of the
working class and the working people which . . . is the most direct and danger-
ous obstacle to socialism."[2] Unlike Gramsci, then, Yugoslav theoreticians
located the source of "unproductive, administrative" labor not in the private
property relations of capitalism but in the bureaucracy created under central
planning. The solution, they argued, was not simply to decentralize initiative
and democratize the planning apparatus, as Gramsci had envisioned. In the
eyes of the Yugoslav leadership, the lessons of the past taught that defining
"productive" labor through political criteria uninformed of relative scarcities
brought results quite the opposite of what was intended: unrealistic targets,
administrative overhead, and the political and economic subordination of the
"direct producer" to the demands of an "unproductive" and often irrespons-
ible bureaucracy.[3]

This was the economic rationale for introducing self-management: the hope
of Yugoslav leaders that workers' councils would stimulate economic
development, productivity increases, and technical innovation. Yet in order
for the workers' councils to mobilize energies successfully and direct them to
the areas where they would show the greatest returns, the councils had to
have the freedom to implement grass-roots initiatives, as well as some way of
evaluating the utility of proposed changes. The answer was to introduce
market mechanisms such that consumer demand would play a role in determining what "production for use" actually meant in practice, while the
microeconomic responses of producers would be the responsibility of the
individual workers' councils and managing boards. Meanwhile, macroeconomic
decisions and general economic policy would continue to be made hierarchically, but through a more decentralized and responsive set of political
institutions. With the Constitution of 1953, the pattern was established:
detailed, political planning of production was abandoned and left to a
regulated market, while political (or "social," to use the Yugoslav euphemism)
planning of "reproduction," or investment, continued on a more decentralized basis, with the national government and the local communes playing
the critical roles in it.

SELF-MANAGEMENT IN OPERATION:
GOVERNMENT RESTRICTIONS ON THE MARKET

By introducing market mechanisms to regulate microeconomic behavior,
Yugoslavia departed substantially from Gramsci's model of worker-controlled

socialism. Nevertheless, enough state intervention and political controls remained to enable us to assimilate Yugoslav self-management in the 1950s with the overall lines of the Gramsci model. Thus, Egon Neuberger writes:

> Whereas in free enterprise countries the firm has control over its profits (except for the effect of a corporate income tax and possibly an excess profits tax), in Yugoslavia its control is severely restricted, and there is a plethora of deductions from its gross profits.[4]

Federally prescribed accounting regulations not only circumscribed what firms could do with their profits, but also defined which items they could include in their costs. As all payments passed through it, the National Bank exercised the function of "social control"; it could both prevent enterprises from transferring to other accounts funds allocated for certain purposes and, to cut investment or excess demand, restrict the use of enterprise funds deposited with it. Tax policy and wage regulations, too, changed almost annually, in a ceaseless search for a suitable system of remuneration and incentives.

At the same time, when the high rate of forced savings and lax credit policies caused inflationary pressures to break out, price ceilings and controls multiplied. Meanwhile, a multiplicity of exchange rates, designed to encourage exports and changeable at the whim of the government, meant that the factors determining the profitability of many products were quite beyond the control of the firms manufacturing them. "Furthermore, exportation was carried out according to lists of exporters, and companies had to use their influence from all sources to achieve a position on the right list."[5] Even then, the foreign exchange acquired through such transactions remained at the disposal of the National Bank. This meant that while firms could and did attempt to shape their business policies and plans to respond to market cues, the shape of the market itself as well as firm responses were as influenced by the decrees of government agencies as they were by consumer demand.

The most critical political interventions in the market, however, occurred in the allocation of capital. While wages and product prices fluctuated to some extent with supply and demand, investment priorities remained centrally determined until 1965.[6] Moreover, the bulk of the funds used to finance investment were not derived from interest charges and voluntary savings but from the taxes of federal and local governments levied on the enterprises themselves. These were then centralized into a General Investment Fund and channeled back into the economy via the politically controlled banking system. In this way, the investment plan "transferred decisions about the rate of capital formation, the distribution of investment funds among economic and geographic sectors and the size of collective consumption expenditures to the political sphere."[7] As a result, firms were left with only a fraction of their gross profits to invest or to redistribute as wages (table 1); any major expenditures had to be financed through the government banks.

Table 1. Profit of the Firms: Percentage Distribution

Year	Total Profit	Federal Profit Tax	Wages Supplemented from Profits	District Budget[a]	Funds of the Firm	Others[b]
1954	100	49.5	4.8	28.7	10.3	16.7
1955	100	44.0	5.8	27.8	12.6	11.8
1956	100	40.0	6.3	11.3	15.0	27.4
1957	100	28.0	9.2	—	9.7	—

Source: R. Bićanić, "Interaction of Macro-and Microeconomic Decisions in Yugoslavia, 1954-1957," in *Value and Plan*, ed. Gregory Grossman (Berkeley: University of California Press, 1960), p. 356. Reprinted by permission of the University of California Press.
[a]Commune revenues.
[b]Not defined.

Accordingly, a series of noncompeting capital markets were set up according to the macroeconomic proportions established by the national plan; within these markets, the Investment Bank, the National Bank, and the various specialized banks were left with wide discretion over specific directions and conditions governing the final allotment of capital. Nor were these intrasectoral allocations necessarily made with a view to the profitability of the investment. As late as 1962, Albert Waterston noted that interest rates "do not play a decisive role in the allocation of investment and are not an important factor in production. . . . Moreover, investment funds are loaned at subsidized rates."[8] In fact, the Investment Bank used multiple criteria, none of which was directly comparable with the others, and "the procedure became so complicated that in the end the decisions were guided by political factors."[9] The National Bank, responsible for short-term loans and circulating capital, was not immune from political influence either. To quote Waterston again: "The National Bank has sometimes been under strong pressure from interested groups to grant credits to enterprises for purposes the National Bank was not always in a position to assess."[10]

In sum, enterprises seeking to respond to the cues of an admittedly imperfect market still "tended to devote a large part of their time away from

questions of productivity and cost, spending it haggling with various governmental organs, exercising pressures, and arranging for subsidies and higher
prices for their products."[11] While firms no longer received administrative
orders telling them what and how to produce, they nonetheless depended on
the goodwill of political authorities to carry out decisions of their own
making. Although the goals of Yugoslav firms may have differed from those
of Gramsci's productive communities because of the former's operation on
the market, their position vis-à-vis political authorities was, in many critical
aspects, fundamentally similar.

SELF-MANAGEMENT IN OPERATION: THE "FIRST CELL" OF THE SOCIALIST STATE

What was different from workers' democracy, however, was the position of
the political authorities in relation to each other and to the enterprises in
Yugoslavia. Whereas Gramsci envisioned a centralized hierarchy of elected
bodies starting from the factory councils, the Yugoslav Constitution of 1953
created a federal system, with a considerable degree of autonomy granted
to the lowest unit of government, the commune (općina). Furthermore, while
Gramsci saw political representation organized around production principles,
in Yugoslavia, units of electoral representation were structured on a territorial
basis.

In certain ways, however, the Yugoslav commune fit well within the outlines
sketched by Gramsci of municipal government in workers' democracy.[12] Its
bicameral legislature, like those of higher political units (district, republic,
and national assemblies), was partially elected on production principles and it
was administratively autonomous but politically supervised by government
organs above it; in other words, it made and executed its own decisions within
the limits set down by higher authorities. Moreover, its legislature elected
representatives to the republic assembly, and so on. Again, the indirect electoral system offers a parallel with the Gramsci model.

In addition, the Yugoslav commune had an important role in economic planning, differentiating itself sharply from the more limited, traditionally service-
oriented role of municipal governments in private enterprise systems. Drawing
it closer to its counterpart in the Gramsci system was the Yugoslav commune's responsibility for the economic development of the territory under
its jurisdiction. Funds for this purpose were supplied by grants-in-aid from
the federal government, loans from the Investment Bank, and local taxes on
enterprises. The commune also drew up its own development plan, based on
local needs and conditions. In doing so, the commune was expected to take
into account the objectives of both the federal plan and the plans prepared

by local firms, insofar as both had a major impact on the nature and amount of funds available for commune expenses.[13] In turn, the economic plans formulated by communes were important factors shaping the annual national plans, as well as critical determinants of the behavior of local enterprises.

These arrangements had several implications for the enterprises. First of all, in Yugoslavia, the commune, a geographically defined unit, *not* the enterprise, defined by what it produced, was the "first cell" of the workers' state. Jovan Dordević, a leading Yugoslav legal theorist, is quite explicit in this respect: "The commune, as a basic socioeconomic community and fundamental organization of self-management, is *the foundation of the entire social and political system.*[14] Even though Yugoslav ideology made a clear distinction between the "economy" (the worker-managed enterprises and cooperatives) and "social" and "sociopolitical" bodies, assigning the performance of "productive labor" and the "creation of value" only to the first of these, the enterprises and workers' councils in Yugoslavia always lacked the direct political power assigned them in Gramsci's model.

The establishment of the Council of Producers did indeed represent an attempt to base political representation more on the "organization of production." In practice, however, it never succeeded in becoming much more than the poor second cousin, if that, of the legislative chamber based on geographical representation.[15] This left the enterprises in a position of relative weakness not only vis-à-vis the state administration, but within the political system itself. For the political system, in turn, it meant that to the degree formal organs of representation were responsive to pressures from below, they were by and large responding to territorially based interests—which, in Yugoslavia, all too often meant ethnically rooted ones.

A second consequence of the commune's role in planning was its function in regulating the business activity of enterprises within its boundaries. It participated in the election and dismissal of enterprise directors, approved the basic regulations—covering everything from salary scales to structuring the self-management organs to production and financial plans—drawn up and adopted by the enterprises themselves, applied within its territory the laws and regulations made by higher political bodies, and guaranteed all long-term loans and credits received by the enterprises. Moreover, its own tax revenues were partially dependent on the incomes of the firms within its jurisdiction. Not surprisingly, cries of commune "meddling" in internal enterprise affairs were frequent.[16]

"Meddling," however, took many forms. At times, it was undoubtedly quite justified in the eyes of all but the work collective affected, as when inflationary wage increases or price hikes were voted in by enterprise self-management organs.[17] At other times, it took less auspicious forms of direct intervention through orders to the firm director, bypassing the workers' council entirely. More frequently, however, one suspects that commune encroachment on enterprise autonomy took the perfectly legitimate and legal channels of "recommendations" of various types.[18]

Not all commune interventions were unwise, and not all were unwelcome to the enterprises. Often, outside pressure was sorely needed for enterprises to clean their own houses, and the fact that communes were, in the last analysis, responsible for enterprise debts in case of bankruptcy was certainly an incentive in this direction. Moreover, the commune's discretionary power in enforcing regulations was often used on behalf of the enterprises when a mutual benefit was to be derived. For example, prior to 1957, the basic wage structure for skill and qualification groups was set down by the federal government. Nevertheless,

> Both the enterprise and the commune frequently had a common interest in attracting labor to their area. If the wages offered were too low to attract the necessary labor, the enterprise and the commune, working together, would "upgrade" workers into skill and qualification categories for which they were not qualified on objective grounds. In this way, the higher wage would be paid, labor could be attracted to the enterprise and the commune, and the enterprise, on the surface, would be acting in conformity with federal wage regulations.[19]

The fact remains, however, that discretion was lodged in the hands of the commune, not the enterprise itself.

The example of local authorities using their discretionary power to benefit their district and the enterprises within it at the expense of federal regulations brings us to the third implication of the commune's role in planning: its tendencies toward a peculiarly Yugoslav analogue to the "subordinate autarky" problem frequently found in planned economies. It was here that the subordination of allocation decisions to political bodies responding to territorially based interests had its most serious consequences, political as well as economic.

Peter Wiles defines "subordinate autarky" as "the desire of every subordinate and intermediate unit to ensure its own supplies" and ascribes it to "planner's tension."[20] When the planning is organized on production principles (as in Soviet ministries or, we might add, Gramsci's workers' democracy), subordinate autarky takes the form of vertical and horizontal integration and a tendency toward regional specialization. But when planning decisions are made and influenced by geographically defined units, "quickly everybody will be producing everything, regardless of cost."[21]

This was precisely what happened in Yugoslavia, where a protracted epidemic of "localism" proved a continual thorn in the economy's side. In the Yugoslav context, "localism" resulted less from "planner's tension" than from the financing of local services and industries from federal funds and was less a desire to ensure local firms needed supplies than an attempt to guarantee them exclusive access to the local market. That is, as long as the federal government could be made to pick up the tab, communes pushed ahead with plans to increase industrial employment and output within their areas regardless of costs, effects on the national economy and its development, or even the consequences for the long-term economic viability of the firms affected. The outcome of pursuing narrowly defined territorial goals for the economy as a whole was a costly duplication of capacities, a loss of economies of scale, a growing number of "political factories," and the burgeoning of intermediate bureaucracies at the subnational level.[22] Paul Shoup gives an apt description of the problem:

> In the Titoist system, particularism was first and foremost due to the fact that the reforms . . . decentralized control over large areas of planning and investment allocation without giving power to the enterprises to determine the flow of capital on the basis of profit considerations. As a result, the local "power elites" came to exercise great discretion in economic matters and invariably used their power to pursue the interests of their own region, which . . . amounted to obtaining investments for the construction of industry and then protecting that industry at any cost.[23]

Apparently, the problem was particularly pronounced in less developed areas where

> the conviction of local officials . . . that it was dangerous to specialize [led] to pressures on factories to produce a wide variety of products for local needs; when such methods tied down the factory and made it uncompetitive, pressures would develop to cut off competition, to give local industry favored treatment, and to integrate trade, industry and agriculture within the boundaries of the local commune at the expense of normal market mechanisms.[24]

Thus, because of the inherent conflict between production and territorial principles of planning organization, the tendency of communes to "meddle" in enterprise affairs for better or worse was not, as Đuro Salaj claimed, simply

the product of the "subjective attitudes of local officials,"[25] but had much
more profound causes. The costs of particularism became so acute that in
1962, a major campaign to "integrate" firms engaged in the same line of production was initiated by the national government and spearheaded by the
League of Communists. Not surprisingly, the chief source of "obstructionism"
to interregional mergers was local officials, who feared that locating enterprise headquarters outside of their jurisdiction would dry up their sources of
tax revenue and diminish local control.[26]

Several patterns of enterprise-commune relationships emerged as characteristic by-products of particularism. On the one hand, there would be a conflict
of interests when communes, in defense of the local standard of living,
obstructed enterprises from specialization and adaptation to a market wider
than that of the immediate district. Direct intervention was only one of many
techniques local authorities could employ: high local taxes, pressures on the
firms to employ more workers than they needed, lack of cooperation in
supplying credit, and so on had, in the last analysis, the same effects. Another
type of conflict emerged out of enterprise particularism: enterprises would
run into difficulty and appeal to political authorities for subsidies, pressure
local officials to maintain and protect local monopolies, and so forth. In such
cases, "the refusal of new credits to inefficient enterprises . . . could easily be
attacked as 'bureaucratic interference with workers' management.' "[27]

On the other hand, a pattern of reciprocal aid based on mutual interests was
common. As noted earlier, commune revenues depended in part on the well-
being of enterprises in the area, while firms required both standard commune
services (schools, roads, and other infrastructure features) and the aid of local
officials to ensure them necessary investment credits. Thus, despite the tendency of market pressures to force enterprises and political authorities apart,
the planned, hierarchical method of investment allocation pushed them right
back together again, often at the expense of the larger national community.

Since the commune was, indeed, the "basic socioeconomic community," it
was simultaneously the closest political body to the enterprises and the
political unit most dependent on their profitability. Hence, it was the logical
ally of local enterprises in the competition for politically dispensed investment credits. While less profitable firms used the commune to garner subsidies
from national funds, communes containing more efficient enterprises pres-
sured for an allocation of resources on more "rational" economic grounds.
Moreover, this regional cleavage all too frequently coincided with the ethnic
cleavages so destructive of Balkan politics in the past; aggregation of interests
on the republic level further encouraged the trend. As Valdimir Bakarić, a
member of the Central Committee of the Yugoslav League of Communists

(LCY), noted, "In the race for funds, which must be gotten from somebody, arguments behind people's backs quickly become nationalistic."[28] Ultimately, these cleavages were to prove fatal to the entire system of investment planning.

SELF-MANAGEMENT IN OPERATION: IDEOLOGY, THE POLITICAL CLIMATE, AND THE LEAGUE OF COMMUNISTS

In theory, hierarchical and market mechanisms of resource allocation in Yugoslavia were to hold each other in equilibrium. In practice, the tensions produced were, in the 1950s, usually resolved in favor of the state. Meanwhile, however, ideology continued to declare "bureaucratism" the major obstacle to socialism and the enemy of the "working class," promising that the state must "increasingly transfer its own functions to the independent agencies and organizations of the workers."[29]

The stress on "productive labor" remained the order of the day, receiving a new impetus in the mid-fifties with the campaign to achieve "distribution according to work," designed to increase labor productivity through the universal application of piece rates and tying workers' incomes more closely to enterprise profitability. The emphasis on "building socialism" continued in full force, with industrial expansion (or, to use Gramsci's terms, "advancing production") the central priority. In fact, the "government posed one main goal to the companies, maximum production, high and above the planned level, if possible."[30] Along with these emphases came repeated reminders of the obligations of work collectives to the larger community, appeals to sacrifice for a better future, and constant affirmations of the progress already made. Collective welfare and equality continued to be important values and raising the standard of living a key goal; "socialist commodity production," "social planning," and "workers' self-management" were seen as the paths to attaining them. The use of market mechanisms notwithstanding, the political climate was one of unity, mobilization, and collectivism, stressing participation and involvement while discouraging nonconformity, be it in the problematic guise of particularism or in the more benign shape of abstract expressionism.[31] If ideology continued to announce the imminent withering away of the state, the frequency of such pronouncements and the authority with which they were made suggested that the state was still very much present.

Making ideology into a reality and bringing the solidaristic political climate into the midst of the individual work collectives was, first and foremost, the task of the Yugoslav League of Communists. After 1950, however, its role was not patterned on the Stalinist "builder of socialism" model but rather was defined in terms much more closely approximating Gramsci's idea of the collective intellectual.

The party's "new role" was revealed both in a tendency to separate party and political officeholding and in an increasing emphasis on the party as a "factor of consciousness," whose members analyzed conditions and convinced others of party positions without "dictating" to them. Thus, the Sixth Congress declared in 1952: "The basic duty and role of Communists is political and ideological work in educating the masses. . . . The League of Communists is not and cannot be the direct operative manager and commander in economic, state, and social life."[32] Thus, for example, while basic party organizations in the enterprises were to continue to exist, meet, and take positions, they were neither to be a substitute for the workers' council nor to make decisions for it. Rather, their obligations consisted in persuading workers' councils that the party position on a given issue was a correct one.

At the same time, party positions, whether of the Central Committee or the enterprise cell, were to be formulated after open debate and in terms of the broad interests of the "producers as a whole" (to use Gramsci's terminology) and not on behalf of any small subgroup, territorial or productive. Tito himself warned in 1955:

> Many Communists have forgotten, many have been taken up too much with day-to-day difficulties, many have isolated themselves in local frameworks and all too often see everything through financial accounts, important enough, but it shouldn't be everything. . . . Communists must have a higher end before them, and that end is the building of socialism.[33]

In practice, direct party intervention in the "day-to-day difficulties" of enterprises did seem to decline. The number of enterprise directors who were not party members increased, and only about one third of those elected to the workers' councils were in the party.[34] Even the composition of local legislatures indicated that the League of Communists no longer felt it had to maintain a monopoly on office holding: only 62.2 percent of the seats in commune councils were held by party members.[35] At the same time, "passivity" of rank-and-file party activists became a noticeable problem.[36]

Nevertheless, the League of Communists retained a profound influence on policy making and on the general political climate in Yugoslavia throughout this period. Although theoretical pronouncements of party leaders were excluded formally from the discipline of democratic centralism, in fact, all were well aware that "with few exceptions, the theoretical views of individual leaders remained binding." Despite the emphasis on persuasion, the authority of higher party echelons and their influence on state and political bodies remained intact.[37]

Even at the grass-roots level, the fact that the allocation of investment funds depended so heavily on political factors undoubtedly meant that basic party organizations played critical roles as go-betweens in facilitating enterprise or commune claims to credit. But if such a role made the party a force to be reckoned with inside the organization to which it rendered aid, it also tied the basic party cell as closely to the environment it operated in as it did to the party hierarchy to whom it was responsible. As Albert Meister observes,

> Self-management . . . had had the effect of creating a much deeper link between the lower echelons of the party and the mass of workers. The democratization of the enterprises gradually eliminates local League autocrats and stronger popular control is exerted on activists inside the firms and the other institutions of the commune. Through elections, the work collectives get rid of unpopular Communists and . . . recruitment into the League is done on a much healthier basis.[38]

Party organizations did indeed serve as "transmission belts" and helped to bring the policies of individual enterprises and communes into line with broader social goals, even when this involved "convincing" nonparty members to accept "socialist" but economically less advantageous stands. But transmission belts can work in two directions, and the element of "popular control" to which Meister alludes served to bring a good many pluralistic influences into the party itself. Decisions were still made above and implemented below, but with decentralization, self-management, and the party's "new role," the factors now entering into decision making were necessarily much more reflective of conditions at the base than in the pre-1952 days.

If this was more democratic, its consequences were not always socially or politically desirable in the eyes of Yugoslav leaders. Significantly, manifestations of nationalism in the party began to be criticized as early as 1953. They continued to crop up throughout the ensuing decade, and the organization of the League of Communists on territorial lines at all levels above the enterprise hardly ameliorated the problem.

Nor was ethnic chauvinism the only difficulty. In 1958, Tito admonished party members:

> They are not supposed to permit bureaucratic methods and various localistic tendencies to obstruct the proper and normal development of the social community as a whole. . . . Communists are not supposed to permit an economic organization or unit, because of its own selfish goals, to operate at the expense of the social community. . . . I say this because today such things occur and the responsibility for such phenomena to

a large extent belongs to Communists, who often not only permit but even support these mistakes.[39]

Economic and political decentralization brought not only the tendencies of particularism and localism into the party, but also the pressures of enterprises for greater autonomy and more control over the "value" their "productive labor" created. The advocates of this latter position were, first and foremost, the younger and better trained cadres, committed to modernization and economic rationalization, frustrated by administrative and political obstacles, and jealous of the power still retained by less qualified former partisans entrenched in political offices. If but a small minority within the party, they were also a growing one (table 2).

Table 2. Skilled and Professional Labor as a Percentage of Total
LCY Membership, 1958–65

Year	Highly Skilled Workers[a]	College or University Degree[a]
1958	5.2	6.1
1961	6.8	8.0
1962	7.5	9.7
1963	8.0	11.1
1964	8.3	12.6
1965	8.9	14.1

Source: Miloš Nikolić, Savez komunista Jugoslavije u uslovima samoupravljanja (Belgrade: Kultura, 1967), pp. 775–76.
[a]Note that not all of these members were employed within the "economy."

Furthermore, based in the enterprises or in associations close to them,[40] such technical and managerial cadres could indeed claim to be closer to the "direct producer" and the "real economic life" of the country than were government bureaucrats. Ultimately, they were to take the ideology of antibureaucratism and productive labor at its word in the 1965 reforms, designed to reduce the state permanently to a highly peripheral economic role at both the microeconomic and macroeconomic level.

SELF-MANAGEMENT IN OPERATION: LIFE IN THE ENTERPRISES

The question, of course, is to what extent the political forces seeking greater enterprise autonomy actually represented both what theoretically should have been enterprise interests and what the interests of the enterprises were as perceived and articulated by the work collectives and the workers' councils elected to represent them. That is, did Yugoslav enterprises internally correspond to Gramsci's prototype of the productive community, and if so, to what extent did solidarity manifest itself in a demand for greater independence?

As in the Gramsci model, solidarity in the firm in Yugoslavia was to rest on collaboration in and rationalization of production. As we have seen, workers' councils were not established as an alternative to the division of labor. Rather than eliminating the highly specialized character of modern technology and labor, workers' councils, in the eyes of Yugoslav leaders, were to be mechanisms through which the workers themselves were expected to adopt and perfect a more rationalized and narrower division of labor. Equality was to be based on each member of the work collective being "equally necessary" to production; it was very definitely not to be the primitive equality of the leveler, who would wipe out all differences between different types of workers.[41]

Similarly, although authority was now to be held by the workers' council of the enterprise and, less directly, by the people's committee of the local government, hierarchy was to remain inside the production process. An elected management, operating in a purely functional capacity, would coordinate day-to-day activities. In other words, formal and legal authority was to be exercised by the elected representatives of the workers; "professional" authority, however, would continue to be a functional prerogative of the firm's management. Hierarchy in the organization would remain, but now the hierarchy would be responsive to the claims of those at the base of the pyramid.

Insofar as Yugoslav work collectives shared these features with Gramsci's productive communities, it is quite understandable and legitimate that unequal rates of participation and unequal degrees of influence characterized enterprise decision making. While inequalities of influence are problematic for the Proudhon model of workers' control, which is based on a quantitative equality of inputs, the framework put forth by Gramsci, where equality is based on a qualitative principle, permits and even encourages the formation of an intraenterprise elite. If the goal of "production for use" is better served by overrepresenting skilled labor or any other subgroup on workers' councils, this is quite permissible within the Gramsci schema. Likewise, it is completely legitimate for managerial personnel to have a disproportionate share of influence. What is important, however, is that influential groups not use their power to transform themselves into closed elites, pursuing their own interests at the expense of the productive unit as a whole. "Solidarity in production" does not preclude leadership, but leadership must not destroy solidarity itself.

That an elite existed in most Yugoslav enterprises seems undeniable. Highly skilled and skilled workers were greatly overrepresented on workers' councils, and the composition of the managing boards was even more highly skewed in favor of more educated categories of labor.[42] Further, available evidence indicates that managerial personnel, while presumably not a large part of the elected membership of the self-management bodies, had a disproportionate degree of de facto influence on decision making.[43] Party members were also elected in disproportionate numbers to self-management bodies; at the same time, more educated cadres tended to join the League of Communists in greater numbers than did workers in lower skill brackets.[44] All these factors contributed to the formation of a technicopolitical elite in the enterprises.[45] Yet Yugoslav leaders were not, it appears, very upset about these trends and, in fact, encouraged them. Duro Salaj, a leader of the Trade Union Federation, explained the disproportionate number of skilled and white-collar workers elected to managing boards: "This shows that experience had taught the work collectives that the managing board's work is very complex and a great deal of knowledge is required for decisions to be made correctly."[46]

Given that an intraenterprise elite, whose social composition was quite similar to what one would expect in a work collective operating along the lines of the Gramsci model, was a general phenomenon, to what extent did this elite actually represent the "interests" of their constituency in Gramsci's sense? An answer would depend primarily on two sets of factors: the extent to which decisions made by this elite met the criteria prescribed by Gramsci as to the "objective" interests of the "producers" (did they lead to industrial expansion, greater productivity, new "modes of production," and a higher standard of living?); and the extent to which decisions represented the subjective wishes of the members of the larger work collective (did they help to create and/or maintain solidarity in the firm? did they reflect and constitute a response to pressures from below?).

Evaluating "Objective" Representation

With regard to the first question, global data on the overall performance of the Yugoslav economy do indeed show a high rate of growth, industrial expansion, an increase in the standard of living, and a shift of employment from the primary into the secondary and tertiary spheres of the economy. The annual growth rate averaged 8.7 percent from 1952 through 1966, and the growth of industrial production outpaced even this, with an average annual rate of increase of 11.7 percent for the same period. The structure of national income changed radically from its prewar composition, with industry accounting for 46.4 percent of the national income in 1961. Employment in

industry also grew at an annual rate of 5.3 percent from 1953 to 1966, and
"during the same period, labor productivity rose an average of about 4.0
percent—a surprising achievement when employment was also rising."[47]

Moreover, even while around 30 percent of the "social product" was invested annually, both public and private standards of living rose continuously.
Real income of workers and employees climbed (table 3), food consumption
increased absolutely while constituting a declining percentage of individual
incomes, and from 1956 to 1960, the number of personal savings deposits rose
by 50 percent and their total value quintupled. Other indices of physical
welfare also show an upward trend. Public welfare also improved. Expanded
health facilities caused mortality rates to drop, while an improved and enlarged education system saw illiteracy decline and the quality of the labor force
rise.[48]

Table 3. Nominal and Real Personal Incomes of
Workers and Employees,
1956-61 (Monthly Averages in Dinars;
1960 = 100 for Real Income)[a]

	Workers[b]			Employees[c]		
	Total		Nominal	Total		Nominal
Year	Nominal	Real	regular[d]	Nominal	Real	regular
1956	9,780	71	9,230	12,770	66	11,730
1957	11,620	83	10,340	16,320	81	13,750
1958	12,270	81	10,960	16,870	83	14,890
1959	13,800	91	12,500	19,620	94	17,220
1960	16,300	100	14,820	23,240	100	20,560
1961	18,860	105	17,190	27,850	110	24,690

Source: George Macesich, *Yugoslavia: The Theory and Practice of Development Planning*
(Charlottesville: The University Press of Virginia, 1964), p. 24. Reprinted by permission
of the University Press of Virginia, Charlottesville.

[a]Data is based on surveys covering 227 selected enterprises engaged in manufacturing,
mining, and quarrying that employ 33 percent of the labor force engaged in industry;
105 agricultural enterprises that employ about 15 percent of those engaged in agriculture;
39 building enterprises with about 26 percent of the persons employed in this sector;
813 trade and board-and-lodging service establishments employing 31 percent of people
engaged in this activity.

[b]Workers are those engaged primarily in manual work in manufacturing processes,
trade, and transportation.

[c]Employees are those engaged in what are considered intellectual activities. Managers,
technicians, and clerical workers are included in the employee category.

[d]Nominal regular refers to income prior to distribution of profit-sharing bonuses.
Neither set of figures includes benefits such as transportation, children's allowances, etc.

To what degree workers' self-management was a factor in producing this impressive record is much more difficult to say, since it is impossible to separate out the effects of workers' councils' decisions from the effects of a host of other variables which may well have had a more significant impact on economic performance. For example, the high growth rate may have been more a function of the politically determined high rate of investment, the lion's share of which was channeled into industry, than of the decisions of workers' councils. Economic decentralization and the limited use of the market also undoubtedly accounted for a more rational allocation of resources than would have been true under central planning, with or without workers' councils.[49]

Nevertheless, Yugoslav leaders clearly believed that the introduction of workers' self-management was a major factor in stimulating economic development,[50] a belief that contributed to the growing influence of the enterprise elites favoring greater plant-level autonomy. Moreover, some empirical evidence supports the contention that the councils were in fact using the discretion they did have to "expand" and "rationalize" production, as Yugoslav leaders wished and Gramsci would have expected.

Partially, this could be seen in the way enterprises chose to allocate the share of profits they disposed of autonomously. Data here leaves a good deal to be desired, but the results of a trade union survey of 101 enterprises from various economic sectors suggests that despite the low standard of living, enterprises nonetheless chose to spend a good portion of these funds on investment in fixed and working capital rather than distributing them back as wages (see table 4). Additional evidence on the orientation of workers' councils (table 5) indicates that the gradual easing up of external regulation of enterprise funds in the late fifties and early sixties was accompanied by increased, if hesitant, self-financing of investment, as well as by an increase in wages.[51] It is also worth noting the conclusion of a study done by the Institute for Social Sciences:

> The largest number of workers sees the positive effects of workers' management in the raising of labor productivity (25%), in its influence on the policy of distribution of personal incomes (25%), in the improvement of the living standard (24%), and in the prevention of the willfulness of some individuals (7%).[52]

The distribution of the bonuses derived from end-year profits (the "variable" portion of wages) would appear to constitute another sign of the workers' councils' tendencies to "rationalize production." Wachtel analyzed interskill differentials for 1956, 1959, and 1961.

Table 4. Enterprise Use of Autonomous Funds, 1954–56

	In 000 Dinars	Percent
For economic investment	4,032,638	41.0
For investment in the social standard (consumption)	2,765,654	28.6
Donations to social and sports organizations	944,950	10.0
Others (donations to commune funds, legal obligations, advertising, etc.)	1,921,635	20.4
Total	9,664,877	100.0

Source: Slavko Luković, "Ekonomsko poslovanje radničkih saveta," in Kongres radničkih saveta, ed. A. DeLeon and L. Mijatović (Belgrade: Rad, 1957), p. 259.

Table 5. Sources of Gross Investment for 1953 and 1960
(In Millions of Dinars)

Sources	1953	Percent	1960	Percent
Autonomous investment[a]	213,405	62.7	465,944	52.9
Internal financing	37,093	10.9	182,691	20.8
Depreciation	74,529	21.8	145,175	16.3
Other social funds	14,652	4.3	50,189	5.7
Total[b]	340,622	100.0	879,450	100.0

Source: Svetozar Pejovich, The Market-Planned Economy of Yugoslavia (Minneapolis: University of Minnesota Press, 1966), p. 70.
[a]General Investment Fund, investment funds of People's Republics, and investments of local governments.
[b]Including investments financed through budgets.

For all years there is a substantially greater interskill wage differential for the variable wage component than there is for the fixed wage component. For example, in 1959, the high-wage category received a variable wage nearly six and one-half times greater than the lowest wage category, but a fixed wage less than three times greater.[53]

Further, he argues, insofar as "the differentials in the variable wage are closer to unemployment rate differentials than are the differentials in the fixed wage,"[54] the favoritism shown to more educated strata in profit distribution was a deliberate attempt to adjust enterprise wage structures to the conditions of a competitive labor market in order to attract specialists rather than a "capricious exercise of power" by the more highly skilled elite predominating in the self-management organs. The large number of courses and scholarships set up by firms to train workers[55] as well as the high degree of labor turnover among more highly qualified workers and employees also suggests that if intraenterprise elites had privileges, they were certainly willing to share them where enterprise development was concerned.

Sociological studies also demonstrate that the dynamics of workers' council meetings corresponded fairly closely with what Gramsci prescribed for his factory councils. Živan Tanić's content analyses of workers' council minutes of seven industrial firms over a ten-year period (1950-60) shows that the frequency of meetings increased, as did the diversity of areas of council concern. While the initial establishment of workers' councils was marked by a great deal of discussion and some hesitation over what the self-management organs were supposed to do, this confusion over tasks and functions gradually receded into the background, and concrete problems of economic operation of the firm took their place.[56] Meister notes the same tendency:

> The workers' council has become less and less an organism of representation (representative of the interests of the various personnel categories)—which corresponded to the egalitarian tendencies of the councils in the first years of their existence—in order to become increasingly a managerial organ, open to the most knowledgeable elements of the work collective, those likely to contribute personally to enterprise management more than to articulate demands from below.[57]

Significantly, Tanić also found that the issues workers' councils devoted the most time to were by and large those connected with "rationalizing production": determining product mixes, setting plan targets, modernizing both the technology and the organization of work, and so on.[58] In view of the many restrictions and regulations on other aspects of firm behavior, this is hardly surprising: determining its production function was the one area in which workers' councils had full autonomy. Again, however, the parallel with Gramsci's factory councils is close.

If, then, we can accept for the most part a willingness on the part of intraenterprise, technicopolitical elites to pursue the "objective" interests of the "working class," as defined by Gramsci (and the Yugoslav leadership), to what extent were workers' "subjective" interests satisfied? Relying again on Gramsci's model of the productive community, the chief criterion would seem to be the level of solidarity prevailing in Yugoslav work collectives, with high solidarity indicating a greater coincidence between subjective and "objective" interests of the work collective.

Evaluating "Subjective" Representation

Behavioral indices of enterprise solidarity indicate that it was well below what Gramsci would have deemed desirable. Labor turnover and absenteeism were extremely high, and civil suits brought by employees against their enterprises increased in these years.[59] Survey research and participant observer studies confirm the impression that the rank-and-file labor force was only peripherally involved in the life of the enterprises. Lack of both information and a general interest in enterprise affairs seem especially pronounced in the case of unskilled workers.[60]

A key cause of this apparent indifference toward the work collective lies in Yugoslavia's past underdevelopment. Where Gramsci by and large assumed workers' democracy would find its chief support in a politically conscious, experienced, industrial working class, Yugoslavia had no such class at the time self-management was introduced. Industrial workers had to be recruited from the peasantry, which meant not only that a large proportion were unskilled and unaccustomed to the rhythms and rigors of industrial life, but also that many retained their ties to the land even while they held full-time jobs outside of agriculture. According to the 1953 census, 21 percent of the labor force in manufacturing were such peasant-workers, as were 38 percent of the miners and 17 percent of the transport workers; all in all, 38 percent of unskilled Yugoslav workers lived in villages but were employed outside of agriculture.[61] Moreover, the expansion of industrial employment, combined with mechanization of agriculture, discrimination against private peasants in the distribution of social benefits, and a severe housing shortage, encouraged the continuation of this state of affairs.

The high proportion of peasant workers in the industrial labor force goes a long way toward explaining the chronic absenteeism and labor turnover in Yugoslav firms. Typically, absenteeism rose during planting and harvest times; turnover was high, in part, because peasants would often accept industrial employment only long enough to qualify for the health and pension benefits guaranteed to industrial workers.[62]

The reasons for the lack of subjective involvement in enterprise life also became clearer. Since most peasant-workers saw even full-time industrial employment as merely a second job, they were understandably much less interested in the firm's operation than were those who depended on it for all of their income. Undoubtedly this led to a certain amount of friction between the two groups, and perhaps the occasional cases of "bureaucratism" in workers' councils were symptomatic of the latent conflict.[63]

The scarcity of educated manpower was only the other side of the under-

development coin and helps to account for the high turnover among the more
highly skilled and urbanized categories of blue-collar and white-collar personnel.[64] Enterprises competed fiercely to attract and hold educated cadres,
causing interskill differentials to widen. Morevoer, necessity forced many firms
to fill higher managerial and technical positions with people who lacked professional qualifications.[65] All too often, authoritarianism substituted for qualifications, causing conflict between workers and management. The dependence of enterprises on external political agents who tended to deal with firm
directors and bypass the workers' councils altogether merely aggravated the
situation.[66]

   If this analysis is correct, what is surprising is not that the kind of cohesiveness predicted by Gramsci failed to materialize in Yugoslav work collectives
but rather that there was any sense of identification at all with the work place.
Judged from this perspective, the evidence is much more encouraging. Given
a plethora of mass organizations and political institutions all attempting to "involve" a highly apathetic "producer" in one way or other, the enterprise
seems to have been the only one that succeeded at all in making its claim
valid. Thus, Miloš Ilić, in a cross-republic study of over five thousand workers,
found that workers of all skill levels were far more willing to "struggle against
inadequacies and negative phenomena" in their enterprises than in the local
government.[67]

   Even unskilled workers generally expressed interest in eventually being
elected to a self-management body; both Meister and Kolaja report high attendance at meetings of the entire work collective.[68] If suits brought against
firms were on the rise, prosecutions for "economic crimes" dropped sharply.[69]
To the degree that simply doing one's job can be interpreted within the
Gramsci definition as an index of solidarity, the productivity increases and
industrial advances cited earlier can legitimately be attributed to the efforts
of the rank-and-file labor force as well as to the managerial capabilities of the
workers' councils and executives. And it is doubtful that the allocation of
profits to capital expenses rather than to wages was accomplished over the
opposition of the work collectives, even if it undoubtedly was not always
accompanied by wild enthusiasm. DeLeon, in fact, cites a survey of nonsupervisory workers made in 1959:

> 38% considered that the enterprise should allocate more to the funds
> for reconstruction, 34% were in favor of the increase of investments for
> other purposes, and only 13% thought that the net income should be
> allocated to personal incomes.[70]

In addition, despite the frequent warnings of the Yugoslav leadership against "bureaucratism" in workers' councils, work collectives appear for the most part to have been satisfied with their operation. This conclusion follows from survey data, case studies, and the fact that representatives were, after all, elected (and reelected) in at least partially competitive elections. Meister reports that most of the workers he interviewed felt that activists had no tendency to isolate themselves, perceived the council as an organ that represented them, and generally did not think that it unduly favored the economic expansion of the firm at the expense of their interests.[71] Other studies confirm these findings.[72]

Management also generally received favorable ratings, another sign of "collaboration in production." Here, however, the social distance from the rank-and-file worker was greater, especially in the case of higher executive personnel, and complaints were more frequent. Nevertheless, for the most part, these complaints took the form of desires for more on-the-job consultation with the work force and for greater expertise on the part of supervisors. They were not, under any interpretation, protests against too narrow a division of labor or the hierarchical organization of production. In fact,

> the majority of workers not only have nothing against strong supervisors but actually show greater sympathy for them than towards "milder" and "softer" supervision. . . . The data in connection with this problem indicate that it is actually a question of realizing the principle of "the right man at the right place."[73]

Note that these complaints suggest a good deal of implicit support for the attempts of workers' councils to attract more highly qualified labor. And despite these complaints, the attachment of work collectives to their executives was dramatically revealed in 1966, when, despite a major party campaign to replace less qualified managerial personnel with the new crop of university graduates, only 2 to 5 percent of all firm directors failed to be reelected.[74]

There are other reasons for suspecting that plant solidarity and elite-base links were better than the turnover and absenteeism rates would imply. If interskill differentials were getting larger, a high rate of increase of real income at all levels undoubtedly blunted their impact on plant solidarity (table 3). As noted earlier, work collectives by and large appear to have been quite supportive of getting "the right man for the right place." In addition, egalitarian ideological pressures, the activity of the trade unions and enterprise party organizations, the supervisory role of the commune, and the pressures from below all worked to keep skill differentials within single enterprises at approximately a 1 : 4 ratio, reasonably small by Western standards.[75] Added to this were the equalizing effects of family allowances, social services, and various fringe benefits. Indeed, if we examine the data displayed on worker-employee differentials in table 3, it seem that although firms probably employed a few very highly paid engineers, economists, and executives, the bulk of the blue-collar and white-collar labor force enjoyed substantial income equality even after the effect of the differential "variable" wage is taken into account. This would presumably tend to minimize the traditional office-plant antagonism and enhance a solidaristic relationship.

Ideology, which stressed "productive" labor, the importance of blue-collar workers, and a spirit of collective sacrifice for a better future, also contributed to a sense of solidarity in the plant; kept in workers' minds by enterprise party cells, it provided a rationale for limiting consumption in favor of investment. The requirement that firms submit an annual plan to local authorities meant that a clear and concrete goal was constantly before the eyes of the work collective. Under the banner of completing and overfulfilling plan targets, a rallying point was easily available for launching periodic campaigns to raise productivity, with the by-product of creating a solidaristic work climate. Adizes gives one description of the atmosphere in the firms in the pre-1965 days:

> In the past, *udarnici* and *heroji rada*, the work heroes who . . . could double and triple the norm, were given special recognition and privileges. The companies' goal had been to complete a specified plan as early as possible, and the heroes were instrumental in this effort. With obvious sorrow in their voices, several workers told the researcher of the era of festivity . . . when the company's siren would announce that a production plan had not only been realized but surpassed.[76]

Workers may well have been uninformed of specific plan targets, but one suspects from this description that it would have been difficult for them to escape knowing whether or not plan goals had been attained. In this sense, even information levels may have been higher than survey research indicates.[77]

SOLIDARITY AND AUTONOMY

While we can conclude from this that self-management succeeded in creating at least an island of involvement amidst a sea of apathy and that the intra-enterprise elites did by and large reflect the underlying wishes of the rank-and-file to the latter's satisfaction, we must also note that plant solidarity in Yugoslavia was not solely the product of "collaboration to produce." To the extent that the market mechanism operated in Yugoslavia—and, as we have seen, it was considerable on the labor market—it was designed to give workers a material incentive to "rationalize production" along with the moral ones ideology supplied. Workers might well be proud of the contribution their labor made to society and the firm, but this clearly was not the reason they arrived at the factory gates in the morning. While they could easily be convinced of the need for newer and more sophisticated machinery, a better trained labor force, higher productivity, and specialization and improvement of the product line, it was much more difficult to persuade them that these "advances" in production had to come out of their own paychecks. Whereas realizing income through more and better production helped to tie the work collective together, distributing it was an apple of discord.

Yet although workers' council members and higher executives tended to take a more indulgent view of low wages and widening differentials, they themselves were hardly unsympathetic to the pressures emanting from below to allocate less of the profits to investment and to introduce more equality.[78] What exacerbated the problem was that firms, after paying a crushing tax burden and allocating required monies to the proper funds, had little left to distribute. Not only did outside interference and regulations directly cause difficulties in the areas of production, investment, and even in self-management processes themselves, but political controls unavoidably took their toll on the pattern of income distribution. Significantly, the demands of the first major worker protest for higher wages, the 1958 strike at Trbovlje, were directed neither at the firm's workers' council nor at its management, but were aimed at the Federal Price Commission, which finally responded by raising the price of coal.

The weight of government was felt not only in the allocation of capital and the regulations affecting wage levels, but also in the growth of what was officially "nonproductive" (tertiary sector) employment,[79] much of which was financed by the taxes levied on the firms. Furthermore, "noneconomic"[80] activities competed with enterprises for skilled labor; as the former tended to be concentrated in urban areas to a greater extent than industry was, they enjoyed a competitive edge in recruitment, aggravating the differentials problem in the "economy." Although ideology continued to assign the creation of "value" to those engaging in "productive" labor, its control was quite another matter—especially in the eyes of the work collectives affected.

As it became increasingly difficult to reconcile the conflicting pressures from above and below while simultaneously insuring the rational and optimal operation of the enterprise, the position of workers' councils, executives, and enterprise sociopolitical leaders became more and more untenable. Faced with legitimate demands for greater material incentives from below and calls for higher productivity from above, seeking to allocate investment and working capital rationally and without external interference, feeling themselves able to deal independently with internal problems when permitted to, and frustrated by continually changing laws and declarations made by a political apparatus paid for by the "value" the enterprises created yet whose actions they could not control, enterprise elites found the obvious solution was to press for greater firm autonomy.[81]

Moreover, insofar as this pressure was itself a response to the demands of the base for higher earnings, it can rightly be considered a manifestation of plant agreement and solidarity. In addition, when presented as an anti-bureaucratic way of allowing the "producers" to control directly the "value" they created and purporting to "rationalize production" more efficiently than a slow-moving and often unpredictable state apparatus would, demands for greater autonomy could indeed strike a strong chord of resonance in the heart of a work collective whose members were traditionally oriented towards blaming distant authorities for their troubles. Thus, while enterprise elites and their political allies may well have articulated the demands for greater enterprise autonomy, they probably had at least the passive support of the work collectives they claimed to represent and undoubtedly made these demands partially in response to the pressures of these same work collectives.

THE END OF INVESTMENT PLANNING

As Yugoslav self-management moved into its second decade, three basic conflicts emerged:

1. Among organizations based on production principles. These conflicts involved firms in favored sectors (those with lower turnover taxes, favorable interest rates, higher product prices, and so on) and those in less favored branches (primarily outside of manufacturing).

2. Between organizations based on production principles and those based on territorial principles. These conflicts occurred between enterprises—allied with economic chambers, professional associations, and to some extent, the trade unions—on the one side, and on the other, various units of government and party at national and subnational levels.

3. Among organizations based on territorial principles. These were disputes between subnational units of government in different regions and at different levels of the federal system.

In the Yugoslav context, the first of these was the least critical for the system as a whole, because, unlike Gramsci's factory councils, Yugoslav enterprises

did not directly wield political power. Hence, not only did they rarely confront each other directly in the race for funds,[82] as territorial units had to,
but more and less successful firms both could often find common cause by
blaming the government for whatever ills afflicted them. The ideology of productive labor, making a neat distinction between the "economy" and other
activities, helped to weld this alliance, which had its material foundations in
the inevitable interdependence between manufacturing industries and raw
material suppliers. That is, the politically chosen policy of favoring manufacturing had resulted, by the 1960s, in a situaiton whereby the

> manufacturing industries developed even though they had no raw material
> basis of their own. Owing to the restricted scope of the home market,
> the inadequate policy of prices and inadequate import value of the dinar,
> most of the manufacturing industries have a low productivity and turn
> out too wide a range of articles.[83]

Furthermore, many plants operated well below capacity because of shortages
of materials or power. In this sense, both favored and nonfavored sectors
came to feel that they stood to gain from an investment and price system that
more fully mirrored market realities.[84]

But if the system's first latent conflict had a happy ending, this was not so
for the other two. The productive-territorial conflict expressed itself most
fully in the debate over incentives, a discussion gradually consuming increasing
amounts of Yugoslavia's political energy.[85] The problem occurred on two
levels: increasing the productivity of individual workers and stimulating enterprises to cut costs, introduce efficient technology, and use capital rationally.
As we have seen, in the eyes of many enterprises, the two aspects of the problem were related and both were best solved by diminishing the scope of
political decision making in the economy. As far as individual workers were
concerned, if there were no longer a politically determined high rate of forced
savings—or if, still politically, the rate were simply reduced and enterprise
autonomy thereby increased—work collectives might be able to devote a larger
part of their earnings to consumption. Theoretically, such a move would put
teeth into the piece-rate bonus system and "income-sharing" plans put into
effect in the late fifties, thus stimulating workers to produce more in the hope
of receiving significantly higher wages. For the enterprises, greater control
over profits meant lower taxes (and hence a greater incentive to make a profit
in the first place), a more predictable source of funding (their own reserves),
and prices more reflective of supply and demand than of the prejudices of
government officials.[86]

Others, however, whose source of power was largely in the state administration and party bureaucracy at both local and national levels,[87] took a less sanguine view of increasing enterprise autonomy. In part, this attitude simply reflected an unwillingness to relinquish the "bureaucratic privileges" many political functionaries enjoyed, although one suspects that this motive was overplayed a good deal by the promarket forces once they emerged victorious. More profoundly, it arose out of serious doubts of the actual ability of the market to produce results in accordance with the social goals that they, as political representatives of society, were responsible for achieving. If raising wages might stimulate individual productivity, it might also produce inflation. Higher labor costs could indeed encourage a more rational allocation of man-power, but local officials would be left with the responsibility for the unemployment it left in its wake. Giving the producers greater control over the "surplus value" they created was a laudable objective, but eliminating bureaucracy might also entail cutting the social standard of living, especially since it was in the areas of culture, education, and social welfare that "noneconomic" employment had expanded in the 1950s.

If the territorial-production conflict had been the only economic dispute, it is doubtful that the 1965 reforms would have ever taken place. Unlike those in the pure Gramsci system, enterprises in Yugoslavia simply lacked the political power needed to push through a change of such magnitude. Even here, they were divided as to the extent of the independence they wanted. The desire for more enterprise autonomy came through loud and clear at the 1957 Workers' Council Congress, but it was equally true that a large number of firms pushing for "augmenting the material base of self-management"[88] simply wanted freer access to government coffers.

Furthermore, although the enactment of the 1963 Constitution and subsequent elections strengthened the political representation in the Federal Assembly of organizations based on production principles, advocates of increased enterprise autonomy in the League of Communists could only bring about a protracted stalemate over economic policy in its highest bodies. In short, it was not enough for the market to appear as a desirable alternative to even the most dynamic and prosperous sectors of Yugoslav society; planning had to become unworkable.

Here the regional debate and the conflicts between subnational units of government assumed critical significance; by the 1960s, competition for funds was becoming increasingly tense and threatened to pull Yugoslavia's deep-rooted ethnic hostilities back onto the political stage. If political leaders could by and large agree on the abstract principle that investment planning was desirable, this meant little if they could no longer agree on investment priorities.[89] While incentive policies were at the heart of the enterprise-government cleavage, the development strategy was at issue in the regional debate.

A key economic goal of Yugoslav development policy had always been to reduce the disparities in regional living standards while maintaining a high rate of growth. The agreed-upon method for doing so had been to inject, through the centralized General Investment Fund, large doses of capital to poorer areas with the intention of helping them to "catch up" with the rest of the country. By the early sixties, however,

> the richer regions appeared to be tiring of the development policy. Despite relatively high investment outlays in relation to the share of the republics in national income . . . the relative position of the less developed republics declined. The advanced regions saw little reason to continue the existing policies of high rates of investment with the attendant high rates of taxes that, in their view, cut incentives and thus resulted in lower national rates of growth than would have been achieved with lower rates of investment used more efficiently.[90]

Accordingly, developed regions argued for allocation of investment funds based on market criteria of profitability, except perhaps for some small portion that would, in effect, be a form of "aid." Poorer areas, however, were much more dubious about the proposed reliance on the market.

It was hardly accidental that the production-territorial conflict coincided at many points with the developed-underdeveloped cleavage. The more successful enterprises tended to be concentrated in the more advanced republics; these were the firms—ironically, some of the chief beneficiaries of past investment policies and politically manipulated prices—who were finding government regulation more and more cumbersome.

The regional conflict between subnational units of representation was complicated by another cleavage among territorial units: the dispute between local planning units and national authorities. We have already seen the serious economic consequences of localism in the "first cell" of the socialist state, consequences increasingly worrisome for national political leaders. Especially after 1961, when decentralization of the banking system in response to local pressures made investment allocation even more vulnerable to narrow territorial demands, indiscriminate expansion of credit precipitated a heavy round of inflation. Centralization at the national level, however, was no longer a viable alternative, thanks to the regional conflict, entrenched local patronage networks, and enterprise pressures for greater autonomy.[91] Nor, at this stage,

were the republics viewed as suitable substitutes for the commune, for it
was feared that strengthening the former's authority would merely intensify
the centrifugal-separatist tendencies already coming to the fore in the regional
dispute. Significantly, although the 1962 integration campaign had a measure of success in breaking the power of local officials over industry, it was
unable to produce any mergers across republic boundaries.

The inability of Yugoslav leaders to agree on how investment funds should
be allocated was thus complemented by a failure to find a viable political
unit to do the allocating. Moreover, the difficulty in achieving a political consensus was threatening the unity of the Yugoslav League of Communists
itself. The party's "new role" and its responsiveness to the territorial and economic divisions meant that even its status as the one truly national force in
Yugoslavia was in jeopardy. Indeed, a letter of the LCY Executive Committee
in 1962 in effect admitted that "opposition of the republic parties to federal
policies which were contrary to local interests had gone so far that the Central
Committee was no longer assured its directives would be obeyed."[92]

At the same time, the chronic inflation, decrease in the growth rate, and
worsening balance of payments that appeared after the compromise reform of
1961 made it clear that the combination of administrative intervention and
market mechanisms in an uncoordinated and arbitrary way was no longer
feasible. The deteriorating economic situation made increasingly urgent the
search for an impersonal mechanism of resource allocation and economic coordination able to break the power of localism without recentralizing it at the
national level.

As the battle lines were drawn, on one side were the forces representing
enterprise aspirations for greater autonomy, generally composed of organizations without direct political power and organized along production principles: firms, economic chambers, professional associations, trade unions.[93]
Not surprisingly, those firms who had been most successful under the system
of the 1950s were most prepared and anxious to move to "a new stage" of
"socialist development." These forces, although increasingly influential within
the party, would not have been strong enough in and of themselves to
overcome the still considerable sentiment for planning and centralized investment planning. Added to them, however, were the political leaders of the
more advanced areas. Because their base was territorial and hence political in
the Yugoslav system, they could more successfully translate the "value" created
within the areas under their jurisdiction into national political influence.
Enhancing their position was ideological self-righteousness: in view of their
contribution to national income, they could indeed claim to speak on behalf
of the interests of "productive labor," and the widely recognized pressures

for higher wages on the part of workers in all regions helped to legitimize them further. In addition, they were able to garner important pockets of support from the underdeveloped regions, where a number of enterprises and political leaders felt that they stood to gain from a price structure that would not discriminate against primary-goods producers. Skillful playing of the nationalist card by veiled allusions to "Serbian hegemony" helped cement the alliance.[94]

On the other side were the centralizers: a good part of the political leaders of the less developed republics and regions, a significant segment of the party apparatus,[95] and many of the firms born of and dependent on political subsidies and favoritism. But, in effect, the mere existence of such a conflict signaled that they were on the losing side. Like central planning in workers' democracy, centrally planned investment was possible in Yugoslavia only as long as there was agreement among political leaders as to investment priorities and agencies. When such agreement evaporated under the pressures of regional and enterprise aspirations for autonomy, there was no other exit than to allow the market "impersonally" to coordinate economic activity.

As in Gramsci's workers' democracy, such tensions arose in part from self-management's apparent success. Economically, it was precisely the high growth rate, widely attributed to the economic wisdom of workers' councils, which gave enterprise elites the moral force and political credit to press for the autonomy they felt necessary to conduct business effectively. Politically, although Yugoslavia was far from a Western democracy, the system's very responsiveness made it impossible for it to continue in its 1950s form. The result was the head-on collision at the Eighth Party Congress between the forces urging decentralization and those arguing on behalf of planning. Here the issue was resolved in theory, with the decentralizing forces victorious. With the ouster of Ranković and his supporters two years later, the "party of the producers" itself was prepared to lead the transition to a market economy, already codified in the economic reforms of 1965.

4

Market Socialism in Yugoslavia:
The 1965 Reforms and Their Effects

The transition to a market economy in Yugoslavia was a gradual process, accomplished over a period of years and through a succession of political compromises. As a result, the Yugoslav economy was increasingly beginning to resemble a market system a good deal prior to 1965.[1] The reforms of that year, however, constitute something of a watershed in Yugoslav economic and political evolution; it was at this time that the cumulative impact of reforms that quantitatively inched away from planning and hierarchical allocation of resources culminated in a qualitative changeover to an altogether new model of workers' control.

The impact of the 1965 reform was felt on two fronts. First, it greatly increased enterprise autonomy, transforming Yugoslav firms into a close equivalent of Proudon's mutualist associations, whose internal and external relations were to be governed by the laws of the market instead of by the priorities of political bodies. Second, it greatly altered the role of the state in the economy to one that shared a number of similarities with the noninterventionist state proposed by Proudhon. Not only did the reform reduce the instruments the government had previously employed to influence economic behavior, but owing partly to the changed ideology that accompanied the reform and partly to the political conflicts connected with its adoption, the national government failed to make coherent use of the fiscal and monetary powers it continued to enjoy.

The consequences of Yugoslav market socialism were also highly analogous to the consequences produced by Proudhon's mutualism: pronounced economic instability, increasingly apparent inequalities, and growing (in Yugoslavia, frequently nationalistic) pressures for the expanded use of political mechanisms in the allocation of resources. Let us examine in some detail the economic and political changes enacted in the 1965 reforms and in the 1963 Constitution that immediately preceded them as well as their effects on economic performance and politicoeconomic relations. Chapter 5 will analyze their effects on economic equality.

REDEFINING THE RIGHTS TO SOCIAL PROPERTY: THE ENTERPRISE AS A COLLECTIVE ENTREPRENEUR

The reforms of the mid-sixties drastically changed the meaning of "social property" by transferring the lion's share of the control, benefits, and risks associated with its management from the shoulders of the state cum investor to the enterprises as collective entrepreneurs.[2]

First of all, enterprise autonomy was considerably increased by a major reduction in tax rates. Whereas up to 1965, 60 percent of enterprise income went to various government units, now only 30 percent was to be allocated for such purposes, leaving 70 percent of enterprise income for consumption and investment, the relative shares to be determined by enterprise self-management bodies.[3] As additional spurs to enterprise self-financing of investment, the depreciation rate was increased while the capital tax on fixed assets was cut from 6 to 4 percent. Enterprises were also permitted to lend directly to other firms and participate in joint capital ventures, a measure designed to enhance capital mobility.

A major price reform was also undertaken in 1965. It entailed an initial across-the-board price freeze and a gradual relaxation of controls as prices were brought into line with those of the world market. Various direct and indirect price subsidies were greatly reduced, making enterprise income—and hence salaries—far more dependent on market performance than it had been, while causing personal consumption to be tied more closely to actual earnings. In foreign trade, a more realistic, uniform exchange rate was introduced, many quantitative restrictions on imports were removed, and customs duties were cut in half. In addition, a renewed "integration" campaign was launched to make Yugoslav firms more competitive on the world market and more capable of financing their own investment; 12 percent of Yugoslav enterprises merged from 1965 to 1967.[4]

Labor was the only production factor that was individually owned, and pooling it gave workers the right to engage in "collective entrepreneurship." Like Proudhon's mutualism, the new version of Yugoslav market socialism envisioned personal income as a return to labor, the size of this return determined by labor productivity.[5] Land and capital came under the rubric of "social property," which collectives of worker-entrepreneurs merely "managed" for society. Hence, work collectives paid a nominal rent to the local government for the land they used in addition to the (below equilibrium) percent tax/"interest rate" paid on their fixed assets. Moreover, the new system assumed that whatever additional returns to capital the collective acquired would go to financing new investment and not to wages or consumption, although some small portion might legitimately be distributed to workers as a reward for good entrepreneurship. Similarly, losses were conceived of as a penalty for poor entrepreneurship and were to be at least partially borne by the work collective in the form of reduced wages.[6] Autonomy of the firm, then, meant not only that enterprises made their own decisions regarding prices, wages, investment, and other business matters, but also that they bore the consequences of these decisions. Although work collectives would not legally "own" social property, and so were required to maintain and replace it, as collective entrepreneurs they could, to use Proudhon's terminology, "use" or "abuse" it as they saw fit, with the economic incentives and penalties provided by the market as their primary guide.

By becoming collective entrepreneurs, Yugoslav work organizations were to correspond internally in many ways with Proudhon's mutualist associations as well. As the entire work collective was now responsible for managing social property, every member was theoretically to have an equal influence in decision making and equal responsibility for executing decisions. All were to share equally in the results of decision making, be it a profit or a loss: "The producer is no longer a wage earner, but a participant in collective entrepreneurship."[7] Solidarity in the firm, then, was to be the result of the enterprise maximizing its income on the market and distributing it "justly" among its employees, much as in mutualism. The old model of the firm, legitimizing the existence of an intraenterprise elite based on skill and knowledge and pursuing the "interests" of the working class by "advancing" production, now gave way to a new one which in theory did away with "that division of society into two basic classes, i.e., the minority of leaders, and the majority of those who execute orders."[8]

Although each member of the work collective was to be equal in his rights and responsibilities for managing social property and free to leave the collective at any time, labor inputs were not equal. Interskill differentials based on qualifications and the amount and quality of work an individual performed were to be an important part of the incentive system. Labor mobility and the assumption that all individuals had an equal opportunity to acquire skills, however, would theoretically act to keep interskill differentials narrow.

Entry to the market, crucial both for maintaining competition and avoiding the negative effects of an economy composed of producer cooperatives,[9] was to be provided for by the expansion of existing enterprises and by bank loans set at competitive interest rates. Accordingly, reforms were made in the banking system to facilitate the conversion from centralized investment planning to a unitary, competitive capital market. The central General Investment Fund was formally abolished in 1963; in its place, a smaller Fund for Accelerated Development (FAD), into which all enterprises paid a small contribution, was set up as a compromise measure to continue a reduced volume of capital transfers to the underdeveloped republics and provinces. At the same time, "banks, previously administrative agencies for government investment funds, became autonomous, profit-sharing enterprises with capital subscribed to by shareholders (enterprises and government agencies) who manage the bank."[10] Meanwhile, a deflationary credit policy was pursued, signifying the transition from "extensive" to "intensive" growth.

Labor and capital mobility between competitive and autonomous producer associations were thus the main mechanisms the reform proposed for allocating resources efficiently and preventing the formation of large income differentials between regions, sectors, and skill categories. As Proudhon would have it, risk was to be "generalized" and society was to be a system of "equilibrium between free forces." Such a change, however, was not without its consequences for economic performance nor without its implications for the role of the state in the postreform period.

THE ROLE OF THE STATE: FEDERAL ECONOMIC POLICY AND ECONOMIC PERFORMANCE AFTER 1965

As we have seen, the decision to use the market as the basic coordinator of Yugoslav economic life was, in effect, more a decision by default than an act of positive policy. Investment planning was abandoned because political leaders could no longer agree on investment priorities and on who should do the planning; political restrictions on the operation of the market were cut because consensus was lacking on how the market should be restricted and to what extent it could be. The result was not just that the role of political factors and the use of social criteria in economic decision making declined at all levels of the federal pyramid. The failure to reach a basic accord over fundamental economic questions also meant that whatever influence was exerted did not form part of a coherent economic policy, but instead constituted an ad hoc response to whatever adverse effects seemed most pressing at the moment. While the importance of government units as direct economic agents of funding and control declined, their significance as political regulators of economic life through fiscal and monetary policy did not rise correspondingly. Yugoslavia certainly never reduced the state to a mere "federative association" of the Proudhonian type, but what authority was left to it liberty all too often helped to hold in equilibrium.

The preamble of the 1963 Constitution notwithstanding, both federal investment planning and commune planning atrophied, partly because they lacked the economic resources to implement their own policy goals (table 6) and partly because the arsenal of instruments at their disposal to influence the economic behavior of nongovernmental units was so greatly restricted. Theoretically, subsidies and rebates were no longer to be distributed by any

Table 6. Participation in Financing of Fixed Assets, by Source

	1961	1962	1963	1964	1965	1966	1967	1968	1969	1970	1971	1972
Total	100.0	100.0	100.0	100.0	100.0	100.0	100.0	100.0	100.0	100.0	100.0	100.0
Funds of economic organizations	29.5	29.7	27.9	25.9	28.9	39.3	32.7	31.2	28.1	27.1	26.8	29.6
Institutes and others	7.9	7.7	6.7	6.2	7.9	6.6	4.7	6.0	6.4	6.2	7.1	3.0
Banks	0.9	2.9	9.0	31.4	36.6	44.8	44.9	47.1	49.4	51.2	50.9	42.5
Sociopolitical communities	61.7	59.7	56.4	36.5	26.6	15.2	17.7	15.7	15.8	15.5	15.2	19.9

Source: Dragomir Vojnić and Mijo Sekulić, "Odnos privrednog sistema i društveno-ekonomskog razvitka u samoupravnom društvu," *Ekonomski pregled* 25, no. 5–7 (1974):350.

governmental agent, while foreign competition was to be encouraged at the expense of the various import restrictions and export credits available earlier. The turnover tax, which had been used to discourage consumption of some items and stimulate the sale of others, was revised into a tax on retail sales, losing most of its ability to discriminate among economic branches. A Federal Price Control Office continued to function and regulate the prices of goods and services sold on the national product market, but the inflation rate following the reform suggests that its effect was to keep some prices artificially low while price levels on the whole showed a continuous rise.[11]

Meanwhile, a Federal Planning Office continued to churn out five-year plans, annual plans, growth targets, market analyses, and so forth, but these were purely informational, lacking either economic policy or political force to back them up. Local and republic governments, enterprises, administrators of semiautonomous funds, and other economic actors would inform planners of their intentions and goals, enabling a national plan to be drawn up in the first place. However, if their intentions and goals were altered in the course of the planning period, it was the plan which changed, not the behavior of the economic unit. Indeed, the federal government itself led the list of offenders by continuing to covertly spend more for investment through its "extrabudgetary" expenditures than had been provided for in the 1965 plan.[12] Plans, in effect, acquired the status of Proudhon's laws, ex post statements describing what is done, rather than ex ante regulations modifying human behavior. Thus, national planning in Yugoslavia after 1965 bore a closer resemblance to a socialist ritual than to a socialist policy guideline. Even in this regard, it fared badly: since plan forecasts were inaccurate and plan goals unattained, planning had a destabilizing impact on the economy rather than supplying it with the reassurance tradition is expected to give.[13]

Nor did federal fiscal policy form an adequate substitute for the atrophy of planning. On the one hand, the decentralization of much of the central government's taxing power out to subnational units and the automatic assignment of a large portion of its revenues to semiautonomous funds raised severe organizational barriers to fiscal coherency. On the other, the influence of the remaining taxes and "obligatory contributions" on economic performance was largely negative. In fact, far from yielding a countercyclical fiscal policy, the fiscal institutions of the postreform years resulted in "an almost *completely inverse movement* of economic activity and taxes."[14] (See figure 1.)

That is, in the 1960s government expenditures at all levels were seen as falling into two broad categories: budgetary accounts, financed by "taxes" spent at the discretion of legislatures, and semiautonomous social service and special funds, financed by "contributions" for specific purposes (from educa-

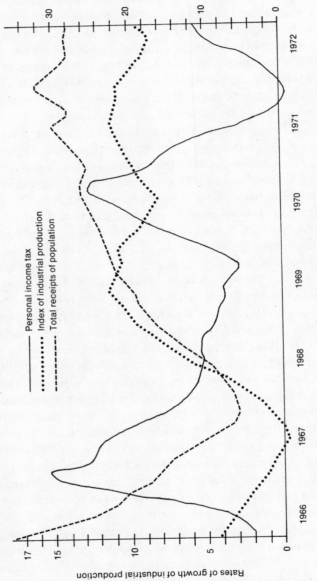

Rates of growth of taxes (contributions)
and receipts

Figure 1. Annual Rates of Growth of Industrial Production, Personal Income Taxes, and Total Receipts of Population

Rates of growth of industrial production

Personal income tax
Index of industrial production
Total receipts of population

Source: M. Kranjec, "An Analysis of the Effects of Yugoslav Fiscal Policy in the Light of Some Newer Theoretical Concepts," *Eastern European Economics* 14 (Fall 1975): 39.

tion and health to disaster relief funds). The main source of revenue for
budgets was the sales tax and a tax on the portion of enterprise earnings allocated to personal income. The federal budget was further augmented by
revenues from customs duties. As for social services and special funds, most
of their revenues came directly out of additional and substantial contributions/
taxes based, again, on the portion of enterprise income going to wages. Supplementary monies were supplied by appropriations from government budgets.
The major exception to this pattern was the Fund for Accelerated Development, financed until 1971 by the tax/interest charge on enterprise assets.[15]

These arrangements had several consequences. In the first place, taxing the
portion of enterprise earnings allocated to personal incomes rather that taxing
enterprise net revenues or individual earnings meant that Yugoslavia had
neither a corporate income tax nor a personal income tax; instead, it had, in
effect, instituted a tax on labor. As a result, firms had an incentive to econo-
mize on the use of labor despite the growth of unemployment, while labor-
intensive branches of the economy found themselves shouldering a disproportionate share of government and social service expenditures. Furthermore, the

> consequences [of] a system of direct taxes . . . based on the factors of
> production independent of business results . . . is a higher cost of labor
> and capital . . . with a resulting higher tax burden in recessions and a
> lower tax burden in upswings. . . . However, in periods of stagnation it
> adds pressure for price increases.[16]

Second, the lion's share of the revenues generated by taxes and contributions from personal incomes went to finance the various semiautonomous
funds kept by each unit of government, most of which were set up to cover
social service expenditures. Since the 1963 Constitution awarded responsibility for most social services to subnational units, the majority of these funds
existed at lower levels of government and are dealt with in that context
below. But for federal fiscal policy, the effects of the geographical and functional decentralization of tax revenues were chaotic.

While the federal government set an overall 10 percent ceiling on the
"taxes" subfederal governments could impose on personal incomes, there was
no ceiling on the size of "contributions" withheld from incomes. These varied
from place to place, at times amounting to 40 to 50 percent of workers' gross
incomes. Hence, not only did quite varied local and republic obligations
have a greater impact on enterprise costs and prices than did national taxation, but tax burdens were not uniform among enterprises in different
regions. Furthermore, the fact that contributions to funds at all levels had to
be spent for specific purposes made it impossible to utilize government and
social service expenditures as part of a coordinated national fiscal policy.

In addition, contributions from personal incomes were not held at a constant rate. Instead, figure 1 indicates that they grew faster in recessions and remained constant or declined in expansions. The dynamic here seems to be that when the various funds each government supported found their real revenues decreasing in times of recession (which, in Yugoslavia, were also times of rising prices), they would pressure governments to increase enterprise contributions. The effect on the economy, according to Kranjec's calculations, was to worsen fluctuations in the business cycle by 214 percent from what they would have been had taxes merely been held constant.[17] A mentality reminiscent of Proudhon's, with its stress on exchanging "a product for a product," reinforced the tendency to view income taxes solely as a way of financing social expenditures without taking their wider economic effects into consideration; the new system of representation set up by the 1963 Constitution helped to perpetuate it.[18]

Nor were budgetary accounts of much use as fiscal instruments. Only about a third of all budgetary revenues were generated from incomes taxes in any case; the main source of government budgets was, instead, the tax on retail sales.[19] Finally, to the degree the government—national and subnational—resorted to deficit financing, this was done "haphazardly" and was accomplished through loans from the National Bank,[20] which then cut into the supply of credit available to firms.

With this we arrive at the role of monetary policy in postreform Yugoslavia. Here, the major obligatory effect of plans on the federal government was to regulate the volume of capital and the emission of money by the National Bank, whose reserve requirements, interest rates, and emission policy was subject to political control. Yet insofar as monetary policy served as the national government's sole general mechanism for regulating aggregate demand, it not surprisingly created more problems than it solved.

In this regard, even the actual rate of money emission can hardly be described as a "planned" phenomenon, despite the fact that it was normally set a year in advance. As Ivan Ribnikar noted in 1973, "The experiences so far reveal that this projection was bound to change during the year and that in spite of these changes, the final increase in the money stock was different, most likely, greater."[21] Moreover, the responses of enterprises to the deflationary credit policy soon brought into question the National Bank's ability to control the money supply altogether. Rather than reducing aggregate demand, "economic organizations replaced bank (emission) credits with mutual credits and . . . replaced money with mutual claims." The result was the widespread illiquidity of firms, which increased pressure on the money supply, and a certain transfer of capital from more efficient to less efficient enterprises: "Those whose debts were increasing relative to increases in claims were taking away capital accumulation from those whose claims were increasing relative to debt increases."[22]

Typically, the government's reaction to these perennial liquidity crises was not to penalize the firms for defaulting on their debts, but rather to ease

> monetary policy to feed bank credit into the illiquid enterprise sector. Ironically, then liquidity crises cause the reversal of the restrictive monetary prices which lead to their appearance in the first place. Unfortunately, however, this reversal also necessitates sacrifice of the macroeconomic goals, most notably price stability, which originally fostered . . . monetary restrictions.[23]

Not only were such policies behind the unplanned increase in the money stock described by Ribnikar, but their regular employment literally encouraged firms to continue falling into debt.

Another factor in the widespread illiquidity problem and the declining capacity of firms to self-finance investment which accompanied it (table 6) was the altered structure of individual and collective incentives resulting from increased enterprise autonomy. Contrary to the hopes of the reform, individual worker-entrepreneurs actually had a disincentive to invest via retained earnings.

Furbotn and Pejovich analyzed the new property rights structure and the pattern of investment incentives in Yugoslavia. They point out:

> Actually, the employees of the Yugoslav firm have two major wealth-increasing alternatives: *joint investment* in physical assets for the firm via retained earnings and *individual* investment in other assets. [The latter] are perhaps best represented by the rate of interest on personal savings accounts.[24]

Insofar as firm assets were not individually owned, workers' returns from investment in them could only take the form of higher wages (increased future labor productivity). Thus, individuals' gains from firm investment were limited to the length of their employment with the firm, as opposed to interest income they could receive from individually owned assets (for instance, savings deposits) or even, we might add, to the utility and savings they might have from the immediate acquisition of durable consumer goods (housing, cars, refrigerators) in a highly inflationary period. Moreover, even the gains in personal income accrued from increased labor productivity would take a certain amount of time to be realized. Hence, "unless the time horizon is very long . . . the expected productivity of capital in the firm would have to be quite high for the collective to have any incentive to invest in the firm."[25]

One result of the new incentive structure was an inflationary tendency to "privatize" accumulation by distributing it as wages. Certainly, the "withering away of the state," with the entailing lack of a countercyclical fiscal policy, was an important factor behind the chronic inflation that characterized the postreform period. So too was Yugoslavia's "integration" into the "international division of labor," manifested in a growing balance-of-payments deficit. Nevertheless, the labor-managed firms' tendency—and, in the sixties, ability—to raise wages faster than productivity was clearly a major contributor to the problem. Branko Horvat explains:

> A single variable accounts for four-fifths of all short-term variations in producer and retail prices. It is a matter of the movement of earnings in relation to the movement of production. . . . When nominal earnings increase up to 6.5 per cent faster than the productivity of labor, industrial producer prices remain unchanged; prices rise if they exceed this limiting per cent and fall if they are less.[26]

A second result of the new incentive structure was the tendency of labor-managed firms to substitute bank credit for self-finance. Encouraging such a pattern was the low interest-rate ceiling on long-term loans set by the Federal Assembly; since annual rates of inflation averaged over 6 percent after 1965, an 8 to 10 percent interest rate actually stimulated borrowing and placed an additional burden on the supply of money as an economic regulator.[27] Indeed, contraction of the money supply appears to have been used instead of a flexible interest rate ceiling to implement the deflationary credit policy. In part, the refusal of federal authorities to employ interest rates as a tool of monetary policy reflected an ideology that, like Proudhon's, saw labor as the sole source of income and hence proscribed high interest rates; in part, the maintenance of below-equilibrium interest rates was caused by the new structure of socialist property in the banks.

That is, according to the reforms, the controlling boards of banks were to be composed of "founder" enterprises and government agencies who subscribed capital to the banks. While conflicts of interest among the members led, for the most part, to domination of policy making by full-time bank executives, as members also borrowed from the banks, the one issue they could agree on was that interest rates should be low.[28] Combined with a contraction in the emission of money and the already noted tendency of Yugoslav firms to overengage in deficit financing, the result was a rapid jump in the

velocity of currency circulation—with the corresponding inflationary effects—
and illiquidity of enterprises—with the consequent piling up of unpaid debts
to each other described earlier.

Moreover, the federally set reserve requirements of the banks led them to
prefer time deposits to demand deposits. Partly for this reason, banks often
required firms to keep their holdings in time deposits as a condition for
receiving long-term credits. Although such procedures generated additional investment funds, they also meant firms had difficulty drawing on their own
accounts to cover working capital needs. Thus, although the value of firms'
monetary assets increased throughout the postreform period, their liquid
"money holdings . . . fell from 35 percent of the money supplied in 1965 to
. . . 20.3 percent in the first 6 months of 1969."[29] In effect, it became easier
for an enterprise to build a new plant than to pay out salaries or cover its
debts to suppliers. While this facilitated the expansion of existing firms into
new markets, it aggravated the capital-intensive/employment effects of labor-
managed firms, and the banks actually helped create the liquidity crises of
Yugoslav firms by contributing to the shortage of working capital.

The final result of the changed property rights and incentive structure was
an increasing concentration of capital in the hands of banks (table 6). Not
only was there a constant flow of capital from industry and government into
banking, but a wave of bank mergers[30] made the possibility of a centralized
financial oligopoly, controlling the vast bulk of Yugoslav capital and strong
enough to withstand the pressures of government and individual industries and
firms alike, seem like more and more of a reality.[31]

Nor were problems with monopolies and oligopolies confined to
banking; they were present in many other branches of industry and commerce
as well. We shall see the effects of concentration and oligopoly on interindustry differentials in chapter 5; they were parallelled by certain distortions
in capital allocation and the efficient use of resources. For example, despite
the existence of unused capacity, plans were made for additional refinery
construction in the highly profitable and concentrated petroleum industry.
Inter-regional jealousies among local electrical power monopolies periodically
led to shortages in some areas and reserves in others without creating economic pressures for greater coordination.

The federal government not only proved unable to formulate a coherent,
countercyclical fiscal and monetary policy; it never made much use of its
authority to pursue an aggressive antitrust policy. Like Proudhon, the Yugoslav government saw competition as the antidote to monopoly; if the narrowness of the Yugoslav market structure and the various integration campaigns

of the early and mid-sixties helped to create highly oliogopolistic domestic market structures, foreign competition was expected to blunt their potential effects on pricing. To some extent, this strategy was successful; a World Bank report suggests, "Yugoslav prices may be fairly well aligned to those on the European Common Market," especially for exportable commodities.[32] Nevertheless, the growth in foreign trade was not without its costs in growing import dependency and in the rise of strong oligopolies in the import-export field.[33]

In part, the dependence on imports was caused by Yugoslav inflation, which, by making even the new exchange rate relatively overvalued, stimulated imports. In part, however, it resulted from the realization of restrictions on foreign borrowing, the domestic credit crunch, and the increased independence of Yugoslav firms. These factors permitted enterprises unable to finance necessary purchases through domestic credits to import materials through credits extended by foreign firms and suppliers. At the same time, firms were now permitted to retain and freely dispose of a portion of the foreign currency earnings acquired through sales abroad. Often firms used these earnings

> to develop import activities above and beyond their needs for production and investment. Moreover, they started importing goods which had no connection with their production. Those imports could be sold on the domestic market with significant profit margins.[34]

Among the chief culprits were the import-export houses licensed by the government to engage in foreign trade. Industrial firms found themselves dependent on these commercial trading companies for access to the foreign market, while the trading companies were in the enviable position of being able to decide autonomously whether to use their hard currency to aid firms wishing to purchase goods abroad or to employ it toward imports they themselves could directly market via retail enterprises in Yugoslavia. On the one hand, industrial firms found themselves paying high commissions for services they were forced to use as well as interest rates on the foreign currency they had borrowed; on the other hand, the trading companies transformed themselves into conglomerates, concentrating their activities in hard-currency-earning industries like tourism. Occasionally, too, they utilized their privileged position on the foreign market to set up or modernize enterprises by providing the necessary foreign-made equipment through their own agencies: "Thus, they [came to] act very much like banks, and in fact frequently grant[ed] loans. In some instances, they share[d] in the profit of new enterprises as well as earning fixed returns on capital invested."[35] In this way, the declining ability of industrial firms to finance investment—and even working capital needs—was paralleled by the rise of what were widely perceived as centers of financial and commercial capital.

One further aspect of the foreign trade problem deserves brief mention: its effect in dramatizing the inequalities present in Yugoslav society. That is, the influx of Western consumer goods and luxuries in the sixties combined with the existence of few private investment outlets led to a wave of conspicuous consumption by those who could afford it. Inflation helped to support a "buy it now" climate, and the requirement for partial participation for those receiving consumer credit or housing loans effectively discriminated against those at the lower end of the income spectrum. Moreover, this was accompanied by the growth of a "petit bourgeois" mentality, social snobbism, and an increase in "exploitation" and "speculation" in semilegal private activities (buying and selling of land and housing, smuggling in articles from Western countries, and so on). Although such activities were encouraged by the individualistic incentive structure created by the reforms, they were sharply attacked by political figures and left-wing dissidents.[36] I shall return to the inequalities issue in chapter 5.

In sum, although the state was very much in existence in postreform Yugoslavia, the net effect of its economic policies—or of the lack of them—appears to have been remarkably similar to that of the federalist nonstate of Proudhon. As a 1970 memorandum to the Federal Executive Council observed:

> In the course [of the state's withdrawal from the economy] a rather dangerous theory and practice developed. . . . It began to be believed that the state apparatus and other organs of the community are responsible only for those actions in which they can intervene administratively by commands. Since the sphere of administrative interventions was substantially reduced, state and political organs in general, but especially federal organs, to a large extent *ceased to consider themselves responsible for economic trends.*[37]

The reaction to this "theory and practice" and the resulting economic instability was also quite analogous to the hypothetical one produced by Proudhon's laissez faire mutualism: growing pressures for hierarchy to correct the workings of the market. That is, a kind of power vacuum in the formulation of national economic policy was created in the aftermath of the 1965 reforms. When this was combined with the poor overall economic performance of the postreform years[38] (table 7), the way was left wide open for Yugoslavia's traditional *bête noires*, administrative intervention and ethnic chauvinism, to rush in to fill it.

Table 7. Statistical Picture of the Yugoslav Economy, 1955-72

	Annual Growth Rates in Percent	
	1955-64	1964-72
1. Production and capacity		
Social product in 1966 prices (entire economy)	8.2	5.7
Social product in 1966 prices (collective sector)	11.1	6.4
Industrial production (physical volume)	12.4	7.1
Agricultural production (physical volume)	4.3	1.3
Fixed assets of the collective sector at beginning of year, 1966 prices	9.4	7.1
2. International trade		
Exports (physical volume)	12.8	8.0
Imports (physical volume)	11.6	7.9
3. Monetary instability[a]		
Producers' prices in industry	1.6	8.3
Producers' prices in agriculture	8.2	15.2
Cost of living	6.9	14.6
4. Standard of living		
Real earnings	7.1	5.6
Personal consumption	7.8	5.9[b]
New housing constructed	16.0[c]	0.5
Employment in the collective sector	5.7	1.8
5. Efficiency of economic activity		
Productivity of labor in the collective sector	5.1	4.6
Efficiency of investment in the collective sector[d]	0.9	-3.6

Source: B. Horvat, "Short-Run Instability and Long-Run Trends in the Yugoslav Economy's Development," Eastern European Economics 14 (Fall 1975): 4.

[a]From 1965 to 1972, industrial prices rose by 6.5 percent, agricultural prices by 10.2 percent, and the cost of living by 10.6 percent.

[b]1964-71

[c]1956-64

[d]Defined as increase of social product per unit of increase of fixed assets the previous year, measured from peak to peak of the business cycle. Rates of growth derived from these absolute quantities expressed in 1966 prices.

Thus, the near paralysis of policy making did not mean that direct regulation of the economy by public and semipublic agencies ceased altogether. To compensate for the negative effects of the market on producers and consumers, various forms of ad hoc administrative intervention were common at all levels of government. In this sense, the Yugoslav economy remained a "mixed" one, although not in the Keynesian sense of the term. Although direct political interventions in the market mechanism undoubtedly occurred on a smaller scale than in the prereform period, their lowered frequency was partially compensated for by their increased arbitrariness, for the guiding hand of the plan was no longer present to direct them.[39] Various subsidies continued through the "extrabudgetary" resources of the federation and of various republic and commune budgets, political pressures were applied to either obstruct or force integrations, price controls were applied on a random basis, wage ceilings were clamped down on occasion, and import restrictions and protective tariffs were voted in. Similarly, regulations needed just to put the reform into effect continued to multiply, and a steady stream of legal changes affecting accounting categories, organizational structure, and other aspects of enterprise operations increased the uncertainty within which enterprises had to conduct business.[40]

Yet whereas prior to the reforms, the pattern had been one of political "meddling" in the affairs of the enterprises, the new dynamic can be more aptly characterized as enterprise meddling in the government, as firms hit hard by the new competition ran to political bodies for bail-outs in the form of subsidies, protective tariffs, special loans, and price increases. Although such political interventions were nominally and practically a departure from allowing the market a full scope in resource allocation, it was nonetheless precisely the effects of the competitive market on the firms which called it forth. Significantly, while one of the goals of the reform was to eliminate the so-called political factories, only two enterprise failures were reported by the end of 1966, and from 1964 to 1970, less that four hundred workers per year lost their jobs owing to bankruptcies.[41] Dirlam and Plummer give numerous examples of the "extremely close" relationships that developed among politicians, banks, and enterprises and indicate that not only firms operating at a permanent or temporary loss sought to pressure the government for favors:

When his bank loans were not renewed in 1966, E. Blum, director of Energoinvest [one of the most successful enterprises in Yugoslavia] issued press releases violently attacking the management of the National Bank. He . . . encouraged the workers to petition Parliament to moderate the central bank policy of credit restriction. Credit terms were not im-

mediately relaxed, but it is significant that Energoinvest believed that
it could influence policy by protest.[42]

As economic conditions continued to decline and enterprise illiquidity to
expand, appeals multiplied and assumed an increasing urgency, resulting in
"ever greater administrative interventions." By mid-1972, "prices were fixed,
earnings were frozen, foreign trade was strictly controlled, and the sphere of
the market and of self-management autonomy was reduced to the lowest point
since 1955."[43]

That enterprises frequently sought protection from the market by bringing
political pressures to bear did not necessarily mean that they invariably addressed their appeals to the national government. On the contrary they sought
the support of the unit of government most likely to come to the rescue.
Typically, this was the unit of government most directly dependent on them
for its revenues: the local or republic governments, which would either aid
the firms directly or, if they lacked the necessary resources or authority, serve
as leverage points for pressuring the national government.[44]

The governments of the republics and autonomous regions began to assume
particular importance in the race for protection for a number of reasons.
Partially, it was because of the integration movement, which had produced a
good number of mergers across commune boundaries but had created relatively few interrepublic enterprises. In part, it was owing to a lack of capital
mobility across republic boundaries—or at least a widespread belief to this
effect[45]—which, ironically but understandably, stimulated demands for further
territorialization of the capital market. The transfer of responsibility for
social services to republics and communes, both ill-equipped to finance them,
and the continued widening of regional inequalities after the reform also led
to a strengthening of republic loyalties. So too did the psychological impact
of the faltering economy: "In conditions of social uncertainty, people identify
with the nation."[46] The indecisiveness of the national government in formulating economic policy fed into the growth of economic nationalism at the
republic level, which occasionally crystallized into political chauvinism in the
form of riots and demonstrations against the national government or other
ethnic groups. At the same time, the rise of the republics' political importance,
formally acknowledged in the 1969 constitutional amendments, reinforced
all the tendencies toward autarchy that had brought economic nationalism
into being: regional inequalities, inability to agree on national economic policy,
territorialization of capital and labor markets, decentralization of taxing
powers, and heightened ethnic tensions. In effect, a gradual tendency for the
republics to replace the communes as the center of "localism" was being
put into motion in the postreform years.[47]

The Role of the State: Local Government

In a 1970 follow-up of his 1960 fieldwork, Albert Meister observed:

> Since the reform, the commune has seen itself supplanted by the banks
> in economic decision making. . . . The present tendency of the commune
> is a return to the activities and competencies of the municipality in our
> western countries: the limited tasks of health, culture, education.[48]

This narrowing of the commune's area of concern, consistent with the goals
of the reform, occurred despite the fact that commune taxing powers and
responsibility for social services and regulation were actually *enlarged* during
the post reform period. Among the reasons for this paradox were the
atrophy of federal planning, the decline of the national government's redistributive role, and the changes enacted in the administration and status of
social service organizations.

Prior to 1965, the importance of the commune in the local economy derived primarily from its position as the lowest unit of the national plan. The
decline in federal planning and the loss of state investment funds allocated to
achieve plan criteria restricted the commune's ability to "direct and har-
monize the development of economic and social services."[49] For example,
Stephen Sacks indicates that after 1965, an increasing proportion of new
entrants on various product markets were new plants established by existing
enterprises, as opposed to new enterprises founded by communes or citizen
groups.[50] The financing of fixed assets by communes also showed a steady
drop: whereas communes financed 18 percent of fixed assets in 1961, the
figure fell to 4 percent in 1968.[51]

The widening scope of the market also restricted the commune's role as an
economic regulator. For example, while communes retained the authority
to impose local price controls, this usually meant that an article whose price
was controlled disappeared from the local market. Thus, the commune's
role in "planning" was more and more defined in terms of traditional urban
planning through zoning laws and land-use requirements;[52] in the economic
sphere, its efforts were increasingly limited to attracting industry within
its territorial boundaries, a limitation of which Proudhon, with his desire to
reduce authority down to incentives, would certainly have approved. Here
the immense advantages of urban areas over rural communes only served to
widen existing regional inequalities.[53]

This brings us to the second factor behind the commune's diminishing importance as a development planner: the reduction of the national government's redistributive role, which accompanied its abandonment of investment
planning. Rudolf Bićanić explains:

[The concept of the reform] greatly differs from that of the welfare
state. The essence of the welfare state is to leave the production machine
capitalist, with some marginal intervention in the public sector, and, by
state taxation, to redistribute the income taken from the richer to the
poorer consumers. The reform in Yugoslavia denies this role of redistribution to the state (even to a socialist one) and endeavors to organize
production on the basis of workers' self-management, in order to
eliminate the roots of exploitation of man by man through income
redistribution. It leaves decisions on income distribution to the workers
who produce the income . . . but takes the world level of productivity
as the objective measurement.[54]

Whereas prior to 1965, the national government had taken the lion's share of
the turnover tax and then redistributed it back to subnational units of government, the reforms reduced the federal government's portion and increased the
share going directly to the communes and republics. At the same time, local
governments directly received the largest share of personal income tax revenues
generated within their territories and used it to finance both social services
and government administration. Meanwhile, the trend toward amalgamating
communes continued: in 1952, there were 3,811 communes; in 1962, 759;
and in 1968, the number had dropped to 501.[55]
These measures were all designed to give local governments a more secure
and reliable source of funding and to free them of their previous dependence
on the national government. Thus, although the commune's significance as an
economic agent was expected to decline, thereby reducing the localism to
which the pre-1965 economy had been subject, theoretically its independence
and importance as a political-administrative unit and as a provider of services
was to grow. Like Proudhon's federative associations, hierarchy between units
of government was to wither away: "Constitutional law . . . requires that the
relationships of federal, republican, district and communal agencies be
based not on hierarchy of authority but on mutual rights and duties formally
established by law."[56]
The only problem, of course, is that it did little good to enlarge commune tax powers and devolve social responsibilities on them by statute
when their tax bases were inadequate to support such activities. Here lies
a primary reason for the lack of commune intervention in the economy:
local governments alone simply lacked the economic resources to develop
the territories in their jurisdiction. Nor did expanding the territorial base
through amalgamation help a great deal. Eugen Pusić, in his study of
Yugoslav communes, concluded that size correlated negatively with

per capita income, especially when size was measured by population.[57]

In addition, the national government's transfer of responsibility for the provision and financing of local services to local governments in a period of extensive rural migration to cities meant that even the wealthier urban areas were unable to keep pace with the demands placed on them. At the same time, local governments in rural areas lacked the resources and personnel to improve the rural environment so as to reduce the flight to the cities.

The federal government, however, did not entirely abandon its redistributive role, which undoubtedly helped to keep differences in the social standard of living from growing intolerable. Supplementary resources were specially allocated to the underdeveloped republics and provinces, while republics had their own system of grants for communes whose budgetary per capita revenue was below a fixed amount. Nevertheless, interregional variations in the social standard of living remained considerable.[58] Note that a good part of these allocations from high-level sociopolitical communities to those on lower levels bypassed local budgets entirely and went directly to the semiautonomous funds through which social services were financed. With this, we arrive at the third major cause for the decline in local planning: the administrative fragmentation that resulted from the introduction of self-management in social service organizations. Although the commune still retained legal responsibility for public services, its authority over their delivery was greatly reduced by the method of financing them through special funds paid for by contributions from enterprise income and administered by the respective social services themselves.[59]

The logic behind this arrangement was quite similar to that underlying Proudhon's description of the relationship between federative associations and mutualist cooperatives: traditional social services were transformed into a near equivalent of public corporations, financed in large part by tax revenues, but semiautonomous, self-managing, and with their own revenues in addition to the government grants or "investments" they received. Under such a system, income taxes came to resemble "charges" for specific services: health, education, and child care, and so on. Symbolically, the official lexicon now defined income taxes as "social contributions," for theoretically they were no longer "taxes" levied by the "state."

Thus, in postreform Yugoslavia, "work organizations" now included schools, hospitals, and city services as well as commercial and manufacturing establishments. The old distinction between "economic/productive" and "noneconomic/necessary" was gradually being legally erased, for all work organizations were beginning to be considered as engaged in "commodity production." Hospitals, for example, charged enterprise employees users'

fees via local withholding taxes on personal incomes; those not working in
the socialist sector and thus not covered by this arrangement, such as small
entrepreneurs and private peasants, paid separately for medical care. The
potential negative effects of these practices on the overall quality of medical
care and the discriminatory delivery of health services soon became all too
apparent.[60] They were avoided largely because social services were a de facto
monopoly supplying limited amounts of a "product" highly in demand at
prices consumers were forced to accept. As such, social service organizations
could avoid the economic pressures to cut wages, shave costs, and increase
productivity (more patients per doctor, more pupils per teacher) to which
other work organizations were subject.

As the amount of money any fund received from local taxes had to be
voted on by the commune assembly, a certain amount of political control
over public services remained: in effect, they were regulated monopolies.
Even here, however, the equating of all types of labor led to a singular situation. The old Council of Producers, symbolizing the predominance of "productive" qua industrial labor, was abolished in the 1963 Constitution to make
way for four separate chambers: economic, educational-cultural, social-health,
and organizational-political, each of which respectively voted along with the
chamber based on geographical representation on matters that directly
concerned it.[61] Thus, as Proudhon would have it, all work organizations were
"equal before the law," and employees in, say, schools and cultural institutions would be relatively overrepresented when voting on their appropriations.[62] While it appears that full-time commune administrators and elected
officials managed to maintain the position of de facto dominance in local
assemblies they had had in the prereform period,[63] and that the state of the
local economy necessarily imposed some ceiling on social service expenditures, such a representational arrangement certainly helps to explain why
"the total withholdings from workers' incomes . . . had reached 40 to 50
percent in some areas and became a source of much public discontent."[64]

Social service organizations not only voted on their own appropriations,
but also autonomously administered them. Given such a fragmentation of
authority combined with an overall scarcity of resources, it is hardly surprising that communes had difficulty in planning their development. Indeed,
by 1970, there were over five thousand separate funds (total) on the local
level.[65] A report of Zagreb's Institute for Social Administration gives this
description of local planning:

> For the citizen, the social plan represents a piece of paper which obli-
> gates no one to do anything . . . With the widening of the areas over

which the producers autonomously decide (in economic and noneconomic spheres) the role of the commune assembly in the adoption and execution of the social plan is increasingly undefined. (From a "plan" we have arrived at a "direction" of development.) The basic characteristic of this direction is its vagueness and nonobligatory character.[66]

As with the national government, the atrophy of planning by no means implied an end to administrative intervention on the part of the commune. Many banks still required commune approval for loans, and commune (as well as republic) officials were certainly not above applying pressure on the banks to obtain loans for favored firms.[62] Moreover, they could be instrumental in getting additional monies from the federation or the republic to help either social services or enterprises experiencing difficulties. High local taxes and close regulation of small entrepreneurs also helped to protect the commune's chief source of revenue, the socialized enterprises. And if the social service obligations of the commune were fragmented by decentralization, its police powers—needed to enforce its own regulations as well as those of higher political bodies—remained concentrated in its administrative apparatus, as both its citizens and the enterprises were well aware.[68] We might cite Eugen Pusić's conclusions:

> To see [the commune] as an autonomous community embodying the free consensus of the citizens . . . is an elusive ideal. . . . Not only is the commune still very much defined by its power role, but there is a tendency toward the formation of local elites, centralized within the communal area, looking toward the central government instead of toward the local population, judging communal affairs, in the last resort, from the institutional point of view of enlarging and stabilizing the commune as a governmental and organizational system. The constructive function of the commune as a service center serves, often probably unconsciously, as a legitimizing ideology.[69]

Thus the Proudhonian elements of Yugoslavia's local and national political system should not be exaggerated, for in practice the system retained many authoritarian features. As distinct from the pre-1965 model, however, commune intervention was now more than likely to be a welcome response to pressures from the enterprises themselves, rather than actions taken over their resistance, as demands for increased political coordination of Yugoslav market socialism continued to build. Contributing to them was what appeared to many to be an unacceptably high degree of social inequality in many spheres of Yugoslav life.

5

Market Socialism in Yugoslavia:
The Inequalities Issue

As we have seen, a major effect of the 1965 reforms was to alter drastically the nature of "social property" by transferring most of the rights associated with it from the state to the individual work collectives. Such a change modified Yugoslav economic and political organization from a variant of workers' control that could be assimilated with Gramsci's workers' democracy to one with many parallels with Proudhon's mutualism. We have already seen the consequences of the reforms for economic performance and the role of the state; they were not without their implications for the distribution of ownership benefits also.

Although in Proudhon's mutualism each member of society started out with equal amounts of labor and property, it was soon characterized by major inequalities in income and capital distribution. In Yugoslavia, social property was far from equally distributed among either individual workers or work collectives even at the outset of the reforms. With the large reduction in taxes on profits, the maintenance of a below equilibrium "interest" rate on social capital (abandoned altogether in 1971), and very generous rental fees, work collectives de facto appropriated a large portion of the return to theoretically "social" property for their own uses, to maximize either current incomes (by allocating profits directly to wages) or future earnings (by plowing profits back as investment). Moreover, the market, left to its own devices, permitted the firms that already enjoyed relative advantages in the distribution of capital to widen their initial lead.

As a result, several inequalities in income and capital distribution became increasingly disturbing in the postreform years. These inequalities interacted in different ways with the ideological battles within the Yugoslav League of Communists and within various units of government. Thus, some inequalities were allowed to widen, while others were corrected by ad hoc intervention, informal political pressures on individual enterprises, and the trade unionization of workers' councils, which then took their toll on overall economic performance and the optimal allocation of resources.

94

INEQUALITIES BETWEEN PRIVATE AGRICULTURE AND THE SOCIALIST SECTOR

Because of prevailing ideology and the political power structure resulting from the 1963 Constitution, Yugoslav political leaders took the least account of the most serious inequalities: those between the socialist sector taken as a whole and the private sector, or more precisely, the private peasant sector. Tables 8 and 9 indicate that although the spread of average incomes between sectors of the socialized area of the economy actually decreased after the reforms, income differentials between the whole socialist sector and peasant agriculture widened by an order of two or three to one.

Table 8. Structure of Average Personal Incomes in the
Major Economic Sectors, Index

	1963	1971
Noneconomic activities	125.9	115.5
Transport	110.2	108.7
Trade and catering	102.5	106.5
All sectors	100.0	100.0
Manufacturing	98.2	95.2
Crafts	93.7	92.3
Construction	91.2	95.3
Housing and utilities	89.5	96.1
Socialized agriculture	76.5	87.1
Peasant agriculture	43.9	38.6[a]
Ratio of highest to lowest	286.6	299.2
Ratio of highest to lowest in the social sector	164.6	132.6

Source: World Bank, *Yugoslavia: Development with Decentralization* (Baltimore: The Johns Hopkins University Press, 1975), p. 108.
[a]Estimated for 1968

Table 9. Value of Annual Net Personal Income per Employed in the
Socialist Sector and per Working Private Farmer, 1971

	Income (dinars)	Level Indices
Per employed in the socialist sector	19,200	100
Per working private farmer	5,700	50

Source: M. Nikolić, "Employment and Temporary Unemployment," *Yugoslav Survey* 14 (May 1974): 17 circa.

Moreover, "growth rates in the incomes of those in the upper 10 per cent
[were] more than double those in the bottom 40 per cent."[1] With 44.2 percent of the labor force engaged in peasant agriculture, with the average size
of individual holdings showing a slight *decline* from 1961 to 1971, and with
labor productivity and investment in private agriculture lagging well behind that in the socialist sector as a whole and socialized agriculture in particular, all the classical elements of a dual economy were present.[2]

Even this situation would not have been so serious—indeed, might not have
arisen at all—had *access* to social property been equal, in other words, had
employment in the socialist sector grown at a rate sufficient to absorb surplus
rural labor. The record prior to 1965 appears much better in this respect
(table 10): "official"[3] unemployment was lower and expansion of employment opportunities in the socialist sector greater than in the sixties. Furthermore, an analysis of table 11 reveals that whereas prior to 1961, employment in industry grew at a higher rate than in services, after 1961 this relation
was reversed; since the qualification structure of tertiary activities was relatively skewed in favor of more educated labor,[4] they were correspondingly
less suited for absorbing manpower from the farms, most of which was unskilled. Trends such as these manifested themselves not only in growing
unemployment and emigration abroad, but also help to explain the drop in
peasant labor productivity after 1961 (table 11), for excess rural laborers were
in effect, forced to remain on the farms.

In addition, the effects of the social welfare system increased the gap between the socialist sector and private agriculture. In fact, private peasants were
not covered at all by health insurance until 1970, when they were permitted
to pay in a certain portion of their personal income to local health services
and receive coverage in return. As peasant incomes in monetary terms were so
much lower to start with, however, it is unclear how high the quality of health
care in rural areas could be. Pensions, too, were available only to those in
the socialist sector, and of course the housing, transportation, and vacation
subsidies and credits that enterprises often extended to their employees were
unavailable in the private sector. Thus, a growing gap in the social standard of
living arose, complementing the urban/rural differentials in personal incomes.

INEQUALITIES BETWEEN PRIVATE NONAGRICULTURAL ACTIVITIES AND THE SOCIALIST SECTOR

Passing note should also be made of what at least were perceived as growing income disparities between the private, nonagricultural sector of small entrepreneurs and the socialist sector of the economy. Deborah Milenkovitch
explains: "The private sector is a highly visible source of extremely high in-

Table 10. Persons Seeking Work, by Professional Qualifications, 1969-72

	1959	1961	1963	1965	1967	1969	1971	1972
University or college	8,277	5,297	8,250	20,727	26,345	43,200	41,800	47,700
Skilled and highly skilled workers	19,790	21,334	30,116	27,704	39,394	45,700	39,900	47,700
Unskilled, semiskilled, or elementary school	133,571	164,682	191,906	198,538	203,028	231,700	209,600	219,900
Unskilled (manual)	n.a.[a]	n.a.	n.a.	n.a.	n.a.	215,200	156,700	159,100
Elementary school (lowest level clerical)	1,553	4,867	12,701	13,255	26,500	n.a.	n.a.	n.a.
Total	161,633	191,283	230,272	236,969	269,067	330,600	291,300	315,300

Source: Statistički Godišnjak SFRJ Belgrade: Savezni zavod za statistiku, 1969), table 104-14, "Lica koja traže zaposlenje prema struč-nom obrazovanju," p. 105; *Statistički godišnjak SFRJ* (Belgrade: Savezni zavod za statistiku, 1973), table 104-14, "Lica koja traže zapo-slenje prema stručnom obrazovanju," p. 107.

Note: "The numbers registering with the Employment Institute for new jobs have varied between 200,000 and 300,000 over the last decade, which equals a rate of between 7 per cent and 8 per cent of the labor force employed in the social sector. These rates, however, considerably understate the total numbers seeking work in the social sector because not all work seekers use the Employment Institute. According to the Institute, not more than half of all new jobs secured each year are found through its reporting system" (World Bank, *Yugoslavia: Development with Decentralization* [Baltimore: The Johns Hopkins University Press, 1975], p. 87).

[a]n.a.= not available.

Table 11. Growth in Value Added, Employment, and Productivity, by Major Economic Sector

	Average Growth Rates (Percent), 1953-61			Average Growth Rates (Percent), 1961-71		
	Value Added	Employment	Labor Productivity	Value Added	Employment	Labor Productivity
Total economy	7.7	0.8[a]	6.9	6.9	-0.1[a]	7.0
Social sector	10.3	7.5	2.8	8.0	2.2	5.8
Private sector	2.7	-2.8	5.5	3.2	-1.6	4.8
Social sector						
Industry	12.3	8.5	3.8	9.3	3.1	6.2
Construction	6.7	3.5	3.2	6.7	0.8	5.9
Services	11.1	7.3	3.9	7.3	3.2	4.1
Agriculture	5.6	10.6	-5.0	8.5	-3.4	11.9
Private sector						
Nonagriculture	0.8	-6.5	7.3	11.0	-2.3	13.3
Agriculture	3.2	-2.4	5.3	2.0	-1.6	3.6
Total agriculture and forestry	3.2	-1.7	4.9	3.1	-1.7	4.8

Source: World Bank, Yugoslavia: Development with Decentralization (Baltimore: The Johns Hopkins University Press, 1975), p. 381.
[a]Total labor force

comes for a few. Long years of restrictive policies meant that too few people entered certain lines of activity and that prices for their services were accordingly high."[5] This impression is substantiated by the data in table 11, which shows that labor productivity growth from 1961 to 1971 in the nonagricultural private sector was the highest in any branch of Yugoslav economic activity.

The same ideological prejudice against private activities which led to the ignoring of the substantially lower incomes and standard of living prevalent in private agriculture caused a continual barrage of political criticism and local harassment to be directed at *privatnici*, the small entrepreneurs. Since a good deal of this criticism had the tone of a campaign, in the absence of hard data, it is difficult to estimate how great these inequalities actually were. Josip Županov, for example, notes in this connection, "Our press publishes a list of so-called "millionaires" every January without bothering to mention how much of their income was paid in taxes."[6] Meanwhile, both the campaigns against the private sector and the high tax rate undoubtedly deterred new private competitors from entering the market, thereby perpetuating the high profits, while encouraging a rash of tax evasion.[7]

INTERREPUBLIC INEQUALITIES

The growing difference between incomes of private peasants and workers employed in the socialist sector meant an increasingly apparent rural-urban dichotomy in all republics.[8] Furthermore, it aggravated interrepublic inequalities insofar as a smaller proportion of the labor force was employed in the socialist sector in the underdeveloped areas.[9] As social services were, after 1965, financed largely on a local and republic basis, this meant not only lower average per capita personal incomes in the less developed republics, but also a lower social standard of living,[10] despite subsidies for "collective consumption" from the federal government.

What is most interesting about interrepublic inequalities, however, is not that they increased, but that they increased so slightly and at rates quite comparable with those of the period in which investment was centrally planned (figure 2 and tables 12 and 13). The explanation, however, appears not to lie with the equalizing effects of the competitive market: even the advantages brought by the 1965–66 price reform, which permitted prices of agricultural products to rise and thus benefited the underdeveloped areas relatively more, were quickly eaten away by an ever greater increase in the cost of agricultural inputs.[11] Nor did capital and skilled labor from the more developed republics—or from abroad, for that matter—rush in to take advantage of investment and employment opportunities.[12] As for labor, migration went in quite the opposite

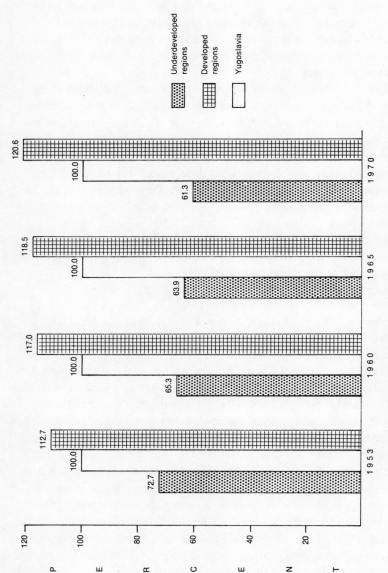

Figure 2. GMP Per Capita by Regions, 1966 Prices

Source: World Bank, *Yugoslavia: Development with Decentralization*
(Baltimore: The Johns Hopkins Press, 1975), p. 190.

Table 12. Index of Per Capita Incomes

	1953 Actual	1971 (1966 Prices)		
		Actual	Same Population Growth[a]	Same GMP Growth[b]
Developed regions	100	100	100	100
Underdeveloped regions	65	50	57	56
Bosnia-Herzegovina	74	53	60	65
Kosovo	42	28	37	29
Macedonia	60	56	62	55
Montenegro	60	58	64	53

Source: World Bank, Yugoslavia: Development with Decentralization (Baltimore: The Johns Hopkins University Press, 1975), p. 193.

[a]Population increase assumed to be the same as that for Yugoslavia, 17.4 percent in both regions. The column indicates the impact of differences in growth rates of GMP on relative per capita income.

[b]GMP increase assumed to be the same as that for Yugoslavia, 240.9 percent, in both regions. The column indicates the impact of differences in growth of population on relative per capita income.

Table 13. Index of Inequality of Per Capita GMP

Year	Current Prices	1966 Prices	Percent Difference
1952	0.3494	0.2603	25.2
1955	0.3360	0.2973	11.5
1960	0.3619	0.3186	12.0
1965	0.3508	0.3585	2.2
1966	0.3296	0.3296	—
1967	0.3486	0.3386	2.8
1968	0.3682	0.3513	4.6
1969	0.3712	0.3553	4.3
1970	0.3918	0.3553	5.6
1971	0.3876	0.3798	2.0

Source: World bank, Yugoslavia: Development with Decentralization, p. 194.

direction, while the bulk of capital inflows came not via enterprise investments and bank loans, but from the Fund for Accelerated Development.

In other words, it was not the market which held interrepublic inequalities in check, but planning done in the form of a political transfer of resources from more developed to less developed areas via federal "extrabudgetary" expenditures and the FAD. The FAD, in turn, merely served as a channel of funds to republic and provincial governments; the latter, political bodies, determined the uses for the funds. As distinct from the pre-1965 period, however, the decisions of subnational units of government in allocating these monies were no longer subject to the priorities set forth in the national plan.

Nor were subnational units of government any longer required to participate in financing the projects they selected. In effect, the governments of Kosovo, Montenegro, Macedonia, and Bosnia-Herzegovina now received a free gift to do with as they liked; in Proudhon's words, "the central power" was indeed quite "insensibly subordinated" to the "departments and provinces," and "social" property was de facto transmuted into (sub)national property.

The vast bulk of FAD funds were used to finance new construction in highly capital-intensive industries, such as electric power and basic metals. Not only were capital output ratios higher in these industries, but they were also ill adapted to absorbing excess rural manpower; partially as a result of this investment pattern, unemployment in Kosovo and Macedonia was three times higher than in Croatia.[13]

High unemployment rates, however, did not necessarily imply lower wages in the underdeveloped areas' socialist sector, as one would expect. In fact, Wachtel reports a gradual narrowing of interrepublic wage differentials in industry between 1963 and 1969.[14] The explanation here would seem to lie less in the "equilibrating effects" of the competitive labor and product market, as Wachtel implies, and more in the effects of the redistribution of social property rights introduced with the 1965 reform.

That is, not only did subnational units of government receive greater authority and independence after the reform; enterprise autonomy was also increased. Moreover, enterprise autonomy in disposing of firm income was not contingent on the sources of enterprise financing: firms receiving loans and credits from the FAD had as much freedom in disposing of their net income as firms who financed their own investment. If anything, enterprises that utilized FAD funds had relatively more freedom, for the amount they had to pay out in interest on social capital was relatively lower, owing to FAD subsidies. Hence, what was saved in interest payments by enterprises in the underdeveloped areas could be used to raise wages to levels comparable with those in the more developed areas.

In addition, that a political transfer of resources was now being effectuated without the high taxes and qualitative restrictions on firm behavior that had accompanied it in the prereform period meant that enterprises in the underdeveloped areas had an incentive to continue this pattern of resource allocation. The resulting higher unit costs in industry served to deter non-FAD sources from investing in these regions and also kept employment growth lower than it could have been. At the same time, tying up large portions of capital in projects that took years to complete and then often failed to generate expected revenue left other sectors—agriculture, light industry, and social services—starved for capital. Meanwhile, the republics not eligible for FAD funds, burdened with their own rural-urban inequalities and their enterprises suffering under the deflationary credit policy, resented what were popularly felt to be political handouts. Ethnic antagonisms were thereby heightened.

The net effect of the FAD does appear to have been to raise the growth rates of the underdeveloped regions and increase industrial employment somewhat more rapidly than in the more developed regions. However, owing both to the factors described above and to higher birth rates, it did not increase them rapidly enough to close the existing gap or even to prevent it from widening. Nor did the injection of FAD funds bring a general growth in the standard of living of the wider population in the poorer areas. Not only did the difference in GMP per capita between developed and underdeveloped regions widen slightly in the postreform period, but dispersion between the poorest economic sectors (private peasants in underdeveloped regions) and the wealthiest (highly trained personnel employed in the socialist sector of the developed republics) increased and was reinforced by the interregional disparities in the social standard of living. Not surprisingly, the resentment of the wealthier areas for the FAD was parallelled by frustration in the poorer republics over what they felt was an insufficient commitment on the part of the socialist community to improving their welfare.

INTERINDUSTRY DIFFERENTIALS[15]

The work collectives in the underdeveloped areas were not alone in their ability to preempt the returns to social property and redistribute them as personal income. Reminiscent of the liberty Proudhon felt essential to mutualist association, the autonomy of all enterprises in Yugoslavia increased as a result of the reform, and all, by definition, "managed" social property. Hence, at the same time the incomes of private peasants fell, those of workers in the socialist sector rose, either because of rising productivity from past social investment or simply because of the decisions of workers' councils to raise wages regardless of productivity gains or losses.

At the same time, social property was not equally distributed among all workers and firms in the socialist sector itself. The past history of planning had deliberately favored some industries over others in the allocation of capital, and economic rationality itself made identical capital-labor ratios for all enterprises neither necessary nor desirable. When the reform transferred the rights over social property to individual work collectives, the inequalities in capital distribution were reflected in growing interindustry differentials.[16] Furthermore, increased enterprise autonomy allowed for higher rates of capital formation in high-wage industries,[17] so that "statistical analyses show that in the period 1960–1969 about 46 per cent of intersectoral [interindustry] variations in personal incomes could be accounted for by the organic composition of capital.[18] Thus, the Yugoslav economy after the reform

appears to have been following a path similar to the one hypothesized earlier
for mutualism.

Like the later stages of mutualism, too, Yugoslavia had its share of oligopolistic market structures. That is, work collectives not only differentiated
themselves by degree of capital intensity but also according to their market
position, a factor whose effect on enterprise profitability became increasingly
important after the 1965–66 price reform. Although concentration does not
appear to have increased a great deal after the reform,[19] the narrowness of the
Yugoslav market and the integration campaigns before and immediately
after the reforms meant that many product markets were highly oligopolistic
at the outset. Theoretically, foreign competition was to correct for the
inefficiencies and inequalities arising from monopolistic concentration;
although this strategy was partially successful,[20] growing balance-of-payments
problems and import dependency made it increasingly costly. Price controls,
occasionally accompanied by covert subsidies (steel), occasionally not (railroads), also attempted to keep prices and hence wages in line. In addition, the
financial weakness of many industrial firms prevented them from taking
advantage of a potentially oligopolistic position.[21] The result was that while
not all monopolies and oligopolies had high wages, with one or two exceptions, high-wage industries all had monopolistic or oligopolistic market
structures.[22] As one observer found, "Capital intensity and monopolistic
behavior accounted for 65 per cent of inter[industry] differences in personal
income" from 1960 to 1969.[23]

Like interrepublic inequalities, what on balance is surprising about wage
differentials in different industries is not that they widened, but that they
widened so slightly. This is particularly remarkable given the high capital-
intensity and concentration ratios of a good number of Yugoslav industries,
plus the fact that they are labor managed and hence, in theory, prone to
raise wages rather than increase employment. True, interindustry differentials
in manufacturing and mining—activities that included over 40 percent of
those employed in the socialist sector and a much higher percentage of the
manual, blue-collar workers employed throughout Yugoslavia—rose. However,
differentials between different *branches* (such as manufacturing and mining,
transport, trade, construction) actually declined (table 8), and in fact, the
position of manufacturing and mining as a whole vis-à-vis the so-called "noneconomic" activities appears to have improved. Also interindustry differentials within the transport, trade, and social service branches narrowed, partially
offsetting their widening in manufacturing and mining.

In part, the competitive market was responsible for these changes, for the
price reform permitted prices of agricultural goods, raw materials, and construction to rise from their earlier, artificially depressed levels. Consequently,

wages and productivity in these branches rose more rapidly than they did in other areas of the economy. In addition, the branching out of existing firms into new fields of activity provided an element of competition in some areas where it had been lacking. More profoundly, however, the narrowness of interindustry and interbranch wage differentials must be explained by political factors that counteracted the effects of the competitive market. To understand the dynamics of this situation, it is necessary to look at the subjective impact of these differentials on both the Yugoslav public and on the political factions feuding over the direction of government economic policy.

In this respect, the significance of interindustry differentials in Yugoslavia cannot be gauged by looking at global wage statistics alone. Their subjective impact in a highly egalitarian political culture was quite out of proportion with whatever their objective dimensions were. Moreover, occurring in the context of a wave of consumerism that followed the sacrifices and asceticism of the 1950s, what income differentials did appear were much more visible than those of the earlier period.

As for wages, table 14, comparing monthly salaries of individual categories of labor in particular industries, gives a better sense of what they looked like to the average Yugoslav. In looking at these figures, it should be kept in mind that they are not controlled for interrepublic differentials and represent *average* wages in a given industry. Thus, individual firms may have had higher or lower salaries, and the fact that the largest four firms in each industry controlled, on average, almost half of all domestic sales suggests that interenterprise differentials may have been considerable.

Moreover, depending on their financial capabilities, enterprises supplied their employees with housing, transportation subsidies, low-cost meals, individual loans for education, consumer credit, and other fringe benefits. As these items constituted a significant portion of individual household budgets, their impact on wage differentials could be substantial. Housing appears to have been a particular problem. High-wage industries could not only afford to buy apartments for their employees, but the apartments—especially those used to substitute for wage incentives for skilled personnel—would also be larger. Since households would often sublet rooms or even whole apartments at high prices, the individual beneficiaries of enterprise collective consumption funds not only saved on their own rents, but acquired a lucrative source of private earnings on the side.[24] Such arrangements effected a de facto transfer of income from individuals with low earnings, forced to be tenants, to those with high earnings.

The effects of the illiquidity crises that periodically ravaged Yugoslav firms also had a differential impact. The more financially stable enterprises and work organizations, with larger cash reserves, typically had less difficulty

Table 14. Interindustry and Interskill Differentials for
Selected Categories of Labor, 1968 (Dinars)

Category	Industry	Average Monthly Wage
Unskilled worker	Petroleum	908
	Chemicals	729
	Textiles	580
	Foreign trade	678
	Elementary school	492
	Banks	703
Highly skilled worker	Petroleum	1,580
	Chemicals	1,077
	Textiles	1,020
	Foreign trade	1,360
	Elementary school	879
	Banks	1,280
Technician-secondary school education	Petroleum	1,499
	Chemicals	1,110
	Textiles	906
	Foreign trade	1,393
	Elementary school	905
	Banks	1,213
University graduate	Petroleum	2,194
	Chemicals	1,752
	Textiles	1,241
	Foreign trade	1,820
	Elementary school	1,124
	Banks	1,868

Source: Statistički godišnjak SFRJ (Belgrade: Savezni zavod za statistiku, 1971),
table 122–6, "Prosečna neto lična primanja prema stepenu stručnog obrazovanja,"
p. 269.

in meeting monthly payrolls. Moreover, since they were more insulated from
the fluctuations of the market, oscillations in the size of monthly paychecks
presumably were smaller. Insofar as these two factors were major causes of
the rash of strikes that afflicted Yugoslavia in the sixties,[25] they must be
considered nonwage benefits of considerable importance, especially for
workers in lower skill brackets.

In addition, table 8 indicates that the position of manufacturing as a whole
deteriorated relative to that of all other "economic" branches in the socialist
sector. That interindustry differentials within manufacturing were growing at
the same time would then suggest that while workers in high-wage industries
were able to maintain or even improve their relative position, those in low-
wage industries perceived their standard of living as rapidly deteriorating.[26]
Interskill differentials undoubtedly compounded the sense of relative depriva-

tion of the unskilled workers who constituted the vast majority of the labor force in the labor-intensive low-wage industries.

Finally, the division of the economy into high-, medium-, and low-wage industries meant that individuals with similar skills in similar jobs received both unequal pay and unequal access to nonwage benefits.[27] Although with labor mobility the economic consequences of these inequalities for resource allocation need not have been serious, ideologically they constituted a direct challenge to the principle of "distribution according to work," or at least to the interpretation of it held by many national and local political leaders. The combination of blue-collar complaints and strikes, overall economic instability, and ideological confusion interacted to make "exploitation" of social property and "groupism" in work collectives key political footballs to be tossed around by warring factions within the League of Communists and the government.

Some saw direct intervention as the means of "equalizing conditions on the market," others argued for general regulation, and yet others favored letting the market take its own course. Meanwhile, the strength of the factions varied from time to time and from place to place, making the outcomes of these political conflicts in any specific context as unpredictable as they were vital to an enterprise's economic future.[28] On the whole, however, the overall effect of the political uncertainty was to narrow interindustry differentials. In contrast with Proudhon's federalist state, then, the impact of political intervention in Yugoslavia—or the threat of it—was not to reinforce the operation of the market, but to counteract it.

On the one hand, high-wage industries dared not raise personal incomes above socially and politically acceptable levels lest, as in 1967, wage ceilings be clamped down on them and/or other, less drastic forms of political harrassment be directed at them.[29] At the same time, egalitarian norms had the effect of forcing a higher rate of accumulation in high-wage industries; while this could have beneficial effects, as when existing firms founded new ones in different product markets,[30] it could just as easily be detrimental by allowing horizontal monopolies to become vertical ones, thereby concentrating vast amounts of capital—and control—in the hands of single enterprises. The rapid expansion of a number of import-export houses into quite unrelated fields of economic activity was a sign that the selfmanaged conglomerate had arrived on the Yugoslav scene.[31] Note that through such arrangements, the possibility of adding interest to income derived from the concentration of social capital and monopolistic market position became a reality.

On the other hand, low-wage industries could use the political uncertainty to raise wages above productivity by rationalizing such decisions as a defense of working-class interests and the principle of distribution according to work. They could then point to the higher wages of workers with similar skills in other industries, blame "monopolies" and "unequal market conditions" for an inability to compete, appeal to the "difficult situation" inflation created for low-income workers, or complain about the "discriminatory" effects of changes in government regulations.[32] Despite the fact that such actions hurt accumulation, jeopardized future incomes, and contributed to inflationary pressures, they were made possible and even encouraged by the aid rendered such firms by politicians at various levels, who would pressure banks to grant special loans or extend repayment terms on loans already due, "find" funds to subsidize losses, join in appeals to better-off firms for acts of "solidarity," and so forth.[33] In this way, bankruptcies and wider interindustry differentials were avoided at the expense of inflation and misallocation.

It is important to emphasize that popular support for this kind of ad hoc intervention—whether to hold down wages in some industries or inflate them in others—was considerable, regardless of the "statist" overtones it carried. Not surprisingly, support was strongest in enterprises hit hardest by the reforms,[34] in particular, among blue-collar workers.[35] In order to understand the situation that led to what Županov terms "the mass base of statism," it is necessary to look at one other source of inequalities in self-managed socialism: those arising within the individual enterprises themselves.

INTERSKILL DIFFERENTIALS AND INEQUALITIES WITHIN THE FIRM[36]

Interskill differentials within single enterprises, legitimized under the "distribution according to work" principle, proved less of an ideological problem than interindustry differentials.[37] Generally, they remained within politically acceptable limits, narrowing in the first years of the reform but widening a bit when a brief economic recovery set in in 1969.[38] Several points should be noted in this connection.

In the first place, for a number of reasons,[39] recessions in Yugoslavia had an inflationary character, and "as always in a period of inflation, there is a tendency to level out the workers' incomes by increasing first those of the lowest paid group."[40] However, as we have seen (table 10), inflation in Yugoslavia did not coincide with full employment, suggesting that the narrowing of interskill differentials from 1963 to 1968 was not owing to the operation of the labor market. On the contrary, it would appear a consequence of the actions of workers' councils, which, out of feelings of *political* solidarity, raised the wages of unskilled groups relatively faster than those of the skilled groups, despite the higher unemployment rates of the former. Moreover, workers' councils were supported and encouraged in these actions by political figures outside the enterprises.[41] In other words, the fluctuating pattern of interskill differentials and the fact that they appear relatively small by Western standards must be traced to political factors and not to the operation of the market. In this, they were essentially similar to interindustry and inter-republic differentials.

Secondly, as do interindustry differentials, global wage statistics tend to underestimate the extent of interskill differentials present, since nonwage benefits also cumulated along skill lines. Housing again was a particular problem, for it was used to attract trained personnel. And whereas high-wage industries might be able to purchase housing or at least supply credit to a large proportion of their employees, thereby ameliorating intraenterprise conflicts over nonwage benefits, low-wage industries were forced to ration the restricted means they did have on the basis of skill in order to retain technical and managerial specialists. Understandably, such policies only demoralized their rank-and-file work force further.[42]

Added to this was the question of "other earnings," a source of great irritation to many blue-collar workers. Vladimir Milanović explains:

> These other earnings constitute an "invisible," socially uncontrolled and usually untaxed portion of income, which accrues mainly to functionaries and various experts. These are the numerous travel allowances . . ., expense accounts, awards for overtime work . . . prizes (usually unmerited), compensations for use of a private automobile, allotments for meals . . . etc. . . . The sums received in this manner are not insignificant, and this can be seen in the data for 1971. With 37,376 million dinars paid out in the name of personal income, there was another 5,100 [million] dinars, fully 20 percent, paid out for "other earnings."[43]

Third, opportunities for part-time employment outside of one's enterprise favored those in higher skill brackets. The growth of the private, nonagricultural sector, the introduction of a forty-two-hour work week, labor laws that made it difficult for firms to hire someone for short periods without taking him on as a permanent employee, and the levelling tendencies of the workers' councils all gave highly trained individuals an incentive to hold down second jobs. Even though unemployment among this group showed a considerable upswing in postreform years (table 9), the contacts employed specialists acquired through their regular job gave them a definite edge in the labor market. This not only widened the income span between them and unskilled workers, but also hurt the employment possibilities of new, highly trained entrants to the labor market.

Differential possibilities for outside employment and fringe benefits help to explain why inequalities tend to cumulate on the household level. Female employment and social stratification also helped make income concentration by households significantly higher than for individuals.[44] Nevertheless, demographic data indicate that wealthier households in Yugoslavia are not smaller than poorer ones.[45] This suggests that individuals of similar skills and income levels tend to marry one another, hardly an unusual sociological phenomenon but one that would perpetuate income differentials over generations. Not surprisingly, the proportion of university students coming from working-class and peasant families dropped dramatically in the 1960s.[46] Ironically, workers found themselves paying high "contributions" for education, which self-managing educational work collectives then allocated to increasing salaries, employment, and capital expenses, while keeping scholarship funds constant.

Finally, wage differentials within enterprises were not the only inequalities. Equally irritating to workers and far more problematic ideologically were the inequalities in influence and power increasingly apparent in the postreform years. Despite the fact that theoretically the new "collective entrepreneur" model of the firm assumed all members of the work collective had an equal voice in decision making and an equal share of the risk, study after study revealed that managerial and technical personnel had a much greater influence than blue-collar workers on the decisions made by self-management organs, regardless of the former's numerical inferiority and regardless of whether or not they were actually elected members of the authorized bodies.[47]

The highly skewed balance of power was partially because the reforms had simply granted greater autonomy to enterprises with essentially oligarchic power structures at the outset. Thus, when the sphere of enterprise discretion was enlarged, the already influential groups were in a far better position to take advantage of it.[48] Illustrative was Amendment XV to the 1963 Constitution. Enacted in 1969, it was designed to give enterprises more internal flexibility and thereby "widen the sphere of worker self-managing action." Most enterprises, however, used it to replace the managing board, a body elected by the workers' council from the firm labor force, with a business board on which only enterprise executives sat.[49]

In part, the oligarchic power structure in Yugoslav firms, like the oligarchic power structure we saw developing in mutualist associations, was a product of the enterprise's new dependence on its market position for its income. Financial and commercial operations began to assume an importance they had lacked before, while production, where blue-collar involvement was highest, lost much of its earlier centrality.[50] Similarly, the need for rapid decisions to respond flexibly to market cues and increased pressures for technological innovation enhanced the influence of executives and specialists over that of manual laborers.

Note that while autonomy increased the power of the already influential groups, dependence on the market simultaneously caused it to be redistributed among them. In this process, the big losers were the "sociopolitical" organizations within the firm, especially the party cell and the trade unions.[51] Sociopolitical organizations had important functions as bridge organizations between political bodies and the enterprises. They helped insure that enterprises conformed internally with regulations and laws made outside the firm and that enterprise interests were represented when political bodies made decisions that affected them. Accordingly, the more important state intervention was for the fortunes of a firm, the more influence the sociopolitical organizations would have inside it. With the withdrawal of the state from the economy, however, enterprise dependence on a unified set of political agents was transformed into dependence on a series of contradictory and pluralistic forces, many of which were not political at all (customers, suppliers, banks). Thus, the influence of the sociopolitical organizations declined, while that of technical, and especially managerial, personnel rose.[52]

The decline of the sociopolitical organizations within Yugoslav enterprises resulted from factors external to the firm as well. While these will be dealt with in chapter 6, at this point it should merely be noted that a decline in influence should not be equated with an eclipse of influence: the presence of and possibility for ad hoc administrative intervention still meant that good activists were an important *economic* asset for an enterprise. At the same time, it also caused the fortunes of enterprise sociopolitical organizations and activists within them to be dependent on enterprise performance, rather than vice versa, as had been the case in the 1950s. The effect of this situation on the national sociopolitical organizations, the League of Communists in particular, was simply to increase the fragmentation of an already highly factionalized political leadership.

Yet another cause for management's concentrated influence lay in the distribution of responsibility in the self-managed enterprise. That is, "the responsibility of self-management organs is in its form, collective, and in its content, moral, while the responsibility of executive organs as a rule is individual and not only moral, but also material and criminal."[53] Not surprisingly, in this situation workers often hesitated to press an issue knowing that the enterprise director would suffer the consequences. At the same time, it meant that managerial personnel had a much greater incentive to see that correct decisions were made than did the elected membership of decision-making bodies. This helps to explain why studies found participation of managerial personnel at *all* levels of the enterprise hierarchy higher than that of workers *or* specialists:[54] while even a specialist's responsibility ended once he had written a report, made recommendations, and submitted the information and conclusions to the authorized self-management body, an executive's job was not completed until a policy recommendation was voted on and put into effect.

Moreover, the need of managerial personnel to get policy decisions formally accepted by self-management bodies within a reasonable time understandably led to attempts to manipulate these bodies, to stock them with "reliable" people, and occasionally even to sanctions and harassment of workers and employees who offered resistance.[55] Management by "contract," threats to resign, mystifying "professional" authority by presenting information in hopelessly technical terms, and other such behavior all became reasonable solutions to overcoming the gap between authority and responsibility in the self-managed firm,[56] while being highly dysfunctional in terms of the egalitarian collective entrepreneur model. Furthermore, while enterprise executives might well get their recommendations formally accepted by the self-management bodies through such techniques, this was not necessarily equivalent to receiving the voluntary consent and adherance of the collective or even of the members of the decision-making bodies themselves to a course of action. Significantly, members of self-management bodies participated in fully 85 percent of all Yugoslav strikes, and Obradović, French, and Rodgers found that workers' council members "with high aspired levels of participation" were *more* alienated than their more apathetic peers, "because reality reveals they do not attain the level of participation they, as members of Workers' Councils, feel they ought to have."[57]

The effects of these inequalities of power and responsibility on the atmosphere in the Yugoslav firm were quite comparable with those produced by similar developments in Proudhon's mutualist associations. When inequalities in influence were compounded with income differentials, unequal educational opportunities, and status differences, a growing sense of social differentiation was created within the walls of the Yugoslav enterprise.

Education and occupational category ("function" in production) became the best single predictors not only of income levels, but also of participation levels, desires to participate, attitudes toward self-management, attitudes toward work, willingness to accept risk, as well as of general social values. For example, while executives felt that the material incentives connected with managerial positions were too low, workers typically felt that the wage span was too great.[58] Although managerial personnel generally felt all the members of the collective should suffer if the enterprise showed losses, workers typically felt only management or the "guilty parties" should bear the brunt of losses.[59] Similarly, executives and specialists were on the whole opposed to price controls and keeping unprofitable enterprises in business, while workers and routine employees tended to take a more favorable view of both.[60] At

Table 15. Value Systems of Unskilled and Semiskilled Workers
and Managers in Yugoslav Industry

Unskilled and Semi-skilled Workers	Average Value[a]	Managers	Average Value
1. Equality	242.3	1. Personal freedom	244.4
2. Equity	220.3	2. Equity	229.2
3. Personal freedom	217.3	3. Honesty	218.3
4. Security	216.2	4. Payment according to work	217.2
5. Standard of living	208.2	5. Standard of living	206.2
6. Honesty	203.8	6. Security	193.2
7. Solidarity	188.8	7. Equality	186.5
8. Self-management	181.6	8. Self-management	182.3
9. Distribution according to work	146.5	9. Solidarity	164.5

Source: Silvano Bolčić, "The Value System of a Participatory Economy," *First International Conference on Participation and Self-Management*, 6 vols. (Zagreb: Institute for Social Research, 1972-73), 1: 111.

[a]Respondents were asked to rank values supplied by the interviewer. "The average values were obtained as follows: for each value a separate grouping of the data was made, so that the ranks 1-3 were interpreted as "very important," ranks 4-6 "important" and ranks 7-9 "of little importance." The percentage distribution of answers were calculated, and then the percentages corresponding to . . . "very important" were multiplied by 3, "important" . . . by 2, and "of little importance" . . . by 1. The cited "average value . . . was obtained by summing these results" (p. 110n).

the same time, directors felt that they lacked authority to perform their tasks, felt they should have more influence on a whole gamut of enterprise policy issues, particularly in choosing the management "team," and generally saw power in the firm distributed much more evenly than the workers perceived it. Workers, in contrast, saw management as monopolizing decision making as it was and felt they themselves should have a much greater input into such matters as personnel decisions, business policy, and distribution of wage and nonwage benefits.[61] Bolčić provides a global index of the social values lying behind these contrasting evaluations and aspirations (table 15).

Understandably, conflict within enterprises increased along with the growing social differentiation. A Slovenian study found the consequences of the new primacy of "distribution according to work" to be the deterioration of interpersonal relations, the division of people into those of greater and lesser worth, encouragement of an unremitting and crudely materialistic struggle among individuals and groups to grab a larger share of personal income (merited or not), and pressures exerted on older or handicapped employees to leave the firm.[62] Horizontal conflicts between divisions and departments within enterprises cross-cut the vertical cleavages between occupational categories, and various cliques created by the fragmentation that decentralization introduced fought ongoing, covert and overt battles for influence.[63] Strikes and work stoppages became regular, covered in the press and on occasion televised.[64] And while executives saw the cause of work stoppages as workers' lack of information and/or inability to understand it, workers ascribed them to low wages, bad labor relations, and poor management.[65] In such a situation of heightened worker-management conflict combined with a certain amount of managerial manipulation of the regular self-management organs, workers quite rationally began turning to the trade unions and, to a lesser extent, the League of Communists and the state as the only organizations capable of defending their interests.[66]

In its broadest lines then, the pattern in many Yugoslav firms was similar to the one that developed inside Proudhon's mutualist associations: specialization and hierarchy in the context of the market and an egalitarian ideology calling for "just distribution" brought an increase in conflict within the firm over exactly what fair distribution meant in practice along with increased politicization and protest by lower-income groups.

Nevertheless, the increase in conflict within the Yugoslav firm did not mean that solidarity vanished entirely. While internal questions such as hiring, distribution of income, allocation of apartments, and similar issues generated a good deal of open dispute or covert grumbling, enterprises typically presented a united front in dealing with outside parties. Whether these external organizations were economic (customers, suppliers, banks) or political (government, party committees), all members of an enterprise work collective shared an interest in successfully concluding their dealings with them.[67] Stane Možina's study of decisions workers would be most interested in participating in is revealing. Workers emphatically wanted a greater voice in decision making and control in questions of income distribution, personnel, work conditions, business policy, plan formulation, work hours, and on-the-job relations. However, their interest in enterprise relations with the commune, economic chambers, and business associations, in "sociopolitical" problems (ideology, democracy, and so forth), price policies, and drawing up factory regulations (internal rules implementing various externally enacted laws applying to firms) was virtually nonexistent.[68] The implication is that insofar as these latter questions had to be handled by someone in the enterprise, management, experts, or the sociopolitical organizations could just as easily represent worker interests as could the workers themselves.

Meanwhile, loyalty to the enterprise in its dealings with outside agencies exacerbated conflicts in Yugoslav society as a whole. It began to lead to a situation in which each one feels exploited by the others: agriculture by industry, industry by the banks, the producers of raw materials by the producers of finished goods, undeveloped areas by developed ones, small entrepreneurs by large ones, advanced firms by less developed ones, etc.[69]

In this regard, "groupism" and internal enterprise conflict could even reinforce each other, as firms would appeal to political authorities to aid them in the name of a "working class" suffering under the burden of low personal incomes.

The gap between workers' control in theory and managerial domination in practice, between the model of a conflictless and united collective entrepreneur and the reality of firms in which strong and often bitter disagreements were a way of life, was not only a source of cynicism among workers, frustration among executives, apathy among specialists, and a whole series of economic dysfunctionalities. It also was an enormous topic of ideological controversy among political leaders in the League of Communists and at all levels of government.[70]

Whereas the pre-1965 self-management model had encouraged managerial and technical oligarchy, the new model disallowed it. Thus, the under-representation of lower skill categories and manual laborers on workers' councils and other self-management bodies was no longer construed as laudable deferrence by blue collar workers to superior knowledge.[71] Rather, it was attacked as a technocratic takeover. Economically, too, the concentration of power in the hands of enterprise managements caused a good deal of consternation when it was added to the highly oligopolistic market structure of so much of Yugoslav industry and commerce: in effect, a handful of executives seemed to be controlling vast amounts of capital and labor.

These features were combined with a declining worker presence on major political bodies, an inability of the League of Communists to enlarge significantly the proportion of blue-collar workers in its membership,[72] and a pyramiding of the various inequalities so that the brunt of the reform appeared to have fallen more on industrial workers than on any other group in the socialist sector. The illiquidity problem, the trade deficit, the disappointing overall economic performance, and the heightened tension among the nationalities all added to a growing sense of crisis as Yugoslav self-management entered its third decade. Thus, when the question of what had gone wrong with the reform became unavoidable, "technocratic-managerialism" provided an all too ready answer.

6

Toward a New Model of
Self-Managing Socialism

IDEOLOGY AND THE POLITICAL CLIMATE

What the 1965 reforms did for the economy, the Eighth Party Congress and the Fourth Plenum of the Central Committee accomplished for the Yugoslav League of Communists. Dennison Rusinow summarizes the line of thought that was to dominate party activity in the postreform years:

> Yugoslavia was to become a non-party—not a single party or a multiparty—"self-managerial socialist democracy. . . ." Pluralism should be achieved, not through the competition of parties based on class or special interests, but through the competition of institutions representing the differing functions performed by citizens and the interests associated with them.[1]

Like Proudhon and Gramsci, Yugoslav communists had long assumed that the principles regulating the economy also governed political life. Accordingly, just as market competition was to regulate economic life after 1965, "the struggle of ideas" was to characterize party life. Hierarchy was to be abolished in economic units, and "bureaucratism" was to be eliminated in political life. Decentralization was to prevail in economic allocation and party policy formulation alike. Economic organizations were to be made autonomous of the state, and government bodies were to be freed from the "dictates" of party committees in order to respond directly to the needs of the "working people." "Equalizing conditions of operation" in the economy meant that all enterprises and work organizations were legally equal; applied politically, it meant that the hegemony the League of Communists had enjoyed over organizations like the Socialist Alliance and the trade unions was to decline as the mass organizations assumed more independent roles in their respective spheres of competence. "Distribution according to work" was not only to encourage firms to hire personnel on the basis of competence, but also to make party offices available on a more meritocratic basis and to break with the apparatchik mentality that had gone hand in hand with the "old methods" of the past.[2] As Proudhon would have it, the "notions of power and authority" were to be replaced by the "notions of labor and exchange" in all spheres of social life.

What was new about the Yugoslav League of Communists in the mid-sixties was not just its ideological pronouncements, many of which can actually be traced back as far as the Sixth Congress in 1952. It was also who was voicing them, how they were implemented, and what interpretations they received.

At the higher levels of party leadership, the purge of Ranković and his supporters in 1966 as well as the internal struggle preceding it shifted the balance of power in favor of the more liberalizing elements. While these could unite around a common distaste for central planning, once they emerged victorious, the winning coalition began to break up into component parts, each of which began to assert its own demands with increasing stridency. At the same time, the climate of tolerance created by the liberal victory and the "struggle of ideas" slogan permitted numerous bastions of support for greater centralization and "strong arm" (čvrsta ruka) policies to remain in the party and the state despite the Ranković ouster. Since the postreform ideology itself contained numerous ambiguities and contradictory elements, these factions could legitimately join the debate over its implementation by simply interpreting the new principles in more traditional terms.[3]

The triumph of the liberals, the conflicts in higher party circles, and the ideological emphasis on control from below also weakened party discipline. This permitted demands for yet greater democratization and decentralization to be heard from below as well as from the party leadership itself, as distinct from the period preceding the Eighth Congress.[4] The 1968 Belgrade student revolt and the way it was handled by political leaders is indicative. But this centralization also made it extremely difficult to eliminate dissenting groups, whether liberal or conservative, by action from above. At the Ninth Congress in 1969, Tito himself was clearly concerned over the situation:

> An energetic opposition must be put up to all those who, paying lip service to socialist democracy, are attempting to underrate the leading ideological-political role of the LCY, as well as to all those for whom reorganization means turning the LCY into some kind of debating club. We must sharpen in the LCY ranks a feeling of responsibility of both the rank and file and the leaders. In this respect, there used to be weaknesses, irresponsibilities, obstinacy and indiscipline with quite a large number of communists and leaderships.[5]

Furthermore, the new resolve to stop "dictating" and the continual con-flict at higher levels translated itself into a lack of concrete directives for

rank-and-file party activists. This, plus the dependence of grass-roots militants
on the nonparty organization with which they were connected, made it easy
for such nonparty organizations to utilize the basic party cells as pressure
groups for particular interests.

The effect of this decentralization and pluralistic fragmentation on the
League of Communists was not only a general diminution of its direct influence over state organs and work organizations.[6] In a manner somewhat
reminiscent of the narrow and shifting interest alignments in Proudhon's
mutualism, the LCY became transformed from a somewhat unorthodox version of a Marxist-Leninist party into a close approximation of what, in effect,
was a union of competing factions.[7]

Although the various interests that surfaced under the LCY umbrella were
fairly homogeneous in terms of their acceptance of the goals of the reform
and of self-management, conflict on particular policy measures was often
extremely sharp. On the one hand, the broad consensus on values meant that
should the highest party leaders take a resolute stand, their position would
become party policy; on the other, the presence of strong disagreements within the ranks of the party on specific questions deterred them from doing so.
In this sense, the retreat of the League of Communists from the political
arena was as much a reflection of its own divisions as of a conscious, ideological decision.[8]

Two broad sets of issues appear to have been the main sources of controversy both within the League of Communists and within government decision-
making bodies. The first centered around the role of the state in the economy,
the second around where the locus of power within the state was to lie.

Although all agreed (at least verbally) that centralized investment planning
had been unsatisfactory, that the enterprises were being taxed too heavily,
that administrative intervention should be reduced, and the "political"
factories should be eliminated, opinions were far from unanimous on what
should replace them. We have already seen the effects on the economy of the
measures finally taken, results considered undesirable by "liberals" and "conservatives" alike.

Debate then entered a second stage. Where the main question in the first
period had been how fast and in what ways the state should withdraw from
the economy, the key question in the second period was what had gone
wrong with the reform. While the first stage, lasting up until about 1968, had
been marked by a "liberal" hegemony, the second stage was one of stalemate,
in which liberals blamed the failure of the reforms to achieve the desired
results on the persistence of "statist" elements, while conservatives argued

that the state had retreated too precipitously from its legitimate responsibilities. The presence of a good deal of administrative intervention, poorly coordinated and illegitimate, lent plausibility to the arguments of both sides. At the same time, the struggles between the factions quickly led to

> promises that we will do more for the underdeveloped areas and that we will take less for them, that we will free up the economy [reduce taxes on firms] but we will give more to the social services than previously, that we will shorten work time [*radni staž*] and increase personal income— and all this simultaneously.[9]

As we shall see, the third stage of the debate involved an overall questioning of some of the central premises of the reform and a transition to a new, more government-heavy model of self-managing socialism.

The second set of issues concerned the division of whatever responsibilities the state was to have between the republic and the national governments. Concessions to those supporting a greater role for the republics were initially made in the course of the party struggle against Ranković.[10] Although such demands were advanced primarily by Slovenia and Croatia at the outset, once they began to be granted, all the republics became highly protective of their own territorial and ethnic interests.

The process of "republicanization" began first in the League of Communists in 1964, when the Eighth Congress allowed republic party congresses to meet before the national congress convened. It quickly spread to the national government, where such an impasse was reached in 1966 over the allocation of federal funds to the underdeveloped areas in the National Assembly that the Chamber of Nationalities had to be brought out of the cold storage it had been in for twenty years to decide the issue. This was followed by the 1968–69 constitutional amendments, giving the republics considerable authority over their own affairs at the national government's expense and promoting the Chamber of Nationalities from an essentially symbolic token of ethnic equality into the first chamber of the national legislature. Nevertheless, as with government economic policy,

> the system as it then operated until 1971 turned out to be a recipe for stalemate. The republics were strong enough to prevent the federal government from taking any step that might infringe republican interests through the Chamber of Nationalities, but on the other hand the federal government retained enough of its power through its control of the country's finances to block any republican initiatives.[11]

The deadlock only began to be broken in 1971, when the Yugoslav state was redefined altogether in the new set of constitutional amendments that saw the republics as the key units of government.

Although it is possible to identify vaguely a "liberal" and "conservative" side in both the economic policy and the decentralization debates, these labels are highly misleading. Those who pushed for a diminution in state regulation of the economy did not necessarily support decentralization down to the republics of whatever state power was left.[12] At the same time, those who wished to see the republics granted greater autonomy often favored a stronger state; indeed, one of the arguments against such a decentralization was precisely that the strong republic governments proposed by some factions would threaten the "unity" of the Yugoslav market by institutionalizing political obstacles to the free circulation of capital.[13]

Moreover, while one can identify two (or more) sides on each issue, labeling them with a common appellation makes each faction in the conflicts appear far more cohesive, homogeneous, and ideologically consistent than any of them really were. There were those who favored withdrawal of the state from the economy in some fields and opposed it in others; some who supported increased republican autonomy in some areas and resisted it in others.

The splits in the Croatian League of Communists are a case in point. While Vladimir Bakarić initially had been a major protagonist of the economic reforms and the dismantling of the General Invesment Fund, by 1971 he could support a purge from above of the more nationalistically inclined leaders of the Croatian party as well as new measures restricting enterprise autonomy. The demands of the Kosovo demonstraters in 1968 offer a parallel illustration. While they insisted on greater autonomy for the province of Kosovo on behalf of the Albanian ethnic minority within it, they also claimed that the Yugoslav community had made an insufficient commitment to economic development in Kosovo and that a greater share of the Fund for Accelerated Development should be allocated to it.

Complicating these divisions further was what came to be known as the "split between theory and practice," the source of a good deal of cynicism toward self-management in general and toward Yugoslav political leaders in particular. This "split" referred first to the difference between the promised effects of the economic reforms and their actual results. Second, although the measures designed to compensate for the imbalances created by the market were largely administrative, they were often taken and supported by political figures who ardently espoused state withdrawal from the economy. Thus, a gap between policy and implementation and between words and deeds grew up to complement the discrepancy between expectations and achievements of the reform. Confidence in political leaders was further eroded by their practice of proclaiming every measure a success regardless of its objective results. The editor of a Zagreb weekly newspaper gave one example:

> A few days ago, Comrade Šabić, a member of the Federal Executive Council, said to the Parliament, "The housing reform is proceeding successfully," and then announced that in the last two years, 20,000 fewer apartments had been built than was planned, while prices had jumped 70 percent.[14]

At the same time, the "size" of the theory-practice discrepancy was not uniform throughout Yugoslavia: in some localities, the reforms brought positive results, in others, negative consequences; some local leaders were more prone to extend aid to struggling enterprises and/or aggrieved workers, others less so. Generally, however, it appears that the closer the political leaders were to the firms hardest hit by the reforms, the greater was their preference for transferring economic risk to the state. Thus, "statist" sentiment was stronger among local politicians than among national leaders, in less developed than in more developed localities.[15]

This brings us to the central factors behind the dynamics of the debates over both economic policy and political decentralization: the economic instability and its effect on the socialized enterprises, and the inequalities question and the reactions of industrial workers. As we have seen, managerial and technical elites and, to some extent, even rank-and-file workers employed in the socialist sector had initially been among the reforms' strongest supporters. As the economic downturn began to threaten an increasing number of enterprises, however, the glamour of their new-found autonomy began to dim considerably.

Furthermore, since few enterprises had interrepublic branches or even national product markets, when appeals for aid were directed to government officials, it was local and republic leaders who felt much of the pressures. Both they and the enterprises understandably resented having to lobby with the national government to protect what both all too conveniently agreed were viable firms suffering under poorly thought out reforms. Moreover, as enterprise branches of the sociopolitical organizations were often the vehicle by which such pressures were exerted, these organizations also became increasingly sympathetic to state intervention and particularly to intervention from the units of government that fell within their spheres of influence: the local and republic governments.

Meanwhile, the work organizations that did appear to be prospering under the reform turned out to be large organizations that had far-flung national and even international operations and were, by and large, concentrated in banking and trade. As they resisted, often unsuccessfully, attempts by any and all state agencies to intervene in their affairs,[16] they were reluctant to come to the aid of the national government when it came under attack, although they hardly saw strong republic governments as a desirable solution.

As for the high-wage industrial enterprises, regardless of whether they had national product markets, their production operations tended to be concentrated in one republic or another: shipbuilding firms were located on the coast (Croatia); the giants of the petroleum industry were based in either Croatia or Serbia; the power industry was carved up into smaller regional monopolies; Kragujevac (Serbia) was the Detroit of Yugoslavia; and so forth. Owing to their high profits, significant capital reserves, and large labor force, such enterprises had considerable influence in the republic and, to a lesser extent, in the national government.[17] Like banks and trading companies, then, they resisted the notion of a strong and independent central government.[18] Yet since a lower-level republic government would be more directly dependent on them for its revenues, they might well have stood to gain from a political decentralization even if it entailed giving the republic government greater regulatory powers.

At the same time, the illiquidity crises made the less solvent firms highly dependent on banks and trading companies for financing both their long-term and short-term capital needs. They thus came to see banks and import-export houses not only as prospering, but as prospering at their own expense.[19] This plus the fact that financial and commercial operations were conducted on a national scale led to demands that banks and trading companies be put under republic control, where locally based industrial firms would have easier access to them. Alternatively, it was argued that large capital concentrations be broken up through political means and the assets distributed back to the enterprises. In effect, the centralization of capital created by the competitive market, the incentive structure of labor-managed social property, and the need for interregional capital mobility became equated in the popular mind with the political centralization of investment funds in the old GIF. When banks and trading companies objected that the various decentralization schemes would obstruct capital mobility and lead to a politicization of investment decisions, their opponents accused them of "technocratic-managerial" deviations and wanting simply to preserve their monopoly positions. Thus, the political prominence and power executives of these organizations had acquired in the course of trying to keep political influences out of the allocation process proved their Achilles heel once the promarket tide had begun to ebb.

Not only financial and commercial executives and employees were labeled "technocrats." All executives and specialists in the socialized enterprises[20] became subject to this accusation once the inequalities campaign really got underway. In this regard, we have already seen how the subjective impact of inequalities in income and power within and between enterprises cumulated to convince blue-collar industrial workers that they were bearing the main brunt of the 1965 reforms. The growing sense of social differentiation between blue-collar workers and managerial personnel meant that the managerial and technical elites who had pushed for the reforms and still continued to support them in principle found themselves increasingly isolated from the base of blue-collar support they had initially enjoyed.

Certainly, the alienation of blue-collar workers from the postreform self-management model never took the form of an organized and conscious protest movement. At its most articulate, it materialized as sporadic work stoppages and wildcat strikes and as individual responses to interviews conducted by social scientists.[21] Even here, there were no generalized or specific demands for greater political controls over the allocation process, but merely expressions of support for values and goals that could only be realized by greater state intervention.

Nonetheless, the mood had definitely changed; continued economic instability provided a golden opportunity for the increasingly influential political factions favoring a greater role for the state in the economy to undercut the support for the competitive market still present in the firms. Moreover, by linking the inequalities issue to the demand to restore "control" over "surplus value" to the "direct producers" (as opposed to banks on the one hand and managerial personnel on the other), they were able to place the defenders of enterprise autonomy in both a politically and ideologically untenable position. In effect, executives had to choose either the "working class" and reduced enterprise autonomy or "technocracy" and the "anarchy" of the market. Not surprisingly, most opted for the former.

The shift in the trade unions' position is somewhat symptomatic of the growing sentiment against the premises of the reform; of all the mass organizations in Yugoslavia, they were perhaps the most directly responsive to the moods of industrial workers. Prominent among the reform proponents in the early sixties, blocking adoption of the 1965 social plan with pressures for higher consumption levels, by 1971 they were exhibiting increasing concern over inequalities and subsequently became strong supporters of the system of self-management agreements limiting the amount of gross income enterprises could allocate to wages.

Thus, similar to the hypothetical sequence of events in Proudhon's mutualism,

economic instability and inequalities in Yugoslavia contributed to growing
pressures for the use of hierarchy in the economy. By the end of 1971,
the lines had hardened in an atmosphere of acute economic and political crisis.
Continued inflation, high unemployment rates, sluggish economic performance,
growing "indebtedness" of enterprises to banks and commercial firms, a
persistent foreign trade deficit, increasing tension among the nationalities,
factional infighting amidst continued stalemate in the party and the government, and a widespread sense of "drifting" were all militating in favor of a
major change taking place.

The riots that shook Zagreb, resurrecting all the old fears of Croatian
separatism and foreign intervention, were the last straw. New constitutional
amendments aimed at breaking the deadlocks over both economic policy and
republic rights had already been adopted; Tito's Letter of 1972 and subsequent party purge attempted to guarantee their rapid and uniform implementation. In 1974, the reorganization process was crowned with a new constitution, signifying the transition to a "higher stage" of "self-management
development," one in which resource allocation would be based on bargaining
between units whose equality would be guaranteed by the state. While
hardly a return to central planning, it was certainly a step away from the competitive market.

THE CONSTITUTION OF 1974

Arrangements established under the 1974 Constitution made bargaining the
central principle of political and economic life in Yugoslavia. "Like hierarchy,
bargaining is clearly an alternative to the price system," and "commonly
means reciprocity among representatives of hierarchies. . . . Bargaining is therefore not the clean-cut alternative to hierarchy that it is sometimes thought
to be; it may in fact avoid few of the evils of hierarchy, at the same time aggravating problems of coordination."[22]

Applied to relationships among the republics and between them and the
federal government, bargaining meant that decisions on a wide range of
issues—the social plan, foreign trade and currency regulations, tax policy, aid
to less developed regions, and financing the federation—were now to be made
at the national level only with the prior assent of all republic and provincial
governments. Moreover, many of the decisions arrived at centrally were to be
implemented in a decentralized manner. At the same time, the single
presidency envisioned in the 1963 Constitution was converted into a collective
one, composed of representatives from the republics and autonomous
provinces with a rotating chairman, which would begin to operate in full force

after Tito's retirement. Thus, the republics became the central actors on the political stage, and decisions binding on all would be arrived at by bargaining among them. Neither the federation nor the commune would form the main counterweight to the centrifugal forces of republic autarky; rather, this function was left to the powers of large, integrated economic combinations and a more highly disciplined League of Communists.

As for the role of the state in the economy, both the Constitution and subsequent legislation emphasized the importance of social planning, while political leaders announced their determination to overcome the "anarchy" of the market by expanding the use of political mechanisms for economic coordination.[23] Significantly, the ever elusive meaning of social property was again revised; rather than implying that property belonged to those who created it (workers in self-managed firms), social property now meant that property belonged to society, regardless of who created it.[24] Thus were laid the ideological bases for limiting enterprise autonomy.

Planning, however, was not to be either the relatively centralized and hierarchic investment planning of the fifties nor the hopeful forecasting of the sixties. Instead, it was to consist of a series of coordinated "social compacts" and "self-management agreements" concluded among firms, industries, units of government, and mass organizations. If the system used terms similar to Proudhon's, its spirit and emphases were reminiscent of the democratic planning put forth by Gramsci.

According to the 1976 Law on Social Planning, planning began in the firms, which were now legally required to draw up medium-term plans on all aspects of their business operations as well as projected requirements government bodies and semigovernmental agencies were to fulfill, such as how housing, city planning, education, credit policy, and so forth should be adapted to enterprise needs.[25] Based on enterprise plans and the plans of subfederal units of government, an economywide plan containing general target figures for a five-year period (growth rates, investment rates, regional and sectoral development goals, and so on) was then adopted by the federal government.

Meanwhile, the policy measures taken by units of government to facilitate realization of plan goals were to be formulated in national, regional, and/or industry-specific social compacts. Essentially, these were agreements reached by bargaining among units of government or between them and economic organizations in which each obligated itself to take the actions necessary to achieve an agreed-upon goal. If the bargaining process provided an institutionalized setting by which enterprises could influence government activities, the social compact system as a whole was designed to give political bodies leverage on the economy in several ways.

First, it provided a framework within which diverse units of government could coordinate economic policy while retaining their autonomy and freedom of action. For example, a social compact between the republics in 1974 obliged each to ensure that the nominal growth of consumption averaged 20 to 30 percent below that of social product, with the most rapid growth being permitted in the least developed areas. What specific measures republics and provinces took to achieve this goal were their own decision, but the compact allowed them to take direct action on personal incomes should it prove necessary.[26] Similarly, one of the most significant innovations in fiscal policy was made through an interrepublic accord to introduce a tax on enterprise income; while all the republics and provinces agreed to levy such a tax, tax rates were set individually by each republic, and revenues went to finance republic government activities.[27]

Second, industry-government compacts supplied a framework in which policy measures could shape the market so that politically influenced signals would encourage firms to move in the desired directions. For example, the Social Plan of 1976-80 proposed drawing up fifteen social compacts in priority sectors, according to which governments, republic or federal, might agree to float public loans and bonds, relax restrictions on equipment imports, arrange easier credit terms and the like in return for industry and enterprise promises to raise productivity, increase output, maintain certain savings rates, or in the case of chemicals—introduce antipollution measures.[28] Similarly, with the new tax on enterprise income, republic governments could use social compacts to grant tax exemptions to industries and regions in whose development they were particularly interested and ensure that the tax-free income would be used in appropriate ways.[29]

Third, social compacts could be used to legitimate more direct forms of political intervention in economic processes, as in the case of "compensation." Designed to "alleviate the negative effects of . . . uniform instruments and economic policy measures adopted at the federal level,"[30] compensation was to be provided for industries placed in an unfavorable market position by government policies (for example, maintenance of artificially low prices) or because "more efficient production opportunities" had been found elsewhere (for instance, the fund for the substitution of coal production). It would be used to financially reorganize firms in difficulty, retrain workers, or "employ a surplus of workers on the basis of a reorganization program."[31] Hence, compensation represents a legitimized version of previously covert subsidies and rebates given out through government extrabudgetary funds. A "political" allocation of resources, compensation appears aimed not only at "equalizing conditions of economic operation," but also at securing the assent of conflicting parties to the bargains adopted in social plans.

Finally, social compacts were a way in which the "socio-political community" could influence enterprise behavior from inside the firm itself. While enterprises continued to make their own decisions, the criteria governing these decisions were formulated in the compacts, with the participation of political authorities and mass organization.[32] This enhanced the role of the state in preventing inflationary wage and price increases, guaranteeing at least a minimum rate of enterprise savings, providing for greater equality, and setting the general direction of the economy, while the discretion of individual firms was circumscribed.

Not surprisingly, the distribution of enterprise income was a prime concern of national and regional social compacts. Thus, a 1975 social compact between the republics, the Federal Executive Council, the trade unions, and the economic chambers directed firms with above-average productivity increases to devote larger portions of enterprise income to savings, so as to keep wage increases within the limits defined by the average rate of growth of labor productivity in each republic. Social compacts within republics prescribed that allocation of enterprise earnings be done within the context of enterprise development programs so that minimum levels of personal incomes and accumulation would be defined in advance of business results. In addition, income derived from monopoly, tariff protection, and so forth was to be separated from general enterprise earnings and earmarked for investment.[33] In contrast with the 1960s, when enterprise autonomy permitted firms to distribute returns to capital and land and the benefits derived from a favorable market position as increments to personal incomes, in the new system only the income arising from current labor and previous investment ("past" labor) could be allocated to wages. Finally, "price intervention through social compacts was accepted as a legitimate means of affecting income distribution."[34]

Social compacts, however, in and of themselves only laid down goals and criteria to guide political and economic action and carried merely "political and moral" obligations. They were to be implemented through policy measures (legislation, regulations, agency decisions) on the part of government and self-management agreements on the part of firms and industries. The latter were indeed enforceable in the courts; they were to regulate internal relations in the firm as well as its dealings with other enterprises in the same or different industries. Self-management agreements were thus another form of bargaining in the new system.

In this regard, enterprises were no longer construed as single units of production. Rather, they reorganized themselves into a number of basic organizations of associated labor (BOAL), units roughly corresponding to divisions in Western firms.[35] A BOAL was defined as a "part of a work organization which constitutes an economic-technological entity the results of whose work (products or services) can be expressed in terms of market value";[36] in many ways, it replaced the firm as the main microeconomic decision-making unit. Each BOAL was legally independent, and an enterprise (organization of associated labor) was the product of a contract "voluntarily" concluded by its component units. Thus, the terms of the self-management agreement by which an enterprise was formed were set by bargaining among the BOALs, each of which had not only its own workers' council and executives, but also its own assets, investment funds, and so forth. Moreover, BOALs allocated personal incomes, based on their share of enterprise earnings. This, in turn, was determined on the basis of the "prices" charged other BOALs for services or products supplied. In this sense, intraenterprise relations continued to be governed by prices and hence by the market; but since the prices were determined by bargaining, they would not necessarily be competitive.[37]

Self-management agreements within the firm regulated the distribution of its earnings, provided for joint capital investment, collective consumption, and other matters of common concern, and outlined the responsibilities of the various self-management bodies. While self-management agreements could delegate power to central administrative and self-management bodies, decisions involving personal income distribution, collective consumption, and investment had to be ratified by the individual BOALs. At the same time, both these decisions and the criteria regulating them had to conform to the social compacts governing such matters in the area or industry. Enterprise sociopolitical organizations were expected to play a more active role in the firm to ensure that enterprise and BOAL decisions did in fact take broader "social" interests into account.

Aside from attempting to involve the "direct producers" more in enterprise decision making by breaking up hierarchy in the firm, the BOAL system also appears to be part of a strategy aimed at disciplining the firms to the (directed) market and forcing them to engage in good entrepreneurial practices. Since personal incomes were to depend on the business results of the BOAL, it was hoped that a more direct link between wages and labor productivity would be established. The provision that a return on "past" labor was to be channeled through the BOAL also encouraged workers to increase savings. Finally, requiring units within the firm to cover at least part of their own capital needs might increase total enterprise investment.[38]

The process of linking together small, specialized units into larger industrial combinations was also designed to facilitate the formation of integrated industry associations, operating on local, republic, and even national scales, and economically powerful enough to exert considerable influence on government. The Law on Associated Labor (1976) sought to further the "associating" process, in effect converting all long-term business arrangements into joint ventures. The statute set forth procedures by which enterprises and BOALs could (and by implication, should) invest in one another ("pool labor and resources") and receive the socialist equivalent of a dividend on their investment; its size would depend on the business results of the firm or BOAL receiving the capital.[39] In addition, the law proposed certain subjects (for instance, research and development) to be covered by joint investment, singled out certain enterprises (foreign trade companies) that had to engage in it, and prescribed detailed criteria for the allocation of income acquired from both joint ventures and regular sales. In this way, it was hoped, firms would be less dependent on banks for investment funds, enterprise savings would be stimulated, interregional and interindustry capital mobility would be enhanced, and firms would exert pressures on each other to be more efficient.

Moreover, such widened economic associations, organized on vertical and horizontal lines, would theoretically counteract the localistic tendencies of political units and protect the "unity" of the Yugoslav market. Simultaneously, they would pose an additional check to the autonomy of the individual firm by requiring it to adhere to the development plans of the association as a whole. Meanwhile, political bodies and the remaining autonomy of the component industrial units were expected to form a counterweight to the monopolistic tendencies such industrial and commercial associations could easily begin to manifest.

The ultimate goal of the institutional changes was to reconstruct a planning mechanism based on polycentric foci of power in which firms, governments, and sociopolitical organizations would participate. If the state—or more concretely, the republic "sociopolitical communities"—was now to appear as a legitimate player in the economic game, industry was to be its partner—at the expense of the old "centers of economic power." Accordingly, the banks were decentralized and reorganized to give enterprises greater influence over credit and lending policy. Similarly, foreign trade companies were mandated to "share risk" with the firms that had been paying their high commissions and interest charges.

By the institution of "interest communities," social services were also to be brought under the more direct control of the firms that financed them. Where previous arrangements had put social services in the position of poorly regulated monopolies, the new interest communities were to be composed of delegates elected by enterprises and the respective services who would bargain over the "price" of services and over how they were to be delivered.[40]

The influence of industry and "associated labor" on government was structured into the new system in other ways as well. On local and republic levels, the 1974 Constitution changed the five-house legislatures into tricameral assemblies. They were composed of a Chamber of Associated Labor, in which all work organizations were represented, a chamber based on geographical representation, and a chamber elected from the sociopolitical organizations. By virtue of their numbers, workers in the primary and secondary sectors of the socialist sector would predominate in the Chamber of Associated Labor over the tertiary sector, seen as the source of "technocratic" and "bureaucratic" deformations in the past. At the same time, the third chamber gave the mass organizations and the League of Communists in particular enlarged representation in the sociopolitical community.

The altered electoral process also attempted to link the activities of legislative bodies more closely with the communities they represented. Under the new delegate system, the basic electoral unit (the BOAL for the Chamber of Associated Labor, the neighborhood for the chamber based on geographic representation, the enterprise or neighborhood party cell, trade union organization, or Socialist Alliance branch for the sociopolitical chamber) no longer would elect a single person to represent it in the local legislature. Rather, a set of delegates was elected, which then would choose a legislative representative from its midst. During the term of office, the delegates would form a kind of workers' or neighborhood "council" for the issues voted on in the legislature. At the same time that they were to prevent the single representative from distancing himself from the rank-and-file constituency, the delegations were also to be a means of insuring that policies enacted in legislatures would be implemented correctly in their own organizations. Moreover, insofar as the delegate system put another "step" between the voter and the parliamentary representative, it was a useful device to screen out the "anti-self-management tendencies" that had previously sat in legislatures under the old, more direct electoral system.

THE NEW ROLE OF THE LEAGUE OF COMMUNISTS AND THE TENTH PARTY CONGRESS

Bargaining, as noted earlier, can aggravate problems of coordination, especially when interests conflict and limited resources are disputed. While the use of authority itself cannot enlarge the size of the pie, it can help to resolve interest conflicts over particular portions, either through arbitration or by simply eliminating some of the interests from the negotiating table. These tasks formed the essence of the new role of the Yugoslav League of Communists.

The first steps toward redefining the role of the party were taken at the Twenty-first Session of the LCY Presidency in December of 1971. At that time, a major purge of nationalist elements in the republic parties was initiated, starting with the Croatian party, where the situation had gotten most dramatically out of hand.[41] This was soon followed by Tito's Letter of 1972, which called for party unity and a weeding out of dissident elements. "Technocracy," "liberalism," "nationalism," "statism," "ultra-leftism," and "unitarism" were all harshly condemned as "anti-self-management tendencies"; the old days of the "struggle of ideas" were abandoned in favor of a "resolute defense" of the "interests of the working class." Kardelj justified the change of position:

> First of all, we are struggling against the illusion that freedom is something above society, above its class antagonisms and ideological and political conflicts. Further, when it is a question of discussion or the struggle of opinions, then freedom consists of the right of the opponent to freely and equally express his opinions. Meanwhile, when it is a question of *social antagonisms*, then it is no longer a question of the struggle of ideas but of conflict between mutually exclusive opposing interests.[42]

Nor was the Letter a call for unity for unity's sake alone. The noninterventionist stance the LCY had maintained vis-à-vis other organizations and institutions was also abandoned in favor of a more activist policy. Rather than seeing itself as the harmonizer of the pluralistic interests of the "working people," the LCY now defined itself as the representative of the interests of the "direct producers," a position much more akin to the "productive labor" ideology of the prereform days.

The new commitment to the direct producers involved increased party action on a variety of fronts. Editors of several major newspapers and journals were changed, an increased emphasis on Marxist studies in universities and schools was put into effect, directors of a number of enterprises came under sharp attack. A major leadership shake-up took place in all of the mass organizations, too.

The new constitution, as we have seen, not only increased the role of the state in the economy, but also enlarged the authority of the party within the state. In this way, a unified party could both arbitrate conflicts that arose in the bargaining process and prevent such conflicts from arising in the first place by limiting the range of interests that could legitimately be expressed. Hence, the party's role in defending the interests of the "direct producers" in the conclusion of self-management agreements and social compacts was to be a critical factor in coordinating the whole system. Similarly, a unified national party, purged of nationalistic elements, was to be the major force in preventing the old interrepublic conflicts from surfacing again.

The Tenth Party Congress, meeting in May 1974, officially confirmed this new orientation. Tito called on the League of Communists to increase its activity in all organizations, strive to implement the new constitution, re-organize itself in conformance with democratic centralism, struggle against factionalism, and reaffirm itself as a specifically class-based political party. He laid special stress on the need to recruit more workers into the party to ensure that "views typical of bourgeois society" would not make "their way into the League of Communists, threatening to change the nature of the organization and to paralyze its activities."[43] As one observer of the Congress noted, "The wheel of Yugoslav Marxist theory in at least one key sector has come, if not full circle, most of the way around."[44] Nevertheless, if the "struggle against factionalism and anti-self-management tendencies" managed to keep some interests out of the newly established bargaining processes, the party's assumption of a "leading role" in implementing the new constitu-tion caused changes that made it all but impossible for it to assume the role of a central arbitrator among the interests that remained.

SELF-MANAGEMENT AND BARGAINING[45]

Perhaps most important among the benefits multilateral bargaining and a more unified party brought Yugoslavia has been an end to the political stale-mate of the early 1970s. Consequently, it became possible to begin planning macroeconomic development at the federal level, reach agreement on regional, sectoral, and national economic goals, and achieve some consensus on the instruments that federal and republic governments would use to attain them.

Nevertheless, the stabilized political situation and enhanced role of social planning do not appear to be producing a corresponding degree of economic stability.[46] Current difficulties can be traced in part to international factors beyond Yugoslavia's control;[47] yet these factors have had to interact with domestic political and economic institutions to have led to the actual results.

Apparently the increased legitimacy and prominence of the "sociopolitical community" in economic development has had the (predictable) consequence of creating tensions between economic units expected to achieve social priorities and the political units determining them. In view of our earlier analysis of Gramsci's workers' democracy, this is hardly surprising, and indeed, several of the contradictions appearing in Gramsci's design of worker-controlled socialism found analogues in Yugoslav practice in the 1970s.

The first set of difficulties stemmed from the sociopolitical community's responsibility to "direct" the course of economic development. As in workers' democracy, fulfilling this responsibility in Yugoslavia required agreement among political and economic units on plan priorities and appropriate mechanisms for achieving them. The polycentric bargaining system, however, made the process of achieving such consensus terribly lengthy and cumbersome. Not only was the 1976–80 social plan adopted after the start of the planning period, but by mid-1977, only three of the fifteen social compacts it proposed had been concluded.[48]

Further, since social compacts left the use of various instruments to the discretion of whichever organ employed them, coordination on behalf of common goals suffered. For example, if republics and provinces agreed to impose a tax on enterprise income, methods and rates of taxation and even the very definition of enterprise income differed by region. In the absence of a national tax to even out the variations, capital mobility was obstructed.[49] Equally serious were the coordination difficulties created by continued use of administrative actions, ranging from price controls and import restrictions to regional "socialization of losses" in bad years.[50] Consequently, social compacts and general policy enactments often gave enterprises one set of signals, while administrative decisions and emergency measures were conveying entirely different messages.

The second set of problems in the 1970s lay in the different vantage points and time horizons of the political units doing the planning and enacting the policy on the one hand and the economic units expected to conform with the goals their representatives had chosen for them on the other. As one might suspect from our analysis of Gramsci's design, what looked like an incentive and a rational business practice from a broad, long-term point of view did not necessarily appear so to individual firms or BOALs.

Thus, firms resisted industrywide self-management agreements that, however desirable from the long-range perspective of increased intraindustry specialization, might involve immediate changes in production programs or require them to "pool resources" with potential competitors.[51] Similarly, when bank credit was available at low interest rates, firms were reluctant to enter into joint ventures, even if this carried fewer inflationary consequences in the long run.[52] Moreover, many firms were so heavily in debt from previous borrowing that they lacked the resources to pool in the first place. Similar problems plagued the social compact process, and inconsistent and uncoordinated government directives and policy measures hardly facilitated matters.

The third set of problems stemmed from the reorganization of Yugoslav firms. Here the intention of the 1974 Constitution was quite different from Gramsci's prescription for production units; whereas Gramsci emphasized hierarchy in the firm, the new Yugoslav system aimed at breaking up existing enterprise hierarchies. In a highly unstable economic environment, the reforms produced not solidarity, but instability and conflict in the firms, as intraenterprise groups struggled to maintain and enhance their control over decisions. Moreover, the more complicated subsequent legislation made the rules of the game, the more difficult and time-consuming it became for firms and BOALs to comply.[53] In effect, the firms' very attempt to conform to the new institutional structures weakened their ability to do so.

To stabilize their internal power structure, enterprises sought to insulate themselves from outside economic and political influences. Such insularity provoked a wave of "formalism" in complying with legislation, greatly complicated the process of arriving at self-management agreements and social compacts, made it extremely difficult to enforce accords that had been concluded, deterred firms from cooperating in joint ventures, and may have prevented them from introducing innovations in product lines, technologies, and personnel structure that might upset the intrafirm balance of power.[54] While increasingly detailed legal measures sought to structure the firms in ways that would lead them to increase productivity, make better use of capacity and personnel, and save more of their earnings, firms found themselves able to pursue these goals only insofar as doing so did not jeopardize the position of intraenterprise groups.

Finally, for reasons similar to those underlying the growth of bureaucracy in Gramsci's system, enterprises in Yugoslavia proved unable or unwilling to shoulder the political burdens assigned them in the new system. Enterprise insularity deterred the firms from assuming too high a political profile; firms also lacked the time and personnel to undertake broad social tasks, whether formulating legislative proposals and economic policy in the sociopolitical communities or planning the activities of social services in the interest communities. More important, enterprises remained essentially productive and economic units; as such, they were ill adapted to take on broad social perspectives or perform the tasks of interest aggregation and policy formulation the new system expected of them.[55]

Consequently, it fell to full-time political leaders and bureaucrats to take the initiative in the sociopolitical communities, while the social services planned their own activities in the way they judged best.[56] Partly as a result, social consumption turned into Yugoslavia's major growth industry of the 1970s, despite the inflationary pressures it generated and enterprise protests over the high taxes it provoked.

The enterprises' default on the economic and political responsibilities awarded them within the new institutional framework thus militated against their becoming the strong bargaining partners the 1974 Constitution had envisioned. Instead, their power was largely negative; they could obstruct the government's attempt to make them play a role they didn't want without having a clear idea of what they did want beyond narrow, particularist benefits. And to the considerable degree that special pleading was effective, it exacerbated the problem of coordination among units of government. Not surprisingly, it became a Herculean task to plan economic development when firms did not conform with the basic assumptions the plan made about their behavior and motivations.

As for the League of Communists, it did indeed succeed in curbing the worst of the nationalistic excesses of earlier years, making social compacts and self-management agreements into the predominant mode of business in Yugoslavia and spearheading the drive to reorganize the firms. Ironically, however, the changes the party's "new role" helped to introduce were the source of the problems. While there could be widespread agreement on what had to be done, doing so required the consent and coordination of so many different agents with such a multiplicity of interests that execution of decisions—either in the firms or in the sociopolitical communities—was frequently beyond the control of even a more disciplined LCY. In short, having led the drive to implement the new system, the League proved unable to contain the fragmentation it brought in its wake.[57]

The best the party could do in such a situation was see that the new procedures were observed, procedures that, as the years went on, were becoming more and more complex and detailed as the economy on its own failed to produce the hoped-for results. It was here that the Eleventh Congress (1978) rested, arguing that the main cause of the economic difficulties had been a failure to fully and/or correctly implement the new institutional framework and contending that the economic situation would improve once the new system really took hold.[58]

Clearly, it is premature to discount this analysis. Yet four years after the adoption of the Constitution and six years after the amendments that signaled the start of the institutional transformation, it appears just as likely that the delays in implementation and compliance with the new rules of the game are part and parcel of the new system rather than a departure from it. As one might expect from a return to planning in a labor-managed politico-economic system, a new impasse between economic units and political units is gradually emerging.

PART III

The Case of the Self-Managed Enterprise

Yugoslavia's thirty-year experience with its own variant of self-management does indeed seem to manifest empirically a tension between the use of planning and the use of the market similar to the one postulated theoretically in our analyses of Gramsci and Proudhon's schemas of workers' control. The tension appears to stem partially from the peculiar characteristics of the labor-managed firm and partially from the responsiveness of political leaders to the pressures exerted by the firms.

An intensive study of a single enterprise can shed some light on the causes of the plan-market conflict in Yugoslavia at the microeconomic level. By examining in depth the reactions of one enterprise and work collective to market controls and the need to make entrepreneurial decisions on the one hand and to hierarchical and political regulations on the other, we can get a sense of the internal dynamics that apparently lead so many self-managed enterprises to have what is, in effect, a split politicoeconomic personality. Similarly, an examination of a single firm's relations with political authorities gives some insight into the mechanisms for political redress available to Yugoslav enterprises at the local level. At the same time, such a case study should indicate that to the degree a Yugoslav enterprise and the environment it operates in replicate features of Proudhon and Gramsci's respective microeconomic models of workers' control, they also manifest the patterns of conflict and consensus found in mutualism and workers' democracy.

The case study presented here is based on field research conducted in a Zagreb machine-tool plant. While the firm was certainly not one of Yugoslavia's showcase enterprises, it can hardly be considered typical either. Its small size, highly skilled and urbanized labor force, well-qualified management, and recently stabilized financial situation suggest that it was, in fact, somewhat above average in its suitability for self-management. This does not, however, affect the value of the study; not only would it be impossible to find a single "typical" enterprise but finding one is not essential for this analysis.

That is, Yugoslav firms are all subject to the same essential regulations regarding their self-management bodies, and all are a hybrid of the Gramsci and Proudhon models of firm organization. Nevertheless, they vary widely in many other ways, including their market position, their political clout, and the degree to which they observe the spirit as well as the letter of the latest variant of self-management. Although the effect of national legislation is to bring them closer to one model or the other, how close an individual enterprise actually gets depends on more than legal regulations alone and differs greatly from firm to firm.[1] This case study explores if and how the behavior patterns of a single firm can be explained in terms of its particular adaptation of the Gramsci and Proudhon models. In other words, the case study is presented because the relationship between behavior and structure may be generalizable, not the behavior or structure itself.

The research was done from March to September of 1974. At the time, the dust had not yet settled from the 1971 constitutional amendments, and the 1974 Constitution had just been adopted. No one in the firm was sure how all these legal changes were to be implemented in the enterprise and what their practical consequences would be. Both the firm and its environment were in a very transitional phase, and as a result, life in the enterprise during the period of the study appeared somewhat more chaotic, frenetic, and conflict prone than usual. Nevertheless, a review of earlier records of enterprise behavior reveals that the issues over which conflicts took place and on which solidarity was generated were the same, so the fact that the field work took place during an atypical period in the enterprise's history should not affect the conclusions of the analysis.

There is a real lack of reliable economic data on the firm, especially for the period prior to 1970. In part, this is due to the incessant legal changes made in accounting methods to insure a better "distribution according to work," in part to the sorry state of the factory archives, and in part to the turnover in finance directors. Symptomatic here was the discovery by the current finance director of a 200,000 dinar discrepancy in the accounts when he was hired in 1970. Even afterward, workers' council minutes are dotted with records of reports and accounts presented to the council, but many of the actual reports are missing, and of those remaining, some are quarterly, some are semiannual, and only two annual accounts were ever appended to the minutes. As a guest in the plant, I could hardly request either the finance or the personnel department to undertake the research necessary to compile a statistical portrait of the firm's economic history. Nevertheless, while I cannot supply specific figures on the firm's rate of growth, increase in labor productivity, and investment activity, the general picture of the enterprise's development is clear enough from the information available. For the purposes of this study, such an overall picture is, in my opinion, sufficient.

The basic method used in the study was participant observation. I was present every day at the main plant, attended meetings, and conversed regularly with workers, employees, and executives. I also had access to a disorganized set of factory archives and was able to use my free time to go over minutes of past workers' council meetings and back issues of the factory bulletin. Most of my questions were answered by members of the work collective; when I suspected the answers were unduly subjective or unreliable,

I checked with several different people in varying occupational categories.

Certainly there are problems with this method. I inevitably missed some meetings, for most did not take place at any regular hour or day and I did not find out about some until after they had met. Occasionally, too, I was not permitted to attend certain meetings because a "sensitive" issue was being discussed. Generally, meetings of the party secretariat (its executive committee) and the political *aktiv* fell into this category, as did occasional encounters with "outside" representatives. On the whole, however, with the exception of party secretariat meetings, these incidents were few and far between, and I witnessed practically eveything that went on in the two divisions that made up the main plant. Even with the secretariat, once a decision had been made, the actions that resulted were quite obvious to myself and the work collective alike; thus, only the decision making process itself was unobserved.

Some members of the collective I never spoke with at any length, simply because the occasion never presented itself. To remedy this, I had planned to do a survey on attitudes toward self-management to validate my impressions in a more systematic way. Although a questionnaire was initially approved, one faction of the party subsequently vetoed it and actually wrote a special letter detailing its fear of foreign snooping to the district party committee. After this, it no longer seemed advisable to pursue the matter, for the strong opposition of a party faction that was becoming increasingly influential in the light of the antitechnocracy campaign and the Tenth Party Congress would have affected the survey results in undetermined ways.

Consequently, I have relied upon private conversations and public statements made at meetings as the raw data for my account of occupational attitudes and values. Such a sample is obviously not a random one and, indeed, is quite biased in favor of the more articulate, opinionated, and outspoken individuals in the work collective. While there was no evidence that these individuals were not actually articulating the sentiments held by their more passive colleagues,[2] and while my personal knowledge of the individuals who spoke privately with me enabled me to discount certain comments of those with particular grievances against the firm, the description of attitudes and values necessarily remains somewhat impressionistic.

In addition, since the various statements I recorded were made at different times, in different contexts, and by different individuals, piecing them together to form a coherent picture of occupational attitudes and values involved a good deal of interpretation on my part. Consequently, the account presented in chapter 8 is probably a good deal more logically consistent, philosophical, and thought out than the attitudes and values are in reality. While I can defend such interpretations on the grounds that the social scientist's task is precisely to find some underlying order in a chaotic reality, doing so invariably involves risks of misrepresentation.

Nevertheless, I do not believe the lack of survey data is a serious defect. The evidence presented below falls well within the range acceptable in a case study, and scholars familiar with Yugoslavia will have little difficulty recognizing many of the views and reactions I describe. Moreover, while an account of attitudes and values based on conversations, public statements, and observed behavior has its limits, these must be weighed against the equally serious, if different, distortions produced by the use of survey research techniques, especially given the situation in which I would have had to use them.

Finally, it is worth bearing in mind the extremely difficult political conditions surrounding this study. I arrived in Yugoslavia in June 1973; the battle then going on over *Praxis*, the controversial philosophical journal, made professors hesitate to work with a student from a Western country. The Chilean coup and the Yom Kippur War did not win any friends for the United States in Yugoslav political circles. Within Yugoslavia, a good deal of jockeying for power accompanied the adoption of the new constitution and the party reorganization confirmed by the Tenth Congress, so that only the truly apolitical were relatively unaffected by the general climate of political uncertainty. Enterprises, thrown into confusion by the constitutional reforms, were reluctant to permit observation of their unsettled internal processes by anyone, let alone a foreigner, and executives, under fire as the antitechnocracy campaign grew heated, were hesitant to vouch for a visitor from the very home of Western capitalism. In such a situation, I was extremely fortunate to accomplish what I did, imperfect as it may be; if the case study is marred by not containing the "best" evidence, it has the singular virtue of containing the only evidence of the internal workings of Yugoslav firms at this time. Moreover, as far as I know, intensive research of this kind is no longer possible in Yugoslavia. Hence, I can only express my profound appreciation to those who put me in contact with the firm and to those in the firm itself who were so very cooperative and helpful. They, of course, bear no responsibility for the line of argument I have developed nor for any errors I have made.

7

Conflict at Klek: The Uses of Autonomy and Their Impact

KLEK, A SELF-MANAGED ENTERPRISE: THE SETTING OF THE STUDY

Klek,[1] a machine-tool plant in New Zagreb, was little more than an artisan's workshop when it was nationalized in 1946. Rapidly transformed into a small industrial enterprise, the firm had begun to assume its modern lines by 1952, employing 240 people and producing machinery for the mining industry.

From that time on, the firm experienced a gradual, if sporadic growth. The economic reforms of 1965 hit the enterprise—indeed, the entire machine-tool industry—hard, for the cost of raw materials jumped, while price controls on capital goods remained in force. At the same time, modernization of the physical plant and the production process appeared imperative if the firm was to compete successfully with foreign competitors. With the election of a new director in 1966, Klek began to manufacture a narrower, but far more technically sophisticated variety of machinery. Meanwhile, it continued to develop its capacity for repairing and servicing the machinery it produced and in 1969 merged with another enterprise whose plant was converted into an enlarged service sector.

Although Klek enjoyed a domestic monopoly on the product market, the persistence of price controls and the deflationary credit policy made it difficult to exploit this advantage. Its domestic customers, being in the economically weak primary sector, were unable to purchase the new, highly elaborate machinery Klek had begun to produce unless credit was extended. Like so many Yugoslav firms in the postreform years, Klek was faced with the choice of selling on credit at the expense of its own liquidity or refusing to do so at the risk that potential customers would buy machinery, even if higher priced, from better-financed foreign competitors who could offer more favorable credit terms. Klek opted for the first solution; such a policy, combined with higher raw materials' cost, channeling savings into the modernization plan, price controls, and the unavailability of outside credit resulted in an increasingly acute shortage of working capital. By 1972, when it was unable to pay its suppliers for over three months, Klek found its bank account "blocked."*

By 1974, however, Klek was among the most successful machine-tool plants in Zagreb and Croatia. The enterprise bank account was no longer blocked, thanks to a loan from the city reserve fund and to approval of a price increase by the Federal Price Commission. The firm had received a license to import and export on its own, enabling it to bypass the trading companies on whose highly priced goodwill, efficiency, and connections it had previously depended. A contract had just been concluded with a German firm under which Klek would use the former's patent to produce and market a new type of mining machinery in Yugoslavia and Eastern Europe. A skilled worker was earning 2,500 to 3,500 dinars a month; not a high salary, but well above average for the machine-tool industry in Zagreb at the time.[2]

The modernization plan, begun in 1969, was just being completed, and plant equipment was new and considerably more automated. Business, both domestic and foreign, had expanded to the point where a new building to house technical and administrative services was being constructed on the plant site. Plans were also being made to move the Service Division there from its current location in another part of Zagreb. In addition, the enterprise was about to introduce a new system of technical organization, streamline the work process and create higher piece-rate incentives. All in all, a rise of 30 percent in labor productivity was anticipated, and current earnings were expected to double by 1978.

Yet too rosy a picture should not be painted. The liquidity problem was still very much in evidence, for Klek continued to grant credit to its customers. Frequently (four out of the seven months of this study) paychecks were late when there was simply no ready cash on hand with which to pay them. At the same time, shortages and surpluses of production materials were a continual problem, and the reorganizations in decision-making processes necessitated by the constitutional reforms were an additional obstacle to maintaining a smoothly running business.

The reproduction cycle** was a good deal longer than it should have been;

---

*That is, the firm was unable to draw on its bank account until its outstanding creditors had been paid; under a recent law, too, it could not pay full salaries to its labor force until its debts were settled.

**The time needed for the firm to produce and sell an amount whose market value covers the wages, depreciation, raw materials, and other costs incurred in its production.

whether this was because of supply bottlenecks, sloppy work discipline, bad overall management, or other factors is unclear and formed one of the chief topics of controversy in the firm. By September, it was clear that the 1974 plan was not going to be completed, and a good deal of overtime work was going on to achieve a hoped-for 95 percent of the plan goals. Meanwhile, a new law had made overtime work illegal, so aside from having to pay higher wages, Klek might well have to pay a fine for permitting overtime in the first place.

A factor perceived as feeding the difficulties was the firm's labor structure. Although the work collective numbered 528, only 250 to 300 were employed in the direct production.[3] The remaining 45 to 50 percent were technicians, clerks, supervisors, or transport and maintenance staff.[4] Despite its expanding labor force, Klek often found itself short of manual production workers. Absenteeism and labor turnover only added to the problem. The situation had become so serious that in September, the Production Division had begun transferring workers who had been "promoted" to technicians' posts back into their machinists' jobs to overcome the production bottleneck.

Personal incomes were allocated on a point scale. Each job was ranked according to the expertise it required, the qualifications of the person holding it, the responsibility it entailed, and so forth. The job was then allocated a certain number of points, each of which was worth a given amount of dinars. At the time of this study, the distribution of points went from 950 for the general director to 250 for a cleaning woman. Production workers were receiving from 350 to 450 points; department heads and university-trained engineers and economists, 700 to 750 points. Since the value of a point rose from year to year, there was a gradual increase in absolute wage differentials. This plus the constant adjustments in the points allocated to individuals[5] meant that every few years a complete revision of the point scales had to be made. Such a revision—the analytical job evaluation—was in fact undertaken while this study was in progress. Yet, where in the past Klek had been free to allocate points as it saw fit, they now had to be allocated within the proportions agreed to in an industrywide self-management agreement concluded the previous year.

In 1973, Klek had organized itself into three basic organizations of associated labor. BOAL I, the Production Division, was the heart of the enterprise and consisted of the production workers in the main plant, the technicians, and their respective supervisors, for a total of 283 members. It was subdivided into twelve departments, eight of which included the skilled and highly skilled machinists (tool and die, lathe operation, grinding, and so on) and four of which were technical services (mechanical design, quality control). The production process was serial, but on a small scale. Each worker had his own machine and individual norms to meet; payment was on a piece-rate basis. Technicians, in contrast, were paid by the hour. Each department had its own supervisor or foreman, and at the top of the division's organizational hierarchy were the plant chief and the assistant director of the enterprise; the latter, a mechanical engineer, also served as the director of BOAL I.

BOAL II, the Production/Service Division, was located in another area of Zagreb and was visited only once during the study. Originally a separate, small enterprise, it proved unable to survive in the postreform economy. By 1969, it had either to merge with another firm or be taken over by the state. At the same time, Klek, at the start of its modernization and expansion plan, was casting about for a solution to the problem of a sorely cramped service department. The idea of integrating with another enterprise was then engineered by Klek's general director and several other Klek executives and shepherded through under the benevolent auspices of the municipal economic chamber.

By 1974, BOAL II was the most efficient division in the firm, completing its 1973 plan by 104 per cent. It was composed of five departments and included the workers who serviced and repaired the equipment Klek produced as well as its own technical, clerical, and supervisory personnel. On a limited scale, it also produced machinery to fill in the slack when repairs were not in great demand. BOAL II's director had once been a skilled worker and had acquired his managerial qualifications at night school. He was currently responsible for 135 workers and employees.

BOAL III, Collective Services, was located at the main plant site and included 110 people. For the most part, it embraced the white-collar clerical and specialist staff: finance, sales, personnel, supplies, R and D, and the amorphous sector for legal and general services. Klek's general director was also a member of BOAL III, although he was not the division director. In fact, because of executive rivalries within it, BOAL III had no director throughout the course of this study. In terms of its labor force, Collective Services was the most rapidly expanding division in the firm. Legally, however, it should not have been a BOAL at all. Insofar as Collective Services did not "directly" produce a marketable commodity, it should have been a "self-managing work community."[6] As such, it would have had no right to funds of its own (for hiring or any other purpose), but instead would depend on the other two BOALs for its revenue for capital and consumption expenditures alike.

Each BOAL elected its own representatives to the central workers' council and managing board as well as its own delegations and representatives to the communal Chamber of Associated Labor. Each BOAL also had its own council and assembly. While the councils met separately, the assemblies of BOAL I and III always convened as one body. Hence, much as in the past, the

clerical staff and the central enterprise management took part in the decisions
that in theory BOAL I should have been making independently. Partly for
this reason, relationships between occupational groups down at the main plant
did not appear to have been altered as a result of the establishment of the
BOALs.

In addition, the enterprise as a whole was at a very early stage in the transition
to the 1974 self-management model. Enterprise assets had not yet been
divided up among the BOALs, and so none of them had funds at their own
disposal. Certainly, the major costs of each division's operation were itemized
by BOAL and provided for in the annual plan approved by representatives of
all three BOALs on the workers' council. However, problems arose when unfor-
seen expenses, such as opening a new job or extra overtime, occurred in one
division during the year, since it could not legally spend any additional money
without approval from the others. Moreover, since the earnings of each BOAL
at the end of the year returned to the center and were then reallocated back
to the divisions, BOAL II wound up subsidizing the other two units.

New enterprise statutes had not been adopted to clarify the responsibilities
of the various self-management bodies, nor did the BOALs have their own
internal statutes to guide their decision-making processes, despite the fact that
all these documents should have been submitted to the courts for approval
before the time this study began. Thus, confusion in the firm's decision-making
process and the assignment of responsibility among executives and between
them and the self-management bodies compounded the traditional difficulties
in the production process. A vicious circle seemed to be operating, for one reason
for the delays in drawing up new statutes was the confusion over who was
supposed to compile them and which self-management body should begin the
adoption process.

In its broadest lines, then, this was the picture Klek presented in the spring
and summer of 1974. On the outside, it appeared a dynamic, growing enterprise; on the inside, it seemed plagued by difficulties, barely muddling through
from crisis to crisis.

THE INSTITUTIONAL FRAMEWORK

Looking inside the Yugoslav firm, one can analytically define three structures whose interaction constitutes the basic internal life of the enterprise.
First is its self-management structure, the complicated system of councils,
commissions, and assemblies through which the work collective, encompassing
everyone who works in the firm, exercises its formal authority to make policy
decisions (Figure 3).[7]

Parallelling the self-management structure is the firm's organizational

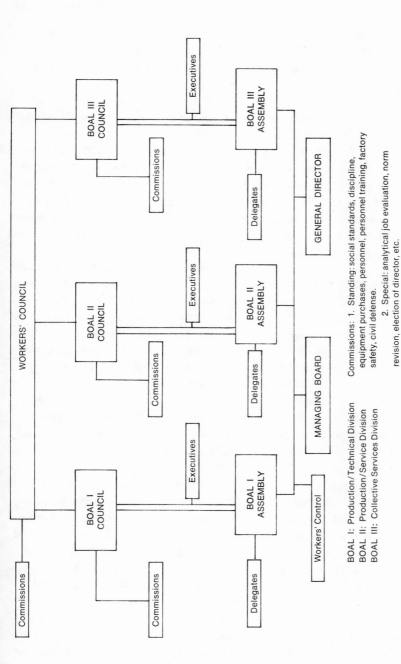

BOAL I: Production/Technical Division
BOAL II: Production/Service Division
BOAL III: Collective Services Division

Commissions: 1. Standing: social standards, discipline, equipment purchases, personnel, personnel training, factory safety, civil defense.

2. Special: analytical job evaluation, norm revision, election of director, etc.

Figure 3. Klek: Self-Management Structure, 1974

structure, the organization of work in the enterprise (figure 4). Like the self-management structure, the organizational structure also comprehends everyone in the firm; one's place in it is simply one's job. But whereas the self-management structure is a political creation and is regulated by laws applying more or less uniformly throughout Yugoslavia, the organizational structure is a productive-economic entity and, at least in theory, is predominantly conditioned by market forces and technology.[8]

Activity in the self-management structure is considered a "right" and carries with it no direct material consequences for the individual actor.[9] Activity in the organizational structure, however, is not voluntary insofar as it is salaried labor, and performance or nonperformance of tasks connected with it does indeed have very direct material consequences for the individual. In addition, all members of the collective are equal as self-managers, and all have a right to participate in decision making regardless of professional qualification. The organizational structure, in contrast, is hierarchical and conditioned by a strict division of labor. Whereas the "sovereign" of the self-management structure is the work collective acting as a whole in the assemblies, the firm's general director and top management stand at the head of the organizational hierarchy.

Yet a third set of institutions comes into play in enterprise decision making: the sociopolitical organizations.[10] Two characteristics distinguish them from both the self-management and the organizational structures. First of all, while the latter are autonomous and contained within the individual enterprise, the sociopolitical organizations are branches of larger, national associations. If the tendency of the self-management and organizational structures is to assert the enterprise's interests as over, and occasionally against, larger social interests, the role of the sociopolitical organizations is precisely to bring overall social considerations to bear on enterprise decision making.

Second, sociopolitical organizations in theory are voluntary associations; while one is automatically a part of the organizational structure by virtue of holding a job and a member of the self-management structure upon entering a work collective, one must make a conscious decision to join a sociopolitical organization. In practice, however, the voluntary character of sociopolitical organizations applies only to the League of Communists, for most individuals feel "expected" to join enterprise branches of other mass organizations.[11] This in part explains why the party is more effective inside the firm than branches of other mass organizations are.

In theory, the self-management structure controls the organizational structure. Supposedly, those who have authority in the self-management structure—the work collective and its elected representatives—should also control the organizational structure; in fact, the sociopolitical organizations are expected

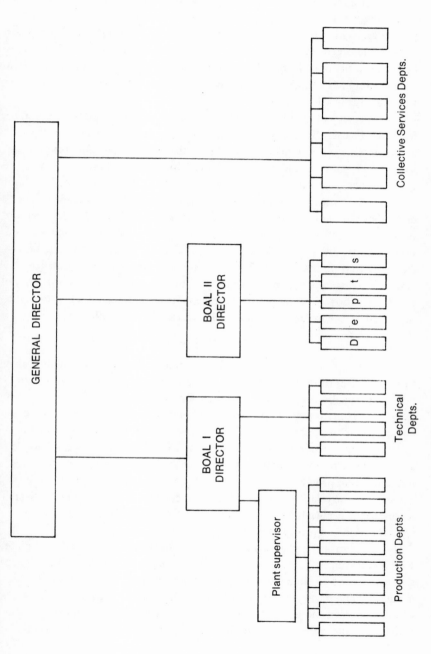

Figure 4. Klek: Organizational Structure

to ensure that the rights of self-managers to make decisions are not violated in this respect. In practice, however, the power equation in Yugoslav enterprises has, legitimately or illegitimately, been quite the opposite: those at the apex of the organizational pyramid—management—have traditionally dominated both the organizational and the self-management structures, and often with the implicit cooperation (and occasional co-optation) of the sociopolitical organizations as well.[12]

Klek, the subject of this study, was no exception to this pattern. Nevertheless, even if real influence was generated in and exercised through its organizational structure, formal authority lay in the self-management structure, while the threat of intervention or the need for favors from outside bodies gave the sociopolitical organizations a share of influence as well. Although power certainly was not distributed equally among all members of Klek's work collective, neither could it be exercised purely arbitrarily by any single group, occupational or political. Even in BOAL II, management's tight hold on influence in the division was highly contingent on the consent subordinates extended to it on the basis of BOAL II's superior economic performance.[13] And at the main plant, if management had the most access to authority in both the organizational and the self-management structures, its use was often quite restricted by the existence—and occasional resistance—of other groups.

KLEK AND THE MARKET: DIFFERENTIATION AND STRATIFICATION[14]

Similar to the effect market competition had on Proudhon's mutualist association, the effect of the market and the 1965 economic reforms on Klek had been to bring about a sharper differentiation in the division of labor. Specifically, the distinction between manual and mental labor, between the blue-collar production workers and technical, clerical, and managerial personnel, appears to have become much more pronounced as a result of the economic and social environment created by the 1965 reforms in general and Klek's modernization program in particular. For the most part, this differentiation occurred at the relative expense of the blue-collar workers, despite the overall increase in wage levels which accompanied the increased efficiency that specialization and professionalization brought.

The modernization plan, whose various stages took eight years to complete, was undertaken to counter the challenge of foreign competition on the Yugoslav market and to eliminate the causes for the growing inventory of unsold machinery and parts piling up in Klek's warehouse. The program not only entailed changes in the product line Klek manufactured, new equipment for the plant itself, and rationalizing the firm's business organization, but also involved recruiting personnel able to master both the new technology and the market Klek was attempting to capture.

One feature was the introduction of a new system of piece-work incentives. The effect was to reinforce existing distinctions between blue-collar workers and white-collar employees by making the former's wages much more dependent on the quantity and quality of individual work than in the past. While a white-collar worker could simply show up for work and put in a minimal amount of effort to receive his pay, a blue-collar worker either kept up with his norms or found himself with a sizable wage cut at the end of the month. Moreover, the modernization program's stress on labor productivity meant that piece-rate norms were higher and more difficult to meet.

Note, however, that the new system in itself did not result in a significant widening in wage differentials; blue-collar production workers could still—and frequently did—earn more than lower-level technicians and clerks.* It was the way in which the members of the two groups spent their time in the plant that was altered, with the blue-collar worker increasingly tied to his machine with each successive analytical job evaluation.

The white-collar worker's status in Yugoslavia had always been somewhat superior to that of the manual laborer, no matter how skilled the latter was. The spirit of the 1965 reforms, with their stress on the importance of the technical intelligentsia in modernization, legitimized this status differential far more than in the past. Also, the labor force in the branches of the economy with the highest salaries and most rapid expansion was predominantly clerical and technical.

Inside Klek, too, once the firm's income began to depend more on sales and finance rather than on simply what was produced, the center of gravity in the firm began to shift off the plant floor and into the offices. Furthermore, with the modernization program's emphasis on technological innovation and improving the quality of production, technical services also assumed a new importance.

Other effects of the modernization program first appeared as it neared completion. Ironically, this was at the time when the premises of the reform, which had made modernization a necessity for Klek, were coming under heavy fire throughout Yugoslavia. Despite the growing uproar in the press over inequalities and technocracy, Klek practically doubled the number of

---

*At the time of this study, the number of points allotted to jobs requiring a skilled worker and to those requiring a high school education technician or clerk were about equal, although the value of a point was lower for blue-collar jobs to provide for incentives.

Table 16. Klek: Qualification Structure, 1965–74[a]

	1965	1966	1967	1968	1969[b]	1970[c]	June 1972	September 1974
Employees	n.a.[d]	77	81	81	88	94	91	126
College or university education	n.a.	27	28	29	34	38	17	30
Secondary or technical school	n.a.	46	49	48	50	52	55	80
Primary school	n.a.	4	4	4	4	4	19	16
Workers	n.a.	274	280	246	221	236	371	402
Highly skilled	n.a.	105	112	104	94	97	37	34
Skilled	n.a.	112	110	90	88	100	235	252
Semiskilled or un-skilled	n.a.	57	58	52	39	39	99	116
Total	335	351	361	327	309	330	452	528

[a]Data from 1966 to 1970 refer to the qualification structure of jobs in the enterprise; those holding these positions did not necessarily have the required qualifications. Data from 1972 and 1974 refer to the qualification structure of the people employed in the enterprise, regardless of the type of work they performed.

[b]Estimates given in 1968 modernization plan.

[c]Planned in 1968; not including those who came to Klek via the integration with another firm. Figures from 1970 to 1974 include workers in the Service Division.

[d]Not available.

highly paid university graduates in its employ between 1972 and 1974 (table 16). Whereas in the past, the few university graduates Klek employed were by and large engineers and supervisory personnel who worked directly with the production workers on a day-to-day basis, the new employees were primarily economists, sales representatives, and research engineers who rarely ventured onto the plant floor. The social distance between manual and mental labor thus appeared to increase, and the various incentives offered the new employees, such as housing or more flexible job definitions, certainly did not help to diminish it.

The sudden influx of highly trained specialists apparently reflects trends that were well underway at Klek in the late sixties, although they are not reflected very well in the firm's statistical data.[15] According to workers' council minutes and the accounts of older employees, a gradual rise in the qualification levels of managerial personnel preceded the professionalization of the staff: for example, the general director, the finance director, and the legal counsel all had more education than the individuals they replaced. So too did their immediate assistants and the lower-level supervisors hired after 1966. The overall impact of these developments was a rise in the average real qualification level of managerial and white-collar employees, with the average qualification level of blue-collar workers remaining constant and even declining slightly (table 16).

This was parallelled by a certain widening of interskill differentials, although it was not reflected in a change in the ratio of the extremes. That is, the salary and point range between the highest-paid and the lowest-paid jobs in the firm continued to hover around four to one. Moreover, the ratio between the points given to higher supervisory personnel and to skilled workers was considerably smaller.

Nevertheless, if interskill differentials at Klek are measured in terms of average monthly earnings for white-collar and blue-collar workers respectively, they widened as white-collar qualification levels rose. If we look at Klek's labor structure in the 1970s (table 16), there is an increase in the number of white-collar workers employed in high point/income jobs and an increase in the number of blue-collar workers employed in low point/income jobs, presumably causing the difference between the mean and median incomes in each category to widen.[16] In addition, there was not only a larger number of jobs requiring higher qualifications, but the proportion of individuals who actually possessed the necessary qualifications for these positions also increased.[17] Despite the rise in personal incomes of all categories of labor in the firm, then, the blue-collar worker's relative position deteriorated, especially in the period immediately preceding this study.

The impact of the market and the modernization plan also brought a sharper distinction between upper management and the rest of the work collective, a distinction that affected white-collar and blue-collar workers alike. In part, this was simply a product of expansion; Klek's labor force doubled in size between 1966 and 1974, which understandably increased the distance between higher executives and the rank-and-file work force. A contributing cause was the increased expertise of Klek's management, expertise acquired at school and at other enterprises rather than through years of hard work at Klek.

In addition, the distance that separated management from the work force was a product of the firm's increased autonomy and its emphasis on higher efficiency. At the same time that the revised organizational and incentive

systems encouraged those in nonsupervisory positions to be occupied exclusively with their immediate tasks, it put a premium on executive concern
with broad policy making, general supervision, and overall coordination. As a
by-product, the different relationships of supervisory and nonsupervisory
personnel with the self-management structure were accentuated: whereas a
cooperative working relationship with the self-management bodies was a pre-
requisite for an executive's fulfilling the requirements of his job, workers and
clerks had little need for contact with the self-management bodies in the
course of their day-to-day activities, and attending meetings was merely an
additional obligation for them. Furthermore, although the impact of management on the decisions of self-management bodies had always been high,[18]
after 1966 the decisions themselves had greater consequences for the economic status of the firm. As this was perceived subjectively by members of
the work collective, both the firm's economic performance and the functioning of its self-management processes seemed to depend more on the quality
of its management than on any other single factor.

Finally the differentiation between executives and nonsupervisory personnel
was accentuated by the change in management "style" which accompanied
the election of the present director in 1966. Where the old director, a war-
time partisan without much higher education and managerial training, was
remembered as one whose day was taken up with getting the goods produced,
his replacement, a mechanical engineer and university graduate, devoted
considerably less energy to routine supervision. Instead, he spent much of his
time with parties external to the enterprise: potential and current customers,
suppliers, finance agents, import-export houses, political officials. Further,
the new director, imbued with the spirit of the 1965 reforms, was as highly
committed to the nonauthoritarian collective entrepreneur model of self-
management as he was to modernizing the firm's work process. On the one
hand, this allowed both the director and the other executives to continue to
hold a position of influence in decision making that formally belonged to the
self-managers; on the other, the new emphasis on participation, toleration of
disagreement, and collective responsibility brought a decline in disciplinary
sanctions and a more open atmosphere to the plant.

Rather than relying on sanctions and commands, the director resorted to
promises and appeals to solidarity to get decisions executed. When he criticized or gave concrete suggestions to specific individuals, he did so privately
in order to spare the individual's feelings and public repute. This was particularly the case with other executives and helped to create a harmonious
management front toward nonsupervisory personnel. So too did the director's
practice of not invervening in the affairs of a subordinate unless he specifically

asked for advice. Yet if such practices guaranteed him the loyalty of each executive, the same warm feelings could hardly be said to characterize the relations of the executives toward each other. Leaving general supervision to essentially unsupervised executives often meant that difficulties in one sector went unnoticed until they became so problematic that they began to affect other departments. At the same time, the combination of public exhortations, private criticisms, and loose supervisory practices led to a widespread feeling among the rest of the collective that it was being called on to perform what was essentially management's job. The new managerial style may have sought to encourage individual initiative on the job and participation in enterprise affairs; in the context of a hierarchical division of labor and an unequal distribution of influence and income, however, what it all too often facilitated was evasion of responsibility and conflict.

The impact of the postreform economic environment reinforced the effects of occupational differentiation and adaptation to the competitive market at Klek. As individuals became more concerned with maximizing their incomes, their loyalty to the enterprise as a center of production apparently dropped. "I remember when we used to work sixty or sixty-five hours a week to meet the plan goals," an older supervisor reminisced. "We would even sleep in the factory if we had to. But people won't do that anymore." Inflation and the arrival of a new generation with only childhood memories of the solidaristic fifties accelerated the process whereby individuals were reluctant to make sacrifices for the work collective and expected reimbursement for any services rendered the firm. The work collective became a "collective entrepreneur" with a vengeance, transforming itself into 528 individual entrepreneurs, each anxious to maximize the return to his individual labor input.

As commitment to the firm as a whole declined, identification with the occupational group seemed to increase. Interfirm and interindustry differentials meant that the road to higher wages was not necessarily through hard work or sacrifices for the sake of investment. On the contrary, it might well be through simply moving to another enterprise—or even another country.

Nevertheless, where a person could move was highly dependent on his or her skills. While Klek's experienced, skilled, and highly skilled production workers had little difficulty finding jobs in other machine-tool plants, locating employment in a different and preferably high-wage industry was another question. Clerical, technical, and managerial personnel, however, had less industry-specific skills and so, having acquired their initial work experience at Klek, had more opportunities for upward mobility. Ironically, those able to garner the highest salaries and have the greatest impact on formulating business policy and development plans also had the highest turnover rates in the firm.[19] Far from increasing the loyalty to the firm of the less mobile strata, however, turnover at the top merely made them more aware of the differences separating them from it.

Not surprisingly, the increased awareness of labor mobility as a means of gaining a higher income had its effects on loyalty to the firm and satisfaction with its operation: "In the old days, people didn't move around so much; there weren't so many differences, and so people just stayed in one place and worked. Now they are always feeling they can do better [in another firm]."[20]

As in Proudhon's mutualist association, the formal egalitarianism of the self-management bodies did little at Klek to create a substitute center of solidarity and loyalty to the firm. Significantly, three of the last seven workers' council presidents at Klek had left the enterprise for better jobs elsewhere; of the four remaining, all but one had been promoted. At the same time, the differentiation and stratification produced by the hierarchical division of labor and the competitive labor market defined the main cleavage lines in the conflicts expressed in the self-management bodies. While the need to remain competitive on the labor and product markets meant that the self-management bodies were unlikely to make decisions that would eliminate these distinctions altogether, the fact that decisions were a product of the interplay of group interests undoubtedly prevented them from becoming even more pronounced than they were.

AN EXCEPTION: BOAL II AND GRAMSCI

Paradoxically perhaps, the one part of the enterprise that seemed to have escaped many of the consequences of both the reform and Klek's reform-inspired modernization program was precisely the unit they had brought into being: the Service Division. Several factors account for this.

In the first place, because of its location and its particular division of labor, the occupational stratification so pronounced at the main plant site was much less apparent within the Service Division. Its blue-collar workers were an elite among the production force, while its small white-collar staff was mainly routine clerical and technical personnel. In contrast with the main plant, where the high-powered specialists and managerial personnel were concentrated, income and status differentials in the Service Division more often than not favored the blue-collar workers.

Second, all the members of the division were drawn together by the fact that they were a subordinate unit in an enterprise whose headquarters were on the other side of the city. Its subordinate status meant that the division handled fewer issues that could form a basis for conflict, and if any group within the division was dissatisfied with a decision, the central enterprise could easily be blamed rather than individuals within the division itself. In addition, the complement to the lack of internal conflict in BOAL II was the growth of a kind of separatist sentiment within it, encouraged by its superior efficiency, physical location, and previous history as an independent enterprise. Thus, its BOAL status was used by the division practically to emancipate itself from the control of other units. When its representatives attended meetings of enterprise-level self-management bodies, they neither requested approval for any decision BOAL II had made on its own nor reported any difficulty the division might be having. In fact, when a young technician in BOAL II appealed a request for a raise to the central workers' council, the BOAL II delegates reacted with indignation at his attempt to get the central enterprise authority involved in a division problem. Normally, however, their participation at meetings was confined to insuring that BOAL II got its share of whatever was being distributed at the enterprise level, and they reacted with some annoyance to the continual discussion of the difficulties plaguing BOALs I and III at workers' council meetings. Similar behavior characterized its executives' relation with the central enterprise *kolegija*. The director of BOAL II frequently missed its meetings, and when required to make a report on the division, he delivered it in two sentences: "The plan is being completed on time. What else do you want to know?"

Third, BOAL II's management, physically insulated from the influence of Klek's general director, employed an approach distinctly different from that of the main plant management. Whereas executives in BOALs I and III were by and large left to their own initiative by both the general director and each other, at BOAL II the three of four executives in charge of the division formed a tight-knit clique. Supervision was more rigorous all down the line, and there was less reliance on the self-management bodies' capacity to solve problems. For example, BOAL I regularly discussed production bottlenecks, hiring problems, and the like at division meetings, and on occasion, difficulties in attaining plan goals came up at workers' council meetings as well; in BOAL II, whatever problems appeared came to the executives' attention first, and only already agreed-on solutions would be presented to the division council for routine approval—if anything was presented at all. Similarly, consultation in BOAL II was on a more informal basis and typically involved the executives and a handful of the more influential nonsupervisory personnel. When a conclusion was arrived at, there were few who were about to take the risk of dissenting from it. In short, not only were there fewer issues for conflicts in BOAL II, but there were fewer opportunities and less tolerance for it.

Finally, BOAL II was the most efficient division in Klek. Its smooth-running operations not only prevented conflicts over who was "really" working from arising, but enhanced the legitimacy of the management's style, helped maintain the division's esprit de corps, and solidified its sense of superiority over the rest of the enterprise.

As a result, if hierarchical relations were more pronounced in BOAL II than at the main plant, they were also more accepted. As an employee who had transferred to BOAL III from the Service Division remarked, "Over in Service, they have technocratic-managerialism, but it works."

While there is evidence [21] that as individuals, the members of BOAL II shared the same occupational attitudes and values that characterized their colleagues in BOALs I and III, there was simply little opportunity for these attitudes to break into open conflicts as they did at the main plant. Insofar as its peculiar characteristics insulated it from many of the consequences the competitive market had on the firm as a whole, BOAL II more closely resembled Gramsci's model of workers' democracy than Proudhon's producer co-op, and solidaristic behavior and suspicion of outside authorities—including the central enterprise—was the result.

CONFLICT AT KLEK*

Solidarity in Proudhon's mutualist association was based on the association's ability to maximize its revenue and distribute it equally. At Klek, the major conflicts that occurred during this study, and apparently in the years preceding it as well, were precisely over whether or not the necessary steps were being taken to maximize the firm's income and over what constituted fair distribution. In addition, the conflicts all occurred in spheres where Klek enjoyed autonomy, involved cleavages between labor and management, and were fought out in terms of contrasting ideological[22] values held by the respective groups.

Distribution questions, whether of wages, profits, or collective funds, were a case in point. Several open and bitter conflicts over such issues occurred during the relatively brief period of this study; the factory bulletin, minutes of workers' council meetings, and accounts of older Klek employees suggested that others had gone on in the past. The observed examples include a major revolt of the blue-collar workers at an assembly held in March 1974 over the issue of retroactive pay for the twenty-four Saturdays Klek had worked without compensation in 1973, a related dispute over profit distribution, and a

---

*This section and the following chapters (8 and 9) refer only to the main plant (BOALs I and III) which, for stylistic simplicity, I will treat as the enterprise. As noted above, BOAL II had a very different pattern of behavior according to all accounts, and so these observations do not refer to the Service Division unless specifically mentioned.

spontaneous mobilization of the production workers for parity with technicians in overtime rates.

In 1973, Klek had received a much-needed loan from the Zagreb Reserve Fund[23] with several conditions attached to it; among them was the requirement that Klek take some concrete step to show it was turning over a new leaf. This condition was satisfied by a decision of the work collective to work on Saturday without pay.[24] Here the problem began: absenteeism climbed, while productivity dropped to the point where one executive later remarked, "Were it not for the political virtues [of working Saturdays], we would have done at least as well without working the extra day." Dissatisfaction in BOAL I in particular mounted to the point where a special assembly had to be called in November 1973. At that meeting, the production workers managed to extract a promise from the general director that, come 1974, they would be paid back for half of the "free" Saturdays if the 1973 plan were completed.

The director's promise quieted things for the rest of the year; 94 percent of the 1973 plan was completed. An expected pay increase for 1974 was effected, and it was agreed that the portion of the 1973 profits earmarked for division among the collective would be distributed as it always had, an equal portion going to each person working at Klek. Meanwhile, January and February came and went with no word on the promised Saturdays pay. Tempers began to rise, and at an assembly called in mid-March, the explosion occurred.

It was quite understandable that the situation broke open when it did. The March assembly, nominally called to approve the 1974 investment plan, was held at a particularly inauspicious moment: a few days after payday, but several days before Klek had been able to get the cash together to meet its payroll. This was certainly neither the first nor the last time paychecks were late at Klek, but it was another reminder of those nagging inefficiencies that hit the lower-income brackets much harder than the upper levels. At the same time, feelings were still rankling over the apartments Klek had purchased for two newly hired engineers despite the long list of less-skilled enterprise personnel who had been waiting years to receive housing.

At the assembly, it became clear the moment the first speaker, a young machinist, was recognized that a worker-management fight was in the making, and its central issue was going to be the interpretation of a key tenet of Yugoslav socialism, "distribution according to work." As the production workers saw the situation, they had come to work on Saturday the previous year and done the work for which they were responsible as best they could. In their eyes, they had created the "value," but when it came time to redistribute it back as personal income, suddenly it had mysteriously disappeared.

This, to the workers, was as impossible as it was unfair; "distribution according to work" for them meant that individuals were entitled to receive in proportion to their contribution, and if they had worked additional days, it should show up in their paychecks. Reasoning from this position, they repeatedly demanded, "Why aren't we receiving pay for the work we did last year?" and consistently refused to accept any of the explanations Klek's management offered. In fact, their refusal was so complete that the first assembly broke up into small groups of workers and executives arguing with each other, without resolving anything after two and a half hours of stormy debate.

Management countered the workers' position by upholding the principle of distribution according to the "results" of work: wages did not depend on the quality and quantity of individual labor performed, but on the overall market performance of the firm. As Klek's general director put it, "You could have worked seven days a week and twenty-four hours a day, but if we don't realize the value on the market, we don't have the funds with which to pay you." He was supported not only by the rest of the executives, but also by the fact that once a share of the 1973 profit had been set aside for redistribution and once a wage increase had gone into effect for 1974, the enterprise simply had no additional funds with which to pay retroactive wages. Thus, faced with a fait accompli, the workers, reluctantly and still unconvinced, conceded their cause as lost at the assembly convened the next week.

Not surprisingly, the same cry of "distribution according to work" was heard again at the next available opportunity, an assembly convened in May 1974 to discuss the distribution of the 1973 profits. Here, the main debate was over who had a right to receive a share of the profits, the size of the shares already having been agreed upon. The workers, undoubtedly recalling the unpaid Saturdays of 1973, contended that only those who had actively worked to create the profits had a right to share in them; all those who had begun working at Klek after January 1974 should not receive a bonus. Management, however, defended the rights of all those currently employed by the firm to share in the 1973 profits. One executive explained, "Well, we want to give an incentive to the people working here now, not to the ones who worked a year ago and then left the firm."

If management appeared ranged on the slide of egalitarianism and the unity of the work collective in this instance, the production workers stuck to their notion of just distribution as both the best long-term guarantee of equality and the surest way of protecting their interests. A highly skilled assembler articulated the sentiments of many: "We work, we live for this factory. Now you're going to tell me that a new guy comes, he gets an apartment, he gets better pay, and he gets a share of the profits we created by coming to work on Saturdays?" Note, in addition, that there was no talk, either publicly at the assembly or privately among the workers before and after the meeting, of getting larger bonuses for themselves by eliminating bonuses for a portion of the collective. The entire debate took place on the assumption that each would receive the same fixed amount regardless of how many bonuses were distributed; the workers' demands seemed to be voiced much more out of a principled concern for equity than from regard for short-term material self-interest.

The issue was finally resolved by invoking the canons of legality. As Croatian law declared that every member of a work organization who had a right to a vacation also had a right to a bonus, and since no one disputed the right of the new employees to their annual vacation, the law was interpreted to mean that they could not be legally denied a share in the 1973 earnings. Thus, management's position was upheld without resolving the rightness or wrongness of the workers' demands; in effect, a conflict was avoided by removing the issue from the sphere of enterprise discretion altogether.

Hardly coincidental to the workers' willingness to do battle on this issue was the fact that the most rapidly expanding sector of Klek's labor force was composed of technical and clerical personnel; most of those hired in 1974 were not production workers. The pervasive feeling among the workers was that while there was certainly a need for engineers and technicians in a mechanically sophisticated production process and for a clerical staff to coordinate business policy, Klek had gone overboard in recruiting white-collar and technical personnel. While several of the higher executives shared this judgment, it was a special source of irritation to the blue-collar workers. Not only was there a shortage of production workers, meaning a greater burden of the work fell on their shoulders, and not only did more highly educated cadres get higher salaries and preferential treatment in apartment allocations, but Yugoslav ideology—as well as the workers themselves—holds that only "direct producers" create value, while "indirect producers" live off it. Hence, even though few contested the "necessary" character of professional, technical, and clerical work, nonmanual employees were still often viewed by the production workers as "parasites."

This was the background to the September confrontation on overtime rates. Again the issue arose in an assembly, and again the predictable worker-management conflict occurred. Here, although workers traditionally received fewer dinars per point than did time-rate technicians, they now protested extending this principle to overtime rates. Instead, they insisted on time-and-a-half wages, just as technicians received.[25] This time, the workers did not simply argue their points; they made it clear that unless their demand was satisfied, they would simply stop doing overtime work. Meanwhile, the plant was already short on production workers, and without overtime, less than 80 percent of the annual plan could be completed. Management was forced to give in; although the change in wage rates had to be approved by the workers' council, both management and workers supported it.[26]

Klek's sociopolitical organizations played almost no role in all three of these confrontations over distribution questions. As for the trade union, its president distinguished himself in the Saturdays pay dispute by being the only blue-collar worker who took management's side in the conflict; not surprisingly, the membership he represented quickly shouted him down. Of greater interest is that Klek's voluntary and, at least in theory, more disciplined LCY organization fell victim to a similar phenomenon: while its leaders tended to support management in the conflicts, its own blue-collar membership led the worker opposition. As we shall see, the LCY at Klek could act as a unified group in representing the firm's interests before external political authorities and it could stand firm on internally implementing decisions and laws made by outside bodies; however, when an issue polarized the collective, the party also split on it. In short, Klek's party organization had a marginal impact on conflicts because it couldn't agree itself on how they should be resolved.

Distribution questions were not the only source of conflict at Klek. "Responsibility" issues came in a close second and chiefly centered around who was at fault for the various inefficiencies that continually plagued Klek's operation. For example, in the Saturdays pay dispute, once the workers had given up hope of actually receiving the retroactive wages, they belligerently accused management of incompetence. They had come in on Saturdays and done their jobs; if the value they had created had not been "realized," that was the fault of management. The executives, in turn, argued for "collective responsibility," asserting that the firm lacked the money with which to pay retroactive wages because no one had worked hard enough.

Collective versus individual responsibility also cropped up frequently in discussions of the firm's progress—or lack of it—in meeting both its plan targets and various program goals. More profoundly, it was the source of an enormous amount of grumbling on the plant floor and of the mistrust that, to a certain degree, ran through both relations between supervisors and subordinates and between the different occupational groups. Each time a machine was late, a cost higher than anticipated, the introduction of an expected change delayed, the cry went up: "Whose fault is it?" Simultaneously, accusations began to fly: if production was behind schedule, the workers blamed the supply department for not getting the parts to the plant on time. The supply department, in turn, pointed to the fact that suppliers would no longer deal with

Klek on credit, and the finance department had not come up with the funds needed if orders were to be filled. Finance would then blame the lack of capital on late delivery of ordered machines and the legal department's failure to prosecute the firms that still owed money to Klek. Meanwhile, those in lower-level positions blamed management for its failure to coordinate the departments, while management called on the labor force to work harder.

Yet the problem was not simply one of passing the buck; a fundamental question of equity was also involved. While the miscalculations a worker might make, such as breaking a tool, represented a relatively small loss to the firm and were easily traceable to the individual responsible for them, executive miscalculations were extremely costly, and responsibility was likely to be shared with a host of other parties, not the least of which were the self-management bodies themselves. Moreover, the resulting loss would be shared by all the members of the work collective. The complaints the workers had about the collective responsibility doctrine were thus all too understandable: "A worker breaks a part and he's got to pay for it, but a director makes a mistake which costs us millions [of dinars] and no one is responsible" (assembler).

A third issue of controversy, if not of open conflict, was personnel policy. Here debate focused on two questions: what the firm's labor structure should look like and what starting salaries for certain categories of labor should be. Significantly, the *size* of the firm's labor force was not a topic of controversy. While everyone was anxious to maximize his or her personal income, no one ever urged restricting the number of people employed by the firm as the way to do this. If a task needed to be done on a regular basis and no existing job definition covered it, the universal reaction was invariably to support opening a new job and hiring someone to do it; altering an existing job description to encompass the added work was never even considered.[27]

What additions to Klek's labor force were needed, however, was another question. While both management and blue-collar workers agreed on the need for additional production workers, a number of the specialists and white-collar personnel suspected that production delays were due to "fooling around" on the plant floor and not to a shortage of help. At the same time, while management and employees laid heavy stress on the need to attract qualified technical and professional specialists, the production workers were distinctly suspicious of the ballooning number of white-collar employees. These suspicions were reinforced by their sense that supply bottlenecks, late paychecks, and various technical delays were not getting any less frequent despite the increased size and expertise of the staff.

This brings us to the second point of controversy surrounding personnel policy: what salary individuals and individual jobs "deserved." Although the

point system and the analytical job evaluation in theory tried to apply "objective" criteria to income distribution, in practice they seemed to reflect the
fact that wage determination at Klek was as much the product of occupational group politics as it was of marginal productivity and prevailing scarcities
in the labor market. Indeed, the need to keep the peace between individuals
and groups in the firm may well have insulated its wage scales against the
fluctuations of the labor market.[28]

While management generally favored setting wage proportions that would
facilitate recruiting competent personnel to the firm, the workers were much
more intent upon using income differentials as a way of measuring on-the-job
performance. The white-collar workers, in turn, were anxious to have education levels reflected in the salary scale. The final product was an uneasy compromise in which point allocations for the different kinds of labor appeared
to be governed by the criteria each respective group preferred: blue-collar
workers were on a piece-rate scale; executives and high-level specialists received
salaries more or less commensurate with what they could get elsewhere; and
white-collar workers were ranked by their skill levels. When each group judged
the others by its own standards, however, it felt underpaid.

Since personnel questions were usually handled on a case-by-case basis, they
did not generate the kind of large-scale disputes to which general distribution
and responsibility issues could give rise. On the contrary, as they were not
played out as zero-sum games, they lent themselves to the solutions in which
the individual or group with the most intense preferences would emerge
victorious. As long as an argument by one group or individual could be made
for hiring an extra person, the others were likely to go along; as long as one
enterprise group supported an individual's request for a raise, the others were
likely to concede it. Certainly a significant factor explaining this behavior
was the fact that it was simply psychologically cheaper for the collective to
add a marginal increment to what were perceived as operating costs than it
was to resist the demands of an insistent individual or group. Indeed, when the
increment looked like it was going to be more than marginal—a new job, for
instance, required a high-salaried university graduate to fill it; raising X's
points meant eventually raising Y's and Z's points as well—it had a much more
difficult time getting the approval of the self-management bodies. Moreover,
when and if it did get through, the response from the rest of the collective
was often complaints over the decision and murmurings about not being
"represented."

Further, personnel questions only went before the elected self-management
bodies, relatively small councils in which representatives from the various
occupational groups were usually about equal in number. In contrast, the

distribution and responsibility debates occurred in the jointly convened assemblies of BOALs I and II, much larger bodies of "direct democracy," which met on the plant floor and were dominated by the production workers.

Yet not all assemblies were marked by conflict and turbulence. In fact, precisely because the assemblies, comprising every member of the two BOALs, had the character of a mass meeting, they tended to oscillate between complete docility, with little or no participation from the collective, or open revolt of the kind described above. The critical factor seemed to be whether a decision involved choosing between mutually exclusive values held by different occupational groups in the firm. When it did, participation was vociferous and involvement high, particularly where the blue-collar production workers were concerned; if one of them started an attack, the others quickly joined in support. At the same time, because the assembly is a mass rather than an elected group, when a proposal did not involve conflicts between occupational groups, the probability of *any* participation from the floor was greatly reduced. In sum, the assembly setting places a premium on conformity to group values, attitudes, and norms of behavior. Let us now examine the fundamentally ideological values characterizing each of the major occupational groups at Klek.

8

Occupational Values and Attitudes
in a Yugoslav Firm

We have already seen[1] that one of the effects of the occupational stratification accelerated by the 1965 economic reforms and combined with a formally
egalitarian model of enterprise decision making was to bring contrasting
values and attitudes among occupational groups into particularly striking relief. At Klek, too, fundamentally different occupational values and approaches
to the enterprise and to the larger society formed the backdrop to the labor-
management conflicts played out in the self-management bodies. At the same
time, these differing occupational value configurations could easily converge
on a number of issues; as we shall see in chapter 9, they could produce
solidarity and consensus on some questions as easily as they could produce
division on others.

The purpose of the following descriptions of occupational values and attitudes
at Klek is not to assert that these particular beliefs are "typical"; since many
of the conversations I had and much of the behavior I observed seemed
grounded on values and beliefs not tapped by survey research with wider
sample populations, there is little hard evidence for believing that the value
patterns found at Klek are representative of workers, executives, and employees throughout Yugoslavia. Nor, however, is there any evidence that they
are not; if anything, the conclusions of the survey research presented in
chapter 5 indicate that the kind of values and attitudes found at Klek and
their distribution among the different occupational groups certainly do not
conflict with what is known about occupational value patterns in other
Yugoslav firms.

Nevertheless, the information I present is primarily exemplary and explanatory. On the one hand, I wish to give an example of the kind of attitude
differences occupational stratification in a Yugoslav firm can cause; as
pointed out earlier, it is the relationship between behavior and structure which
may be generalizable, not the behavior (in this case, the particular attitudes and
beliefs) or structure (here, the kind of occupational differentiation found in
a small, highly urbanized and well-educated work collective) itself. On the other

hand, I wish to show that the differences and similarities in occupational value configurations at Klek form a key factor in explaining the enterprise's particular patterns of conflict and solidarity.

The descriptions presented below are based on observation and conversations with members of BOALs I and III; occasional conversations with individuals from BOAL II revealed that fundamental occupational orientations in that division were similar, but for the reasons already dealt with,[2] they never surfaced in open conflict.

It should also be noted that despite differences in group attitudes and values, these contrasting viewpoints rarely spilled over into relations between individuals at Klek. While management and workers may have been at each others' throats in the Saturdays debate, social relations and plant interaction were normally quite cordial.[3] Similarly, whatever technicians and employees as a group thought of the workers' behavior at meetings and their work habits on the job, these feelings never prevented the organization of a brief soccer game involving mixed teams of both groups during the half-hour daily break.

OCCUPATIONAL VALUES AT KLEK: PRODUCTION WORKERS[4]

The most cohesive group in the firm was the blue-collar production workers in the main plant. They possessed a strong sense of shared values and aspirations which were in many ways rather similar to those Gramsci attempted to institutionalize in his vision of workers' democracy. As in Proudhon's mutualist association, the group that perceived itself to be in a relatively disadvantaged position—both in the enterprise and in the larger society—held attitudes dysfunctional for a market economy and the successful operation of the "collective entrepreneur" model of self-management, while implicitly embracing values supportive of a hierarchical form of resource allocation.

Like Gramsci, the blue-collar workers at Klek made a strict distinction between what they perceived as "productive" and "nonproductive" labor. As they seemed to apply the distinction to the division of labor in the firm, it referred partially to the specific job an individual held and partially to the actual performance of the individual on the job.

On the one hand, the more a given job was regarded by the workers as technically essential to the physical manufacture of the finished product, the more it was considered intrinsically "productive." Not surprisingly, such a view placed the blue-collar workers at the very heart of the production process:

The workers know that they don't need the engineer as much as the

engineer needs them. Without an engineer, they would still be able to
work, but without workers, an engineer is useless. They need him to
make things better, but he's not essential to running a factory the way
workers are (former machinist, currently a staff specialist).

On the other hand, whether or not an individual was "productive" rested
not only on the specific tasks to which he or she was assigned, but also on
how well they were actually performed:

I know we need engineers. Some of the guys don't agree with me, but
underneath it, they know an engineer can contribute a lot. But he's got
to be good. I don't mind if he gets paid more, either. After all, he has to
have a lot more education and has far greater responsibilities. But if he
wants to get paid, he has to work, like we do. If he doesn't do anything,
what do we need him for? (machinist)

Like Gramsci, then, the blue-collar workers at Klek envisioned the factory
as a center of production where, to use Gramsci's phrase, "every worker
represents a definite necessity of the labor process and of production." Klek's
blue-collar workers were not a priori opposed to specialization or even hierarchy, but merely demanded that they be functionally and closely related to
the factory's "real business," producing goods. Indeed, one of the main
worker complaints was that the plant management was not authoritarian
enough:

Our people work, but they have to have a heavy hand (*čvrsta ruka*) over
them. That's why they do well in Germany. (machinist)

We all know what's wrong around here but no one does anything about
it. When I come to work late, does anyone say to me, "Pero, you're late,
you're docked for the day, come back tomorrow on time"? If nothing
happens, why should I come to work on time ever? (assembler)

Repeatedly they would complain, "Around here, everybody is busy with
everything, everyone is responsible for everything, and in the end, nobody
does anything. If everyone would just do his work, we wouldn't have so many
problems."

The view of the factory as a center of production seems to have been an
important factor behind the substantial worker support for Klek's modernization program. Even though the program was financed primarily out of
internal savings and envisioned a long-term reduction in the blue-collar work
force, the workers were anxious to bring more modern equipment to the
plant and complained about having to work on "machinery that [was]

totally depreciated ten years ago" (machinist). Indeed, if they reluctantly came to accept the hiring of a larger number of white-collar and technical personnel, it was largely because they saw it as the necessary cost of getting newer and more technically advanced machinery. In effect, measures to raise labor productivity were as strongly supported by the workers as by management; such support was related partially to what the worker perceived as the proper relation between labor and income.

Labor, for Klek's blue-collar workers, was not primarily a source of enjoyment or self-realization; work was something one did out of necessity, in order to provide oneself with the tangible and intangible means of survival. This did not mean that work had to be a painful, back-breaking experience, but merely that it did not represent a freely chosen activity. As one worker said simply, "Work is work. You have to do it, so why complain about it?" And another: "Everyone has to work, that's all there is to it. Otherwise, how can you live?"

Nor did such a perception of labor as a necessity of human life mean that work was not an important activity, one essential for the continuation of social life and, if productive, a definite social contribution. Like Gramsci, Klek's blue-collar workers felt it was the product of labor that gave work its individual and social significance, not the labor process itself. Moreover, it was precisely because the products of one's labor did represent something useful to society that one had the right to receive something useful from society in return: an income.

Accordingly, "distribution according to work" was interpreted by the workers in its most literal sense: one received in proportion to what one contributed, and the "value" of what one contributed, of the product, was measured by the labor power expended in its production. It followed that the more one produced or contributed, the more one should receive: hence, the worker support for productivity-increasing measures. Note that, like Gramsci, the workers assumed the social "usefulness" of the particular product by virtue of its being produced in the first place. Neither a notion of entrepreneurial risk nor of demand as registered on the market entered into their calculations.

Thus to the extent that the market was accepted by the workers, it was perceived largely as a system for measuring labor values, rewarding those who "worked" and penalizing those who did not. Interfirm differentials, for example, were seen as a result of how efficient a firm's production process was and not as traceable to the demand for the product manufactured, marketing strategies employed, price policies, market position, or other such factors. One worker contrasted a highly profitable enterprise down the road with Klek: "Well, sure they make money. Down there the management manages and the people work. That's how it should be."

Furthermore, the same logic meant that when actual prices differed from the expected, subjectively determined "labor values" and the firm's income departed from what the workers felt it should be, there was going to be trouble. The debate over the free Saturdays was but one example of the workers' commitment to their notion of "distribution according to work." Another was the widespread belief among Klek's blue-collar workers that the executives were stealing from the firm and falsifying the accounts,[5] a convenient excuse for why incomes were lower than the workers felt they should be.

The workers' emphasis on "productive" labor, their view of the enterprise as a center of production, and their notion of "distribution according to work" also help to explain their strong support of piece rates: "Sure, piece rates are fine. This way the people who work get paid, and the ones that don't do anything don't get paid. That's the way it should be" (machinist). In fact, their main complaint over piece rates was that incentives prevailing at Klek were not large enough; many were incensed at the white-collar staff for the delays accompanying the compilation of new incentive regulations to provide greater stimulation. Thus, during the overtime debate, a tool-and-die mechanic added to his criticisms of the current state of affairs at Klek:

> And when are these promised incentive regulations going to be ready? They were promised for January, then June, and here it's September and there's still nothing. I produce twice as much as I'm required to, and all I have to show for it is a miserable 30 dinars [per month].

Indeed, not only did the workers endorse the use of piece rates in determining their own wages, they felt that their use should be extended to cover all categories of labor in the firm. Equality, for Klek's production workers, did not mean the absolute economic equality of the leveler. Rather, it was an equality based on being equally "necessary" to production, an equality that permitted hierarchy, specialization, and wage differentials insofar as they reflected the individual's actual on-the-job performance, his "contribution" to production.

"Distribution according to work" to the production workers thus meant that wage differentials within the firm should reflect actual differences in labor productivity, ideally measured by some universally applicable system of piece rates. An engineer might well receive higher pay than a worker as a consequence, but it would be because he somehow "contributed" more to production and not simply because his skills were scarcer on the labor market. Yet although income differentials would remain under such a system, it was clearly the workers' expectation that they would be smaller and more justified than in the current situation. Indeed, when several were asked whether the present problem was overly large differentials or unmerited differentials, they unhesitatingly answered, "Both."

At the same time, the production workers were intuitively convinced that if payment were "really" on the basis of work, the individuals who "sit in the offices . . . drinking coffee all day" (machinist) would be weeded out and penalized by receiving lower salaries. This belief in the possibility of measuring all labor on a piece-rate scale undoubtedly lay behind the support Klek's workers initially gave to the analytical job evaluations the enterprise periodically undertook; that this belief was largely unfounded explains their subsequent discontent with the wage scales the job evaluations finally produced.

On the surface, the workers' equation of "distribution according to work" with the application of piece rates seems to smack of the elitism of which skilled and highly skilled workers are so often accused. However, given the workers' perception of the actual situation in the firm, in context the demands for precise measurement of on-the-job performance had highly egalitarian overtones. "We have distribution according to work now," a young electrician remarked sarcastically. "The less work you do, the more you get paid— especially if you're in some high position."

This brings us to the wider ramifications of the distinction between "productive" and "nonproductive" labor. That is, as the workers seemed to use the distinction, it applied not only to the division of labor within the firm but also, and perhaps more important, to the division of labor within society as well. In this wider, social context, those who performed productive labor were first and foremost those employed in industry and, secondarily, those working in agriculture and social services. And within these branches, it was particularly the "direct producers" who performed productive labor: the workers, peasants, doctors, teachers—as opposed to those who held administrative positions within them.

In their emphasis on industry as the main source of productive activity and of national wealth, the workers' view is reminiscent of both Gramsci's ideas and the overall philosophy that guided Yugoslav planners in the industrialization efforts of the 1950's:

If it weren't for industry, there wouldn't be anything (electrician).

We [industrial] workers have to create all the wealth. We not only have to produce enough for ourselves, but we have to produce enough to take care of everyone else (welder).

The whole problem is that you have a few million people in industry providing for everyone. How can we earn as much as we produce when it's like that? (assembler)

Significantly, in the workers' eyes, productive labor, an activity that resulted in or at least contributed to the production of a definite product or service satisfying social needs, was not performed at all by the state, political organizations ("Politicians," muttered one worker, "when have they ever produced anything besides talk?"), banks, trading companies, or other such administrative and financial institutions. Nevertheless, it was in the hands of these "nonproductive" institutions that the workers perceived money as being most concentrated. In a thinly veiled allusion, one worker commented, "It [wealth] never winds up where it's produced. It always goes somewhere else, into someone else's pocket. And the workers get what's left over." In an assembly called to discuss the formation of the new interest communities, an assembler burst out:

So much for what it's supposed to do. And how do we know this is not just another one of those schemes for getting the funds away from the direct producer who creates them and channeling them into the bureaucracy? Who's really going to have control in all of this? We all know what's going to happen.

Again, "distribution according to work" was the workers' preferred solution. In a broader socioeconomic context, however, it meant not only favoring the "direct producer" in the distribution of personal incomes, but also channeling resources into the branches of the economy where they would be most "productive." It is here that the egalitarian implications of the endorsement of piece rates became apparent: "politicians" and "bureaucrats" would, presumably, be unable to receive the high salaries, desirable housing, private automobiles, and other privileges they currently had access to (or at least were believed to have access to) once the "productive" effects of their activities were measured on the same scale that applied to everyone else's labor. Indeed, in the workers' view, as politics produced nothing but talk, politicians would find themselves at the low end of the income scale.

At the same time, observation of the principle of "distribution according to work" would also guarantee that the enterprises and branches of economic activity that contributed the most to national wealth would receive the largest share of it in return. This, indeed, was the proper role of the state, in the workers' eyes; rather than consuming the resources that others produced, government's task was to ensure that resources went to those who "deserved" to dispose of them.

Nevertheless, the workers were all too aware that the government in actuality was far from meeting these expectations. In fact, they had little positive to say regarding current government economic policy and generally seemed to feel the net effect of political intervention in the economy had merely been to make life more difficult for those who were "doing their work." They resented having to conform to regulations formulated by political bodies ("Here they are, making this law, that law, and they've never been inside a factory," complained a machinist) and were as quick to blame political authorities for the enterprise's economic difficulties and for low incomes as they were to find fault with the firm management. Significantly, they did not trace either their own or Klek's problems to the operation of the "impersonal" market, as Yugoslav economic reformers of the sixties had hoped. For Klek's workers, specific human agents were the cause of problems, not the abstract workings of an allocation system. One worker gave this analysis of the causes of low productivity:

> It's all these peasant workers. They pushed all the peasants into industry and hurt agriculture and made it harder for people who live in the city to find work. And the peasants don't make good workers. So instead of having one poor person, we have two.

More typically, they criticized the state for placing the burden of economic development on industry and on the "working class" and then depriving both of the material means necessary for such development:

> In America, when something happens, the government helps. Here, when there's an earthquake, they come to us for contributions. Industry and the workers are supposed to pay for everything. So no wonder we have no capital (lathe operator).

The view of the state as a bumbling bureaucracy, as an entity that consumed resources without contributing to their production, was closely related to the workers' overall view of politics. For the workers, work and politics were two entirely separate spheres of activity. Whereas work was something everyone had to do and indeed should do, politics was "only for the people who don't want to work" (tool and die mechanic). Significantly, even the most seemingly politicized workers—those who were most outspoken in the assemblies and former and present party members—never saw themselves as having anything to do with politics, and many were highly critical of enterprise activists for spending their time at meetings in the plant and outside it instead of "doing the work they get paid for" (machinist).

Such a view of politics was not without its consequences for the workers' perception of self-management, seen by many as little more than a way of bringing politics inside the enterprise itself. "It's all talk," said one worker, "Just a lot of meetings and noise," said another. Yet a third elaborated this feeling: "I'm a real socialist. I don't hang out in the director's office and I don't spend the whole day running around to a lot of meetings. I do my job, and if everyone did the same, we'd be a lot better off."

The evaluation of the changes introduced by the 1971 constitutional amendments and the 1974 Constitution was consistent with these attitudes. Most of the workers saw the BOALs as a purely cosmetic change and a purely formal reform. No one felt anything at Klek had changed with the establishment of BOALs, and many even resented the need to go through such a complex reorganization to satisfy the wishes of authorities external to the enterprise. This resentment, however, never materialized as opposition, partly because the changes were viewed as so purely procedural.

Ironically, many of the workers who expressed the most cynical views on self-management were themselves elected representatives on self-management bodies or had been representatives in the not very distant past. Many of the workers who had most actively participated in the assembly conflicts were equally negative. In short, the most active, articulate, and interested workers were also the most critical of self-management.

What such a contradiction between behavior and attitudes seems to suggest is not opposition to self-management among workers or lack of commitment, but frustration with its actual operation.[6] To the workers, self-management did not represent a set of institutions in which workers could participate, but a mechanism through which their interests should be satisfied. Participation, for the workers, was not a value in itself, but merely a means to get the results they wanted, from "distribution according to work" to individual accountability. When it did not bring about the desired results, self-management was, quite literally, "all talk" to them. Yet because many of the results they sought were inconsistent with the firm's operation on a competitive market and/or with the decisions made by political bodies outside the firm, their participation in self-management often appeared of little avail. Viewed in this light, their apathetic reaction to the constitutional reforms is hardly surprising. As far as the workers could see, the main changes the reforms brought to the firm were in decision-making *processes*; this in no way guaranteed that decisions themselves would now reflect the preferences of rank-and-file workers, nor even that different decisions would be made at all.

A similar ambivalency characterized the workers' attitudes toward Klek's League of Communists organization. On the one hand, there probably would have been a good deal of worker support for a strong enterprise party organization that would take their side and supply organized leadership in the labor-management conflicts that periodically wracked the collective. This sense of what the "party of the working class" was "supposed" to be helps to explain why a disproportionate share of the more articulate and more rebellious workers were also highly committed party members.

On the other hand, as Klek's party organization normally remained neutral in intraenterprise conflicts and occupied itself more with procedural rather than substantive issues, there was little general worker confidence in it. For example, in the Saturdays debate, several workers publicly appealed for support to the secretary of the LCY organization at Klek; when he responded, "You have misinterpreted my words," he was shouted down. In this context, it is perhaps significant that although the older workers active in the conflicts were party members, the younger rebels were not. Furthermore, when Klek's party organization did begin to play a more aggressive role inside the firm, it was mainly in response to pressures from outside the enterprise. As a result, even though the party organization was attempting to take concrete steps to "put things in order," it wound up doing so by, in effect, "telling" people what to do rather than by "leading" the workers, as they would have wished.

Given frustration with self-management, suspicion of the state, and a party organization tied to the firm as a whole and to society at large rather than to the specific workers within it, it was hardly surprising that there was a significant amount of sotto voce sentiment among the workers for "real unions," in other words, Western-type trade unions. In their absence, the Klek workers were less prone to turn to the existing union branch in the firm, which at Klek was tied up with mainly social welfare functions, than to the self-management bodies. To the workers at Klek, the self-management bodies represented the one alternative in which at least the level of spontaneous organization they had attained on the plant floor could express itself. Hence, elections were taken quite seriously, and insufficient choice on the ballot would be the subject of protests. Whatever cynicism the practical operation of self-management provoked, then, it did not spill over into a condemnation of workers' councils or workers' control per se. Precisely because of their high expectations, the workers at Klek took care to elect their more aggressive and articulate colleagues to represent them; they would then explain away their representatives' inability to bring about the desired results as "The directors control everything," or "The executives cover up for each other," or "It's all politics," and so forth.

The problem, of course, was that the results the workers wanted, what they felt "workers' control" should be, constituted a different vision of socialism from the market-oriented version Klek was still functioning under even in

1974. Although it did not correspond with what they knew were the realities
of state planning, it was clearly a vision of socialism with distinct similarities
with Gramsci's idea of workers' democracy, where "productive" labor would
be given its due, where enterprises would be solidaristic, if hierarchical,
work communities, where each would "do his job" and carry his share of
individual responsibility, where the state would be subordinated to the needs
of "production," and where "work," rather than the market, would deter-
mine individual and collective "contributions" to society.

OCCUPATIONAL VALUES AT KLEK: MANAGEMENT

While the workers considered themselves responsible for producing the
goods, Klek's management was responsible for the overall performance of the
firm, both economically, as measured by its gross earnings, and politically,
as shown in its compliance with the various laws and regulations made outside
the firm. On the whole, management at Klek had values far more adapted to
and supportive of the collective entrepreneur variant of self-management than
the workers did; as we have seen, this difference in their respective approaches
to decisions and decision making formed a key source of the labor-management conflicts at Klek. At the same time, however, management was quite
as protective of firm autonomy vis-à-vis external political bodies as were the
workers, although generally for very different reasons.

Both management and workers saw labor productivity and earnings as related; as a consequence, both groups supported measures to increase productivity, and both wanted the firm to make money. Yet the reasoning of
each group was distinctly different. The workers defined the enterprise as a
center of production and felt that higher earnings were (or should be) a
function of higher output; a "profitable" enterprise to the workers was one
that maximized output per enterprise employee, an enterprise where management "managed" and workers "worked." Klek's management, in contrast,
saw productivity as a function of overall earnings, and earnings depended as
much on the firm's ability to sell what it produced as on its actual output.
Although increasing output per worker was an important factor affecting the
enterprise's ability to compete on the market, management was well aware
that it was far from the only factor affecting the firm's gross income.

Accordingly, while the executives spoke in terms of "productive labor"
as much as the workers did, they attributed a rather different meaning to it.
For management, productive labor was any labor that helped the firm make
money, and it was more than likely to be performed by a university graduate
in a specialist or managerial position. Thus, Klek's modernization plan, as
drawn up by the *kolegija* in the late sixties, foresaw a (never realized) cut in

the number of blue-collar positions along with an increase in the number of highly qualified specialists employed by the firm. In the seventies, it was management who drew up the plans and pushed through the hiring of the new technical and financial experts; it was management who helped secure apartments for those who required them and guaranteed them attractive wage levels. And later, it was management, led by the general director, who defended the experts judged "incompetent" or "unproductive" by the workers.

Similarly, "distribution according to work" was as well-worn a phrase among the executives as it was among workers, but again, its meaning in any given context was quite different. In the first place, it was clear to management that what the firm had to "distribute" to start with was contingent on its earnings and investment needs and not, as the workers had argued in the Saturdays dispute, on simply how much "labor" went into the production process. Second, while management's definition of "distribution according to work" certainly did not exclude giving adequate material incentives and reviewing individual performance, it also meant adapting wage scales and apartment allocation criteria to attract and keep individuals whose skills the firm needed. Whereas workers stressed on-the-job performance in estimating the "value" of an individual's labor, management emphasized ability and previous training. Finally, since the workers sought to maximize total output and defined it, in effect, as the sum total of individual outputs, they had a highly individualistic notion of distribution: to each according to his "contribution." Management, in contrast, occupied with coordinating and supervisory functions and concerned with overall performance, was less interested in whether or not specific individuals were "doing their job" and more involved with seeing that the collective as a whole was working together. For an executive, it was praiseworthy but unimportant to know that X was overfulfilling his quotas when Y, grinding out a complementary part, was hopelessly behind schedule and the plant was running low on semifabricated steel because the supply department had not been able to get it delivered on time.

Management's responsibilities and value patterns thus led it to identify with the firm as a whole. Unlike the workers, it did not see itself as an occupational group with its own specific interests inside and outside the enterprise. More precisely, management simply equated what other groups perceived as managerial interests with those of the enterprise itself. The critical factor in this equation, of course, was enterprise autonomy, for management's entrepreneurial judgments and values could only be defended as being in the best interests of the collective as long as the enterprise was in fact responsible for its own decisions and responses to the cues of the market. Indeed, for the executives, self-management and enterprise autonomy were practically synonymous.

It was in this context that the postreform, collective entrepreneur model of self-management assumed its importance for Klek's executives. As we have seen, the workers did not have entrepreneurial values and regarded the imputation of such values to them as little more than a way of being blamed for managerial incompetence. While the executives had values consistent with the operation of the market, they lacked the formal authority to impose them on the collective. Management's endorsement of collective entrepreneurship thus stemmed not from a rejection of its managerial responsibilities, but from accepting them while finding itself without the legal authority to carry them out.[7] Instead, executives at Klek's main plant continually had to "convince" subordinates to behave and make decisions in ways that would strengthen the firm's market position. Moreover, the behavior management desired from the collective often ran directly counter to the short-run, individual interests of its members (working on Saturdays, investing in modernization, and so on). Hence, by stressing collective incentives and collective responsibility, Klek's management hoped to instill the discipline, coordination, loyalty to the firm, and willingness to invest that it could not instill by using individual rewards and penalties alone. In effect, getting the work collective to accept the role of collective entrepreneur was essentially equivalent to getting it to behave in accordance with what management believed to be good for the enterprise by collectivizing the values management itself held.

Yet because these values reflected management's own peculiar responsibilities and functions, extending them to nonsupervisory personnel was not easy. While the general director and the other executives appealed to the collective to rally around the firm, promised a blissful future, and deplored the "wage-earning mentality," the workers continued to insist just as fervently on individual responsibility and higher individual incentives in the present. And although on many of the most critical issues of business policy, occupational groups in the collective went along with management's recommendations without a word of dissent, this was normally because management's choices coincided with the preferences that stemmed from their own occupational values and not because they accepted the role of collective entrepreneur.

Management's emphasis on enterprise autonomy, its definition of the enterprise's goal as making money, and its stress on collective entrepreneurship were the main factors influencing its approach to self-management. Unlike the workers, who felt self-management should be a political mechanism for redressing grievances and putting the firm "in order," the executives at Klek saw self-management as both an economic system whereby enterprises were autonomous and a way of making decisions within the firm to make it

more profitable. According to management, the members of the collective
would learn to accept equal responsibility for the firm's performance by
participating in decision making; at the same time, they would learn to make
correct entrepreneurial decisions and be more willing to cooperate in carry-
ing them out. As one executive urged: "We must get rid of the wage-earning
mentality if we are to move forward. That is what self-management means.
Everyone must understand that they are responsible for our firm."

In addition to educating the collective to its entrepreneurial functions and
responsibilities, many of Klek's executives hoped self-management would
stimulate higher productivity by making information available:

> When people don't want to work, it's because they're dissatisfied. And
> they're dissatisfied because they are uninformed. That is why we must have
> self-management. Once people understand the problems, once they are
> informed, they will want to work harder and better (general director).

Essentially, meetings of self-management bodies were to serve as a source of
official information to counteract the grinding of Klek's rumor mill.

Ironically perhaps, management was the only group in the collective that
saw anything positive at all in the conflicts that occurred at Klek during this
study. Nevertheless, the executives generally did not regard the fact that
such conflicts could come out in the open and that such frank disagreement
could be expressed between labor and management as testimony to the vitality
of self-management. Rather, they regarded the conflicts as outlets for worker
frustration and attributed them to "misinformation," which was fortunately
corrected in the nick of time. In short, in management's view, as long as
self-management was not fully "realized" ("It's a process that takes years and
years," said one executive) such conflicts would occur; in the meantime, it
was the role of management and the socio-political organizations to utilize
such conflicts to make the workers "understand" what being a "self-manager"
entailed. In contrast, the workers, wanting their version of "self-management
now," reacted to the conflicts with anger and dismay. They were frustrated
because, despite their formal "self-management rights," they were normally
unable to get their demands satisfied over management resistance. Moreover, even when they emerged victorious on the overtime issue, they were un-
happy that such a conflict ever had to take place; in their view, if the "direct
producers" really ran the factory, there would never have been any question of the justice of their demands in the first place.

Participation in decision making was also stressed by management as a source
of job satisfaction. Although the production workers perceived labor as a
necessity, management typically had a much more voluntaristic notion of

work.[8] In the latter's view, people had to want to work; collective entrepreneurship might give them material incentives, but self-management played a critical role in providing psychological and social incentives. Hence, while the workers were chiefly interested in the results they might achieve through control of the self-management bodies, management stressed the benefits participation itself brought. "It's a good idea," said a sector head. "People can get up and say what's on their mind and then they feel better. This way they're more willing to work." Although these benefits could only be derived at the cost of managerial authority, in theory they made the use of authority less necessary. The general director explained:

> Management cannot dictate decisions. Then nobody will carry them out; people are angry and they won't work. When there is resistance, it must be overcome by arguments. When everyone is convinced that a decision is for the good of the firm, they willingly approve it and carry it out.

Not all the executives at Klek took such a positive view of self-management. Privately, several expressed grave doubts about its efficacy as a decision-making system and resented having to undergo the constant review and criticism of workers whom they felt were "ignorant" or unable to evaluate the quality of an executive's work. Some felt self-management had a detrimental effect on the firm's ability to compete. "Self-management might be all right if we had the money to self-manage," remarked one, "but how can we ever make money if all they do is sit around and talk?" A department supervisor was also skeptical: "In the end, the director does what he wants anyway. So why have all this time lost in something with no effect?" These executives were typically those who took the least active roles in meetings and were usually the least popular among the workers as well—despite the fact that their "less talk, more work" attitude in many ways reflected the workers' own sentiments.

Even the executives at Klek who believed in self-management, participated at meetings, and were careful to abide by the canons of legality were often disturbed by the time and energy the system's operation at Klek seemed to require. The general director, for example, was fond of saying, "We can only progress through the struggle of ideas." Yet even he made a distinction between "constructive" and "unconstructive" conflicts, the latter being those in which the collective, particularly the blue-collar workers, continually refused to go along with management's recommendations. Moreover, all the executives were frustrated by the confusion in lines of authority which appeared to be endemic to sharing responsibility between individual managers and elected bodies. It was not always clear which proposals had to go before which bodies, and if a proposal was not approved in time, an executive was usually blamed for not doing his job. Yet if he went ahead without the self-management bodies, he might well come in for equally heavy criticism and even disciplinary sanctions.[9] Thus, while the workers perceived management as having all the power and little responsibility, the executives felt they had all the responsibility without possessing adequate authority or discretion.

Management's approach to self-management was closely connected with its approach to politics in general. If self-management served to make the firm more profitable, the role of the state was to help "realize" self-management. This was not to be done by dictating to the firms or saddling them with detailed regulations and political responsibilities. On the contrary, in management's view, self-management as an overall politicoeconomic system entailed guaranteeing enterprise autonomy and aiding the firms in the achievement of their own economic objectives: letting them retain their earnings to use as they wished, keeping out of their internal affairs, encouraging them to modernize and raise labor productivity by making capital available, and insuring economic conditions favorable to enterprise expansion. The role of a state ideologically committed to socialism and self-management was to help self-managed firms increase their earnings and personal income levels in ways that they, as autonomous collective entrepreneurs, deemed best. Significantly, the state's role in management's eyes was not to redistribute income, maximize employment, channel resources into politically desirable activities, or guarantee fixed wage levels. The state's objectives were the firms' self-determined objectives, not vice versa, and the firms' objectives, in management's opinion, were to make money. Similar to Proudhon, management felt economic incentives must be the main form of control in self-managed socialism; the state, to use Proudhon's terminology, should neither be an "authority" nor an "entrepreneur" but should play the role of a voluntary "association" to insure the ability of autonomous work collectives to respond successfully to the cues of the market.

Providing the state kept to this role, in theory there was no conflict between it and the enterprise as far as Klek's executives were concerned. Hence, although they hardly welcomed intervention and regulation by political authorities any more than the workers did, Klek's executives never had the same degree of suspicion of and antagonism to "politicians" the workers had. While the workers implicitly demanded a great deal from the government and explicitly expected very little, management demanded little of the state but expected it to conform with and be responsive to the enterprise's needs.

In practice, however, the state rarely lived up to management's noninterventionist hopes. Government regulations and the agencies enforcing them often posed obstacles to Klek's plans and to its smooth operation. On many of these occasions, management was no less frustrated than the rest of the collective and actually helped to mobilize the collective to get unfavorable laws and decisions altered to meet the firm's needs. Moreover, when the enterprise found itself in difficulty on the market, management not only joined, but actually led the workers in pressuring government authorities to come to Klek's aid.

Because executives had to deal with government officials so frequently in the course of conducting firm business, management could not afford to be openly antagonistic to the state bureaucracy. Whether they helped to steer the 1969 integration to a successful conclusion, to obtain an import-export license, to secure a building permit, to get the work force excused from attending courses on plant safety, or to forestall political meddling, good "sociopolitical relations" were an important economic asset for Klek. Furthermore, since management was responsible for the firm's legal operation, both in its business and self-management practices, the burden of defending and enforcing the laws that did regulate Klek's internal and external operations often fell on the executives' shoulders. If this put them in the position of having to defend regulations about which they themselves were not always enthusiastic, interpreting and upholding the laws also gave management an additional source of influence over decisions; the conclusion reached on distributing the 1973 profits was a case in point. This, in turn, reinforced the workers' sense that "management, politicians, they're all in it together and the worker pays for it all" (electrician).

Maintaining good "sociopolitical relations" and protecting "socialist legality" in the enterprise were responsibilities management shared with Klek's League of Communists' organization, which perhaps helps to explain why so many executives were party members. Note that when this study began, party membership was not required of all executives at Klek, and several members of the *kolegija* had never joined the LCY. Nevertheless, for an executive who wished, or was forced by virtue of his position, to play an active role in enterprise decision making or in dealings with political authorities, party membership was certainly an asset.

In relations with outside authorities, possession of a party card had little positive impact on an executive's effectiveness. However, the lack of one could eventually cause serious doubts to be raised about his "moral and political qualifications," which would understandably have detrimental consequences for the firm as well as for the individual executive. Significantly, by April

1974, Klek's party organization began to actively recruit into its ranks the executives who had never bothered to join the LCY. In part, this served to weed out and isolate those who disagreed with its line strongly enough to refuse to join; more important, it was a way of protecting the firm and the executives as a whole against the political fallout of the antitechnocracy campaign.

Moreover, dealings with political bodies were often conducted through the party organization itself, rather than on a direct executive-public official basis. In this case, it was important for executives to be on good terms with Klek's own party leaders, and being a party member oneself certainly helped. Furthermore, the enterprise party organization's capacity to mobilize itself and the collective around agreed-upon objectives inside the firm was a useful supplement to weak managerial authority. So too was the LCY's preoccupation with insuring that the formal, procedural regulations affecting the self-management structure were conformed to within the firm. Again, it was easier and more acceptable for an executive who was a comrade to call on the party to perform these tasks—or, even more important, to criticize it for its failure to do so—than it was for a manager who refused to join the ranks.

Generally, however, the executives at Klek saw themselves as businessmen and managers, not as political functionaries; if most of them were party members, only one was in any sense a party activist.[10] Their notion of what the party should be and what role it should play was quite predictable and consistent with their other views. Inside the firm, its role was to contribute to the firm's profitability and productivity; outside the firm, it was to protect enterprise autonomy and ensure that Klek received a sympathetic hearing from political authorities. For management, the League of Communists was indeed a political organization that utilized political means to achieve its goals, but the goals themselves were defined as essentially economic ones: "Socialism," the general director declared, "is the battle to raise the standard of living of the working class." Hence, the executives could join the LCY out of genuine commitment to self-management and socialism while holding a vision of self-management and socialism that often contrasted sharply with that of the workers.

OCCUPATIONAL VALUES AT KLEK: WHITE-COLLAR EMPLOYEES

The white-collar employees at Klek played a very passive, docile role in labor-management conflicts at Klek. Even when directly implicated in the issues at hand, as in the overtime dispute, they did not participate very actively in the struggle and generally left management to fight the battles on their behalf. In part, this was because a large proportion of the clerical staff at Klek was female and "expected" to take a bystander's role;[11] in part, it was a product of the ambiguous status of white-collar work in Yugoslav industrial enterprises.

As a group, the white-collar employees were the least cohesive and politically involved occupational strata at Klek. They were divided into the predominantly female clerical help, the technicians in BOAL I, and the highly educated staff specialists. All differentiated themselves from the blue-collar workers by their education, their opportunities for upward mobility inside and outside the plant, their cleaner and lighter work load, and their somewhat higher social status. At the same time, even if some of them were more highly educated than several of the managerial cadres, they were all in nonsupervisory roles and hence responsible for little beyond the performance of their immediate tasks. If the workers' values centered around the principle of distribution according to productive work and management's around distribution according to the results of work, white-collar attitudes were centered around a principle that can be described as "distribution according to skill."

All of Klek's white-collar workers were characterized by a great respect for expertise. It was manifested in a tendency to look up to management matched by an equally strong propensity to look down on the blue-collar workers. They rarely exhibited the kind of face-to-face irreverence towards supervisory personnel so frequent among the workers; while the workers would suspect and even accuse the executives of dishonesty when their words did not match the workers' perception of a given state of affairs, the employees seldom expressed even private doubts of management's professionalism and truthfulness. They did, however, frequently criticize the production workers for their rebelliousness and professionally unbecoming conduct:

> They don't know anything and they think they know everything (specialist).

> They complain about the low pay and all they do is fool around on the job (technician).

> They should be quiet and let management manage (specialist).

> All this complaining and uproar is just silliness. . . . They just aren't educated (clerk).

With such views, it is hardly surprising that the white-collar staff sided with management when intraenterprise conflicts occurred at Klek.

"Distribution according to skill" meant, of course, that salary scales should favor those with education; particularly among the young technicians, there was a strong undercurrent of resentment that their pay was at the same level as that of a skilled worker. "Here I went to school all these years," grumbled one, "only to come here and find out I should have been a worker." At the same time, their relatively higher education and social status led them to expect greater consideration from management; when they did not receive it, feelings were bitter.

That their salaries were commensurate with those of the production workers and their day-to-day influence on enterprise life not much greater did little to make lower-level technical and clerical personnel sympathetic to the workers' outlook. On the contrary, it merely contributed to their sense of status insecurity and diminished their already weak loyalty to the firm.

Nor did the white-collar workers identify very much with each other, despite their similarity in attitudes. In part, this was because of the objective divisions among them. In addition to their functional differentiation as technicians, clerks, and specialists, they were women whose main concern was their family life and ambitious, career-oriented men; older, former workers and young graduates fresh out of technical schools and colleges; semiskilled warehouse personnel and experts who participated at *kolegija* meetings and were de facto accepted as management.[12] In part, lack of identification among white-collar employees was also a product of the exaggerated subjective importance given these distinctions by the value the white-collar workers attributed to skill; the more that qualification as a general criterion of evaluation was emphasized, the clearer specific individual differences in qualification levels became.

Although the white-collar workers were well represented on self-management bodies at Klek and attended and participated at meetings, their comments never articulated a group interest. Rather, they were expressions of individual opinion, and white-collar employees rarely supported each other's point of view the way workers and executives did. Significantly, white-collar participation was highest when relatively technical and noncontroversial questions were up for discussion; they did not even make a suggestion or ask a question when the head-on conflicts between blue-collar workers and management occurred.

Partly because of their inability to see themselves as a distinct constituency with specific interests, as a group and even as subgroups, Klek's white-collar employees were highly peripheral to the self-management processes of the firm and perceived themselves as such. When several were asked: "Who is most interested in self-management here?" all responded, "The workers," and a few added, "Management"; none felt that they or their occupational group had much to benefit from the system's operation in the enterprise or even that they should expect to get something out of it.

This sense of "Self-management? It doesn't really concern me" (clerk) was reinforced by the white-collar employees' respect for skill. To them, decisions should be made first and foremost by those most competent to make them ("How can a lot of workers who just came off the farm be expected to run a factory? It's crazy," said one technician), and self-management, with its emphasis on egalitarian collaboration of nonspecialists in decision making, ran directly counter to this belief.

As a result, many white-collar workers at Klek held a view of self-management quite similar in some ways to that held by the production workers: It was "politics," and time devoted to it was merely time lost from work. In contrast to the blue-collar workers, however, the employees seemed to lack a collective sense of what self-management could or should be. Hence, where the workers participated in decision making on behalf of their perceived interests, seeking "results" from self-management processes, many of their white-collar colleagues simply wished to not get involved. The inability of the BOAL III council to meet and make decisions throughout most of this study was one consequence of this attitude. Only when a former executive became council president did it begin to convene regularly, and even then, its decisions by and large consisted of rubber-stamping his recommendations.

The white-collar employee's status insecurity was a contributing factor here. In the first place, noninvolvement was motivated by the employees' feeling that they were too sophisticated to bother with the "stupidity" that went on at meetings; as noted above, self-management was for the workers, not for them. Second, if not measuring their work on a piece-rate scale allowed them easier work rhythms and lighter jobs, it also meant that as white-collar employees in industry, they were always open to the accusation that they were not really "working." As we have seen, Klek's blue-collar workers did not hesitate to make this accusation. Significantly, too, the phrase used by management and workers alike to describe technical and clerical help at Klek was *režijski radnici*, or "overhead workers," a phrase that hardly carried very favorable connotations. Given this situation, many of the white-collar employees simply chose not to intervene too aggressively in decision making; whatever their private thoughts on their ability to contribute to Klek, it often seemed wiser not to rock the boat. Indeed, even when their own positions were at stake, as in the overtime dispute, they were all too willing to let management bear the brunt of their defense. Finally, the above situation, combined with the white-collar worker's respect for individual qualifications and his feelings that he was not appreciated enough, led him to seek avenues of individual advancement in the organizational structure rather than militate for policy changes in the self-management bodies.

Status insecurity, however, worked in two directions, and it also appears to have been a prime explanation of why some white-collar employees at Klek were quite active in the self-management bodies. For those interested in advancing up the rungs of the organizational hierarchy, either within Klek or by transferring to another firm, "good moral and political character" was normally a requirement for a supervisory position, and being elected to a self-management body was one way of demonstrating it. Others simply missed the cohesiveness of an occupational community like that of the production workers and reacted to the connotations of the "overhead" label by wanting to become more involved with the firm. Others, particularly middle-level technicians and clerks, felt they as individuals had something positive to contribute to the enterprise and might be listened to more if they were elected to a self-management body. Finally, of course, there were those who were politically committed to the idea of self-management and participated out of ideological belief. All of the motives, however, were highly individualistic and stemmed from an individual's aspirations for himself rather than from the aspirations of his or her occupational group.

Similar reasons explain why well over half of Klek's League of Communists' organization was composed of white-collar employees; indeed, nearly all of its activists were drawn from their ranks. Ironically, while the white-collar workers as an occupational group had the least articulate sense of their own interests and the most apolitical approach to decision making, as individuals, some of the most politically active members of the work collective were technicians and clerical personnel. In fact, it would seem that precisely because they were not wedded to a highly cohesive group within the enterprise, it was easier for individual white-collar workers to identify with a nonoccupational group interest, be it that of the firm, the party, the trade union, or their own particular professional or political ambitions.

Finally, the white-collar employees' status ambiguity and lack of occupational cohesiveness meant that they simply went along with the prevailing political winds in the firm. When there was conflict, they tended to side with management, partly because it represented the voice of expertise, but partly because its point of view was likely to be the winning one. Alternatively, when the entire work collective agreed on an issue, the white-collar employees easily fell into line with everyone else.

9

Consensus, Solidarity, and Apathy:
The Sources of Unity at Klek

Up to now, I have emphasized the differences in values and attitudes held by occupational groups at Klek. Yet there were important issues on which the occupational group values and attitudes converged. Despite the strong cleavages on distribution and responsibility issues and the arguments that punctuated personnel questions, the Klek collective adopted a unified outlook on actions that did not involve choosing between mutually exclusive group-value premises. Such a unified outlook took three different forms: consensus, when all the groups concurred on the value premises underlying a decision on internal matters; solidarity, when resistance to or a demand for government action was at stake; and apathy, when decisions made outside the enterprise had to be implemented within it.

CONSENSUS AND INTERNAL ISSUES

Not all internal questions at Klek aroused the strong antagonisms that distribution and responsibility questions did. Indeed, some of the most important items considered by the self-management bodies normally passed through without a word of dissent.

The most glaring exceptions to the pattern of conflict on internal issues were business policy (the formulation and adoption of annual production, financial, and investment plans) and the organization of work (what to do about bottlenecks, shortages, etc., as opposed to who or what had caused them). At Klek, a major reason for this appears to lie in the peculiar configurations of attitudes and values held by the separate occupational groups. While these attitudes and values came into sharp conflict on distribution and responsibility questions and bypassed each other on personnel policy, they converged when organizing the work process itself was at issue. As in Gramsci's productive community, Klek had a unified outlook toward production questions.

Regarding business policy, the main plans which had to be drawn up and approved each year were in production, finance, and investment. The production plan, drawn up by the executives of BOAL I and II, the engineers in R & D, and the sales department, basically listed the costs, quantity, type, and specifications of the machinery to be manufactured and the time estimated to produce it. The financial plan, written by the finance director and his staff in consultation with the sales and supply departments, calculated the firm's anticipated earnings on the basis of the production plan and divided them into wages, taxes, interest on loans, investment, funds, and so forth.[1] While the finance plan divided up the total pie, the investment plan, compiled by the director of R & D in consultation with the other sector heads, detailed how the slice of it allocated to capital investment was to be spent. Each plan was discussed first by the *kolegija* and then submitted to the self-management bodies for approval. While individuals might make comments and suggestions all through the process, there was never any group conflict over adopting a plan. Basically, the lack of conflict appears to be related to the attitudes and values held by Klek's occupational groups.

As we have seen, everyone wanted the firm to make money, everyone wanted it to increase productivity, and everyone was in favor of higher incomes. Given a general consensus on goals, the workers' view that everyone should do his job, the white-collar employees' attitude that the most competent to decide should make the decisions, and management's feeling that it was responsible for convincing the collective to take the most profitable course of action, all the groups were willing to go along with the policy recommendations proposed by management. Since there was no internal conflict over what the firm's economic interests were, managerial recommendations on business policy were simply not subject to the suspicions provoked by managerial judgments on other questions.

Conflict was absent even when Klek found it had to undergo a production cutback owing to a sales slump in 1968. In that year, four variants of the production and financial plans, each suggesting a different strategy for making the cutback, were submitted to the workers' council. The managing board recommended the variant requiring layoffs, and the workers' council agreed. Most of the discussion, however, was devoted to how the layoffs should be made rather than to which variant of the plan should be adopted.

The 1968 example should serve as an indication that the lack of conflict over business policy at Klek was not because no alternatives to the management-favored solution normally were presented. Indeed, even if the lack of alternatives left the self-management bodies in a "take-it-or-leave-it" position in policy formulation, there was no pressure at all in the Klek work collective for requiring plan variants to be submitted to the self-management bodies. In fact, most members of the collective probably would have rejected such a suggestion. For the workers and employees, executives and specialists were paid and paid well for the time they devoted to formulating the plans they thought best; requiring them to draw up alternatives they felt were inferior or ill-advised just for the sake of stimulating discussion in the self-management bodies would have been viewed as simply a waste of the firm's resources. As we have seen, as far as the production workers were concerned, there was "too much talking" in the self-management bodies already.

Nor does it appear that the ease with which major decisions passed through the self-management bodies at Klek was primarily owing to the collective's inability to understand what it was approving. Certainly, plans were highly complex, esoteric documents, and even in a firm with a relatively well educated and urbanized labor force like Klek, it is doubtful that every member of the work collective or its self-management bodies understood all the ramifications a plan entailed.

Yet as far as production plans went, Klek's blue-collar workers understood more about the kind of machinery the enterprise produced than the university-trained economists in BOAL III did. The workers were less at home with financial plans, but they were certainly clear on whether or not the value of a point was increasing over the previous year and, as we have seen, understood without really accepting the enterprise's obligations to pay taxes and interest charges. Neither did the production workers or the bulk of the white-collar employees show any great concern for the details of the investment plan; its general lines and main items (in 1974, for instance, these were the new machinery and the construction of a prefabricated office building) were hard for anyone to miss. And as noted earlier, all groups—albeit for different reasons—agreed in principle that modernization and expansion were necessary for the economic and productive health of the firm.

Lack of interest, not inability to understand, seems a more persuasive explanation for the absence of discussion and group conflict in business policy decisions at Klek. "Interest," however, is a function of the values and attitudes individuals and groups bring to the decision making process, values and attitudes that affect how they perceive the questions up for discussion as well as their reactions to them. In this sense, insofar as no group in the Klek collective perceived a threat to its particular interests and values in the normal course of formulating business policy (indeed, the whole collective saw itself as having a unified interest in making the "best" decisions), there was simply no need to suspect the recommendations management offered or even to pay a great deal of attention to them. In effect, the low participation rate of nonsupervisory personnel in business policy decisions at Klek was less a sign of alienation and powerlessness than a sign of consensus on management's goals and confidence in its intentions and ability to protect the collective's best interests.

Certainly there were some costs resulting from this happy entente over enterprise goals. First of all, agreement was grounded on the assumption that productivity gains would be reflected in wage increases. Productivity, however, did not always reach expected levels, while wages still had to be paid at their planned rates. For example, when Klek's general director was accused of going back on his "promise" to provide back pay for Saturdays at the March 1974 assembly, he responded by pointing out, "And you promised to work harder this year when personal incomes were increased. But we're as behind on the plan as ever." Moreover, when overtime had to be done at the end of the year—a regular tradition at Klek—the financial burden was greater. In these ways, Klek not only made its contribution to Yugoslav inflation but also aggravated its already severe shortage of liquid capital. At the same time, a pattern was being established whereby wage levels rose with each new plan, and it is not at all certain that the collective would have accepted management policy recommendations so quickly if that tradition had been broken.

Second, although paying little heed to plan details may well have been a sign of confidence in management, it could easily result in the collective as a whole committing itself to a course of action its members as individuals were unwilling to undertake. The production workers, for example, may indeed have supported higher productivity in principle, but their actual output did not always keep pace with their verbal statements. A frequently cited proverb is illuminating: "You can't pay me so little that I can't work less."

As with business policy, questions regarding the organization of work at Klek also tended to be resolved consensually. Everyone wanted a smooth-running production process, and everyone was anxious to eliminate whatever difficulties plagued it as rapidly as possible. Job and shift assignments, the organizational flow of authority, equipment purchases, making up for delays, work hours, plant safety, and other technical and on-the-job issues were routine questions that rarely provoked any disputes in the self-management bodies. Like business policy, the legitimacy of managerial influence on questions relating to the organization of work was virtually unquestioned; in fact, many of the decisions in this category were increasingly being made in the organizational structure altogether rather than by the self-management bodies, as they once had been.

SOLIDARITY AT KLEK: PRESSURE AND RESISTANCE

Solidarity arose at Klek under two conditions: when the firm's market position was threatened, and when decisions or actions by political bodies negatively affected the ability of the enterprise to conduct what the collective felt were rational business operations. In both cases, the firm's relations with political institutions and agencies were involved, Klek either petitioning for some action or resisting an action already taken.

As an example of the Klek collective's reaction to a deterioration in its market position, the resolution of the enterprise's liquidity crisis is instructive. Capital shortages first began to be mentioned in Klek's workers' council minutes and factory bulletins round 1969; the firm's liquidity crisis continued to worsen well into 1973. Its causes were several. In part, it was owing to government economic policy or, more precisely, the lack of it. I have already dealt with the consequences of Yugoslav monetary policy after the 1965 reforms (chapter 4), and in this respect, Klek's situation was certainly not unusual. It was aggravated by administrative intervention in the form of price controls on heavy machinery unaccompanied by corresponding controls on raw materials. Nevertheless, Klek still decided to embark on an ambitious modernization program requiring a heavy outlay of capital investment at a time when inflation was creating pressures from workers for wage increases and its customers could not afford to buy its new product line without the extension of credit. Meanwhile, no bank was able or willing to supply Klek with the funds to achieve its goals.

The response of the Klek collective to its difficulties on the product and capital markets was articulated belligerently by the general director in a September 1970 article in the factory bulletin:

> We will not say, as some do, either give us the funds or we will close the plant and go off to work in Germany. We say that in current conditions you [political authorities] have obligation to guarantee us normal working conditions. Either insure them or resign from your positions to make way for others who will conduct our economic policy with greater comprehension.

Getting political authorities to recognize their "obligation" was another question, and the years of the liquidity crisis were marked by the continual attempts of Klek's management and sociopolitical organizations to get some form of aid from the government. Appeals were made and meetings held with the municipal and republic economic chambers, the city trade union federation, the industrial associations of the mining industry for which Klek was a major equipment supplier, and the city and republic legislatures. Attention was drawn to the steps forward Klek had taken against insurmountable odds ("Today we are the foremost factory in Yugoslavia for [mining] machinery . . . and our own machinery is depreciated to 85 per cent of its

value"),[2] to its profitability on paper ("Surely you would extend credit to
those to whom a million dinars is owed than to those who pile up debts on all
sides"),[3] to its contribution to the mining industry ("The collective . . . came
to the conclusion that it must . . . modernize the [mining] industry";[4] "We
need a solution not only for us, but for the [mining] industry, which cannot
operate without us"),[5] to its help in establishing Yugoslavia on the world
market ("The production of [machine X] puts our factory in the elite among
world producers of [mining] machinery.")[6]

Significantly, while the sociopolitical organizations were typically neutral-
ized when there was conflict within the firm, once the entire collective united
around a cause, LCY and trade union activists could play—and were expected
to play—a leading role in pushing it before external political bodies. Their
efforts, combined with those of the executives, began to pay off in 1971,
when Klek received a credit guarantee from the Bosnian mining industry
association. The guarantee covered half of the 15,000,000 dinars in outstanding debts that Klek had accumulated.

Yet even this aid proved insufficient, and complaints of the unfair burden
outside agencies were imposing on Klek through their inaction and/or incompetence became so common that Klek's trade union president, among others,
took it upon himself to respond to the collective:

> When we try to discuss the things that aren't right with us, we imme-
> diately start off by blaming it on the outside, we criticize both the sys-
> tem and the society that has brought us to this state. . . . All our LCY
> and Union Executive Council meetings always look for the guilty parties
> outside the factory, but whether everything is so great in the factory . . .
> whether despite the difficulties under which every work organization
> is struggling we can improve our work by ourselves, whether we have
> used all the reserves at our disposal . . . of these things no one wants to
> talk.[7]

Certainly, the work climate had not improved when Klek was prohibited in
early 1972 from paying out full salaries because of its blocked bank account;
continually late paychecks had only caused plant morale to drop further.
It was becoming increasingly difficult for management to urge the collective
to work harder by arguing the collective entrepreneur strategy ("Real people
know that they hold their fate in their own hands," wrote the director in
the June 1972 factory bulletin) when it was simultaneously claiming that
Klek would be in excellent shape were it not for the "incomprehension" of
political authorities.

The enterprise party organization and trade union branch, caught between representing the demands of the work collective and justifying a "system and society" that did not respond to them, were also finding themselves increasingly compromised. At the end of May 1972, a special issue of the factory bulletin appeared, written by the party secretary and intended, as he wrote, to be "an answer to those comrades who attacked our LCY organization at the May 26th assembly on the grounds that it was not taking the necessary steps to stabilize our financial situation." As evidence of the concrete action the party was taking, a letter the party secretary had sent to the Central Committee of the Croatian League of Communists, on advice of the local party committee, was reprinted in full.

The letter elaborated Klek's financial difficulties while dwelling on the organizational and technological innovations Klek had made in recent years, taking due note of the concern the mining industry felt for the solvency of one of its main equipment suppliers. It then reviewed the most important political meetings that had already been held to deal with the fate of Klek, and there had been many. Klek had even come up at a session of the Executive Council of the Croatian Parliament, where two of its vice presidents had praised the enterprise's "business orientation."

Yet although all the meetings had concluded that Klek must be saved, the letter noted, the enterprise was nonetheless in the same serious financial position it had been in at the start. The result, the party secretary warned, was that

> The position of the LC in the factory is increasingly difficult . . . [Wages] have been late for months already. This time, pay was a month late, and the director had to explain the difficulties at an assembly where he appealed for higher morale. The workers then began to ask questions: Why were other structures [an allusion to government bureaucracies] paid on time? And what were the communists doing and to whom have they spoken about the situation? I answered that we had met with the municipal [party] committee and that we had tried to solve the problem there and at other meetings.

The tale was concluded with a fervent appeal by the party secretary:

> I managed to save the work climate for the time being, but I don't know for how long. The workers are waiting for an answer. We cannot find a way out alone, yet a solution must be found—in the name of the party's authority.

This appeal was successful; in early 1973, Klek received a substantial loan from the Zagreb Reserve Fund to be paid back over a three-year period. At

about the same time, the Federal Price Commission approved Klek's request
for a price increase that had been pending for well over a year. Klek paid a
price for this aid, however, over and above whatever interest charges accompanied the loan. In the first place, the firm had to draw up and adhere to a
financial stabilization plan acceptable to the city government and the administrators of the Reserve Fund. As a result, a good deal of its discretion in
future investment policies was curtailed. Second, Klek was required to do
something "special" to show that it was really turning over a new leaf; as it
turned out, this was the decision to work on Saturdays without pay.

It should be noted that although the entire work collective at Klek was
fully convinced that the liquidity crisis was the "fault" of the government,
the decisions the enterprise made on its own to counter foreign competition
on the domestic market certainly contributed to the problem. No one ordered
Klek to change its product line; no one commanded it to modernize its plant;
no one forced it to extend credit when its capital reserves were insufficient.
Nor did any external authority prevent the collective from accepting the risk
a "collective entrepreneur" is supposed to bear and from deciding to lower
wages in order to clean up its debts. Indeed, when the government required it
to adopt this entrepreneurial solution in early 1972, protests against the
"outside" seem to have increased. It was the market and Klek's response to it
as much as the government which precipitated the firm's financial crisis; like
Proudhon's mutualist association, the enterprise's reaction was to seek an
administrative intervention to counteract the effects of the market.

Klek's work collective did not only rally around the enterprise when
hierarchical action was sought; it also united when administrative decisions
interfered with a course of action it had already agreed upon. For example,
Klek's modernization program hinged on the importation of new machinery
from Czechoslovakia. To cover the cost of the imports, an agreement was
worked out with a Czech firm and approved by the relevant Yugoslav state
authorities. According to the contract, Klek would export its own manufactured machinery to partly cover the costs of importing the Czech equipment.
The first stage of the import-export agreement was to be effectuated by
December 1970, and Klek, faithful to its contract obligations, sent off some
machinery to Czechoslovakia that month.

Under Yugoslav foreign trade laws, however, a bank had to guarantee the
enterprise's credit before any import could be made, and it was here that the
problem arose. Even though Klek had initiated the procedure for getting
the necessary approval from its Zagreb bank in early December, by mid-
January the managing board of the bank, for unknown reasons, had still not
granted what, in the Klek collective's eyes, should have been a purely routine

guarantee. Anxiously, the collective awaited a scheduled January 25 meeting of the bank's managing board at which the credit guarantee was to have been approved, only to discover that same Friday afternoon that the meeting had been canceled.

The reaction of the work collective at Klek was quick and decisive: the workers' council met in emergency Saturday session and called a strike, to begin on Monday and "to last until this problem is solved." The strike resolution explained: "The workers' council cannot permit the fate of the development, modernization, and advancement of our factory as well as of the people working in it to depend on whether or not the managing board of a bank wants to meet." The resolution noted that the "municipal political bodies have been notified of our decision," thereby implying that if the bank would not answer to Klek, it might well have to reply to higher political authorities, whose vigilance was easily aroused by the prospect of a strike. The threat worked, and the strike itself never had to take place. Monday morning, the bank's managing board quickly approved the import credit and dashed off a letter to Klek apologizing for not doing so earlier.

Note that the strike threat made sense and proved effective in such a situation only because the bank was operating in an essentially political capacity, as an enforcement agency regulating foreign trade. Had the bank's economic functions as a dispenser of capital been in question, the threat of a strike by an enterprise not only would have been highly ineffective, but might well have put the firm itself in a bad light for being unable to attract capital through "normal" channels. Significantly, despite Klek's inability to borrow money to cover its working and long-term capital needs, the possibility of striking against the bank never was considered.

A more recent example concerns Klek's reaction to the limitations imposed by the industrywide self-management agreement concluded in 1973. In order to deter borrowing and encourage investment, the agreement had restricted enterprise discretion in redistributing annual profits by setting a ceiling on individual bonuses. At Klek, the firm was not permitted to pay over 1000 dinars to any member of the collective out of its 1973 profits, even though it was able and willing to do so.

The restrictive clause was brought up by the finance director at the May assembly called to deal with redistributing the 1973 profits. The assembly's initial reaction was to protest this infringement of its self-management rights ("First they tell you that you can make your own decisions, and then every decision you make is illegal," complained a machinist), and then to offer suggestions on how to evade the conditions imposed by the agreement. One worker suggested "donating" the entire sum to the enterprise trade union branch, with the understanding that the union would redistribute it back to the collective. As the union president began to nod his head, the finance director pointed out, "You can do that, but if I approve paying out that money, I go to jail." Despite the fact that a number of workers firmly believed that the finance director was "stealing left and right" from the firm and probably belonged in jail, on this occasion his comments evoked a wave of sympathy, and the trade union solution was discarded.

The result was that a delegation from Klek's political *aktiv* was sent off to ask the proper authorities to declare Klek a special case under the self-management agreement. The appeal was successful, and the full sum set aside for bonuses was distributed to the work collective.

It is interesting to note how the distinct values and attitudes of the various occupational groups managed to coalesce on these issues. For example, in the enterprise liquidity crisis, management's tendency to equate Klek's goals with those of society allowed it to argue cogently on behalf of Klek's "right" to receive credit and even to mobilize the entire collective around what it perceived as a simple demand for justice. Nor was a receptive audience lacking. To the blue-collar workers, it was absurd that a highly productive industrial enterprise should be starved for capital when it was industry that created "value" in the first place. The white-collar workers, too, were all too ready to believe that the crisis resulted from the incompetence of politicians managing the economy.

Similarly, in the conflict with the bank and the changing of the self-management agreement, everyone concurred on the need for resistance when the firm's decisions were jeopardized by actions of outside bodies. Management thought such actions not only interfered with the legitimate rights of the enterprise to make its own decisions, but also damaged the work climate in the plant and the enterprise's market position; the workers saw these outside actions as threatening their rights to their wages and thus violating the principle of distribution according to work; the employees viewed them as but another irrationality in the system.

As in Gramsci's productive community, guaranteeing the work collective's ability to make its own decisions where the resources it produced were concerned was a popular concept at Klek; politically, it was a highly legitimate one as well. Yet not all laws and regulations to which Klek had to conform directly affected its economic operations, and even among those that did, not all were perceived by the work collective as negatively affecting its interests. For example, despite the work collective's reaction to the limitations imposed on it by the industrywide self-management agreement, there had not even been any debate over the initial decision to send the assistant finance director to represent Klek in the 1973 negotiations that concluded the agreement. Nor was there much discussion over signing the agreement that was finally drawn up, once the representative and management recommended approval. Despite the production workers' intuitive suspicion of management where questions of internal policy were concerned, when Klek's relations with outside agencies were at stake, a cloak of solidarity dropped over the work collective. If those considered most competent to judge declared that the firm's interests were being protected, the entire collective fell into line behind them.

APATHY AT KLEK: LEGALISM AND LEGITIMACY

A variant of this unified reaction occurred when external regulations did not directly affect Klek's economic operations, but instead introduced some alteration in its formal decision making processes, in other words, in the self-management structure. Here the entire work collective responded with compliance, and it was accompanied by widespread apathy for several reasons.

In the first place, as power in the enterprise by and large followed the lines of the organizational structure, changes in the self-management structure appeared to the Klek collective as purely formal, procedural reforms. Significantly, not a word of protest or even discussion was raised at the workers' council meeting in 1971 that substituted a business board on which only executives sat for an elected, representative managing board, undoubtedly because no one at Klek felt such a change would make much difference in practice.

Furthermore, whether described as increasing the firm's earnings, performing productive labor, or doing a professionally competent job, the primary interest of everyone in the collective was devoted to the firm as a business and a work place, and not as a decision-making entity. Thus, while all the occupational groups could get incensed over something like the liquidity crisis, a problem that spilled over into the work process itself, they could just as easily ignore procedural revisions in the self-management structure.

General apathy toward changes in the self-management structure was helped along by the role of the sociopolitical organizations at Klek, in particular, by its LCY branch. If most of the members of the collective were concerned with doing their work as defined in the organizational structure, the party organization was responsible to its higher organs for the legal and efficient operation of the self-management structure. Further, in guaranteeing that Klek's self-management structure conformed to legal requirements, the party was fulfilling its obligations to an authority outside the firm itself and so was not subject to the cleavages that occurred within its own ranks when the collective was divided over some internal issue. Hence, Klek's LCY organization was able to act as a unified body in "creating a climate" that paved the road for the change. However, if one by-product of creating a climate was convincing a part of the collective that a given reform would make a great improvement, another was making it perfectly clear to everyone else that the change was going to be enacted regardless of opposition. As in Gramsci's productive community, when decisions made by outside bodies were simply imposed on the collective and pushed through by agents acting on the former's behalf, apathy in the work collective was the understandable result.

The illegitimacy of resisting externally mandated changes in the self-management structure was certainly a factor in the work collective's reaction to the 1971–74 reforms. Open resistance on the part of a single firm to constitutional reforms was hardly a viable alternative and simply never entered the realm of possibilities at Klek. As a firm in the midst of being bailed out by a politically allocated loan, the entire work collective was well aware of the importance of maintaining "good sociopolitical relations" as well as how much significance keeping its self-management structure up to date and in apparent working order had for that process.

Moreover, if political authorities were not satisfied with the firm's compliance with the latest reforms, they might well intervene directly in the affairs of the firm or impose penalties. Indeed, as October 1974 rolled around and Klek's statutes had still not been submitted to the courts for review, local officials started to phone Klek's director and party leaders to find out what the problem was and if any "help" was needed. Meanwhile, Zagreb newspapers were studded with accounts of "technocratic resistance" to the new principles of self-management and full of praise for the valiant attempts of party organizations and outside bodies to "convince" work collectives to oust the elected management in such cases.

Thus, even if the total impact of the reforms of the 1970s may have been somewhat to restrict enterprise autonomy, noncompliance resulted in far more drastic incursions on enterprise independence. In short, to the Klek collective, despite the inconvenience, complexity, and time-consuming nature of implementing the reforms, the cost of noncompliance appeared much higher. As a result, everyone at Klek was equally anxious to get what they perceived as the legal formalities over with, despite a singular lack of interest in what they involved.

Finally, no one, from management down to the cleaning staff, was ever really sure what the practical ramifications of a legal change in the self-management structure would be until after the change was actually implemented. This was particularly the case with the extremely complicated reorganization put into motion by the 1971 amendments and the 1974

Constitution. Enterprise statutes were traditionally arcane documents, written in highly legalistic and ambiguous terms; many provisions remained dead letters, and others were observed purely formally. As part of the firm's public record, however, statutes did serve to reassure political authorities that the enterprise was conforming to current standards. At the same time, they formed a basis on which to establish the self-management bodies, which could then proceed to define concretely their vaguely worded responsibilities in practice. Thus, only after a legal change had been in effect for some time could its practical impact on the enterprise's operation be felt, and by then, everyone had grown accustomed to the new framework. Thus, resistance to a change at the time it was initiated was minimized, and the probability that a legal reform would simply be adapted to meet the work collective's exigencies was maximized.

For example, when the BOALs were set up at Klek in 1973 and the first BOAL councils elected, even the elected representatives were not clear what their powers and functions would be. As the new system evolved and adapted itself to existing conditions in the firm, the BOAL councils varied substantially in what they interpreted as their grant of authority, even though legally they all had the same power, and financially none had its own funds at its disposal. In practice, BOAL II used its authority to emancipate itself administratively from the rest of the enterprise, BOAL I largely confined itself to ironing out problems in production, and for most of the period of this study, the BOAL III council simply avoided meeting at all unless under pressure from other self-management bodies. By the time the difficulties of coordinating the actions of the BOALs became apparent, the change had already been assimilated into both Klek's self-management and organizational structures; the members of the collective had already begun to think of themselves as belonging to a BOAL. Coordination problems thus were not blamed on "political paper scheming" as were other difficulties, but instead were considered an internal problem and attributed to a BOAL or an occupational group other than one's own.

AFTERWARDS: THE 1974 CONSTITUTION AND ITS IMPACT AT KLEK*

Bearing in mind the patterns of conflict and consensus at Klek, we can begin to analyze what effect the 1974 Constitution and the political developments surrounding it should have on behavior in the Yugoslav firm.

*Since circumstances prevented me from doing a follow-up study in Klek itself, what follows are predictions made in 1974–75 based on the situation in the firm at that time. Anecdotal and macroeconomic evidence since then suggests that these predictions are basically sound, although it appears that the actual operation of the new institutional

First of all, if Klek is typical, by making distribution of income and inter-skill differentials subject to self-management agreements made on a multi-enterprise level, supervised by industry associations and economic chambers and backed up by the local and/or republic government, the new institutional arrangements may diminish the impact of distribution questions as a source of intraenterprise conflict. Also, insofar as industrywide self-management agreements set wage ceilings and social compacts prescribe regional incomes policies, incentives to find jobs in other enterprises should presumably diminish. Accordingly, identification with the firm or, more precisely, the BOAL should increase. Furthermore, at least in Zagreb, moves had been made to eliminate some of the dissatisfaction surrounding apartment allocation as well. Each enterprise made an annual contribution to a citywide Solidarity Fund, administered by the municipal trade union federation, which purchased apartments and distributed them among the firms to be allocated on the basis of need. Thus, regardless of how an enterprise or BOAL chose to spend its own collective consumption funds, the lower strata within it now at least had some hope of receiving housing. Moreover, since seniority was recognized as a criterion of "need" for the Solidarity Fund apartments, another disincentive to labor turnover was created.

Nevertheless, just as these developments should work to reduce conflict and increase loyalty to the firm beyond the ranks of management, the various restrictions they pose for firm autonomy may well increase conflict between enterprises and outside bodies. Klek's handling of the limits imposed on profit distribution by the industrywide self-management agreement is a case in point.

A second institutional arrangement that appears designed to lessen occupational conflict, especially worker-management conflict within enterprises, is the BOAL system. By organizing enterprises into solidaristic units whose boundaries are determined by the product or service they produce, horizontal cleavages would cross-cut the vertical ones of the hierarchical organizational structure. At the same time, influence in the organizational structure would shift from top management to middle-management, the supervisory personnel usually in much more direct contact with the rank-and-file labor force. Moreover, since the central enterprise administration was supposed to consti-tute a "self-managing work community" with no funds of its own, top management would in theory be at the mercy of the BOALs for even its monthly salary.

---

arrangements has been much spottier and less consistent than this analysis assumed. See chapter 6, "Self-Management and Bargaining," pp. 132–36.

Correspondingly, formal authority in the self-management structure would shift from the central workers' council to the BOAL councils, smaller bodies more closely acquainted with specific individuals and their problems. Thus, although a BOAL was expected to be occupationally heterogeneous and hierarchically ordered internally, it would be smaller and composed of individuals who worked with each other on a day-to-day basis. In theory, not only should the members of a BOAL have less difficulty understanding where each of them fit into the production process that was the BOAL's raison d'être, but it would also be easier to exert social pressure on individuals who were slacking off on the job. As a result, the disputes over "whose fault it is" and the antagonisms aroused by the accusations as to whether individuals or groups were "really" working would presumably diminish in number and intensity.

At Klek, BOAL II, the Service Division, seemed to represent the kind of productive community the new system was designed to create. In part, this was because of the peculiar conditions that made BOAL II the equivalent of a BOAL long before it received legal recognition as one. Meanwhile, in its relations with the main plant, BOAL II behaved much as Klek itself behaved toward political authorities. On the one hand, it sought to maximize its autonomy from the rest of the firm and to keep both the central management and self-management bodies from meddling in its affairs. On the other, its superior efficiency supplied it with a justification for pressing whatever claims on the firm it had.

If the behavior of BOAL II is any indiciation of the potential effects of the 1974 Constitution, it would seem that if the new system is successful in creating solidarity within the BOAL, it may also increase conflict between BOALs. To a certain extent, allowing BOALs to have their own funds should help to diminish infighting. Nevertheless, as BOALs assume certain obligations toward each other when they sign the initial enterprise self-management agreement of association, obligations that are often unclear at the outset, horizontal cleavages between BOALs may simply replace occupational divisions within the Yugoslav firm. Moreover, should BOAL lines coincide with occupational lines, as they did in the case of BOALs I and III at Klek, the situation may hardly be very different from the present one.

To some degree, conflicts between BOALs were already occurring at Klek at the time of this study. For example, after the production workers in BOAL I had won their demand for time-and-a-half overtime rates, the decision still had to be approved by the central enterprise workers' council. Since no BOAL at Klek legally had funds at its own disposal, any special expenditure by one division had to be approved by the others. More important for future times when enterprise assets will be divided up, wages for a given type of work were to be the same throughout the enterprise according to Klek's agreement of association. Hence, if skilled workers in BOAL I were to receive higher overtime rates, BOAL II would have to grant the same increase to its production workers.

Significantly, despite the support of Klek's general director, the executives of BOAL I, the finance director, and the presence of a special contingent of workers from BOAL I who had come to the workers' council meeting to "make sure [they] were represented," the entire BOAL II delegation refused to go along with the proposed increase in overtime rates. They argued that any such increase would simply be a reward to BOAL I for being late in plan completion and pointed out that even if BOAL II workers would also have higher overtime rates, their own plan was going ahead on time and very little, if any, overtime work would be necessary. One of the BOAL II representatives took the opportunity to launch a general attack on what he perceived as the "disorganization" endemic to the main plant:

> We've been waiting for the new statutes, and nothing has come. Our analytical job evaluation is finished, and we're ready to move on the new norms and the new system of technical organization, but you won't be ready for another month or two. Why is nothing here ever ready on time? We come all the way over here for meetings and all we discuss are your delays.

The debate over overtime rates went on for a good two hours, with the BOAL I production workers threatening not to work overtime and declaring that they were "not represented" on the workers' council and the BOAL II workers and employees refusing to go along with the raise. Finally, the general director proposed a compromise involving an overall wage increase for blue-collar workers in both BOAL I and II without special overtime rates, a proposal that fortunately proved acceptable to both sides.

The establishment of BOALs may thus diminish occupational and labor-management conflict within the Yugoslav firm but may replace it with conflicts between BOALs. At the same time, it may lead to increased tension between enterprises, BOALs, and outside authorities.* Here we come to the third change that accompanied the reforms of the seventies: the increased activity and influence of the sociopolitical organizations, in particular, of the League of Communists and the trade unions. By making "society's " influence

---

*From what evidence was available in 1978, both of these developments appear to have taken place.

more pronounced within the firm and the BOALs, the sociopolitical organizations were expected to counter "technocratic" impulses on the one hand and arbitrate conflicts on the other. In essence, the sociopolitical organizations were to become the glue to prevent the whole system from coming unstuck.

The trade unions, for example, were expected to play a major role in negotiating the various self-management agreements affecting distribution of incomes, housing, and other benefits. They were also to be responsible for implementing the agreements within the firm and insuring that their provisions were respected in practice. Thus, issues that had once been resolved through the give-and-take of occupational groups now fell to the trade unions, who, as representatives of "society," were expected to press for reducing interfirm and interskill differentials and to protect the "direct producer" in the allocation of other benefits.

At Klek, however, whatever the union's role in negotiating the industrywide self-management agreement had been, its activity inside the firm appeared unchanged despite the fanfare in the press over its "new role" in self-management. A young mechanical designer was elected trade union president toward the end of this study, replacing the former union president who had been "promoted" to the party secretariat. That the new president was honest, upright, without any great political ambitions, and totally without influence in the enterprise seemed to insure that the union would continue to play as marginal a role in Klek as it had in the past. In the new president's opening letter to the collective, he advised those who had complaints to take them to their representative on the Union Executive Committee, who would then forward them on to the "proper authorities" in the enterprise. Eventually, he promised, "you will receive an answer." It was hardly a strategy geared to the aggressive defense of the interests of the "direct producers."

In contrast to the trade union, Klek's party organization did seem to be making attempts to strike out in new directions; at the time of this study, it was still too early to tell whether these presaged a more permanent change in the party's role. Clearly, however, there were strong internal forces present at Klek to prevent it from ever playing too heavy-handed a role in decision making.

In this respect, the cumulative effects of the Tenth Congress, the anti-technocracy campaign, and the return of democratic centralism were to encourage enterprise party organizations to act on behalf of outside bodies in the firm and the BOALs independently of both management and the general work force. At Klek, this was manifested in a slight but perceptible estrangement between the party—and especially the party leadership—and the rest of the collective, including management. At the same time, the locus of power in the party branch appeared to shift somewhat from the party organization as a whole to its executive committee, the secretariat, a smaller and more cohesive body. Moreover, within the secretariat itself, the "hardliners," those who were suspicious of the "struggle of ideas" climate favored by the more influential executives and who were anxious to "put things in order" in the firm, were becoming increasingly powerful in party counsels.

These developments in the party were favored by the rather chaotic climate at Klek caused by the firm's seeming inability to meet all the new legal obligations imposed on it by the constitutional changes. The firm's statutes had not even been revised, let alone adopted by the self-management bodies and submitted to the courts for approval; the regulations governing Solidarity Fund apartment allocations were not ready in September, although they should have been drawn up months earlier. Added to this were the economic difficulties Klek still found itself in: firms that owed it money still refused to pay their debts; BOAL I was lagging in plan completion; the analytic job evaluation was far behind schedule; the new incentive regulations were in limbo. The impact of these legal and economic pressures on Klek was to demoralize the collective, discredit the management, and open the party organization to criticism from the regional committee.

The time was ripe for strong leadership, and in June, just after the Tenth Congress, the secretariat called for new elections to all the self-management bodies, the trade union executive committee, and to the secretariat itself. In doing so, the secretariat hoped to create a new "climate" in the plant which would enable the firm to escape the chaos it was in, allow greater coordination between the BOALs, and unite the entire collective behind the leadership of the party organization.

The action of the secretariat was somewhat high-handed, to say the least. The elections to the self-management bodies were entirely illegal, for the terms of the current council members had not expired, and only the assemblies were empowered to alter enterprise statutes.[8] Furthermore, the election commissions were stacked with party loyalists to ensure the election of party-favored candidates.[9] Finally, in an apparent departure from previous practice, the party leadership did not even bother to inform management that elections were being held, much less the reason why they were being called, even though nearly all the executives were themselves party members.

The June elections suggest that when Klek's party leadership was determined, it was certainly able to push a decision through the collective, even if it had to step on everyone's toes in the process. Strong party action of this type in Yugoslav firms might well diminish labor-management conflict[10] and stem the centripetal tendencies of BOALs simply by making any conflict illegitimate and excluding politically undesirable interests from the decision-making process altogether.

Yet if Klek is typical, there are strong forces that prevent enterprise party organizations from engaging in this type of action on a regular basis: the party's legitimacy as a protector of socialist legality, the injunction not to dictate, its need to be responsive to the collective if it wishes to be more than superficially effective,[11] and its difficulty in disciplining its own membership when the collective is strongly divided on an issue. The party may succeed in lowering the number and intensity of occupational and BOAL clashes insofar as the institutional arrangements it must implement do so. If it is strongly unified, the party may even succeed in creating a "back to work; enough discussion" climate which would deter occupational and BOAL conflicts; this, indeed, was what the hardline faction in Klek's party organization was trying to do, with only limited success.[12]

Yet should conflicts between BOALs begin to replace conflicts between occupational groups, there is little reason to suspect that enterprise party organizations will not mirror these cleavages as faithfully as they have mirrored the occupational divisions. At Klek, the party organization's decision to divide itself into three "Basic Organizations of the League of Communists" with their memberships drawn separately from each BOAL suggests that such a development is not unlikely. In that case, the ability of the enterprise LCY organization to step in to arbitrate conflicts and coordinate the BOALs, as it is apparently expected to do, is highly questionable.

As a result, the need to coordinate the BOALs may very well lead to a resurgence of Yugoslav self-management's bête noire—the central enterprise administration—despite its very tenuous new legal position. The areas open to management's influence will be more limited, for the sphere of autonomy of the enterprise as a whole will be restricted by the self-management agreements and social compacts. Yet within the still rather substantial areas left to enterprise discretion, the division of the firm into BOALs, none of whom has an overview of total business operations, may eventually allow management to emerge stronger than in the past.

PART IV

Conclusion

10

Planning, Markets, and Workers' Councils

In its origins and conceptions, this study was largely inspired by the concerns of radical political economists and left-wing activists in the United States and Europe.[1] In its analysis and conclusions, however, it has departed sharply from the all too idealized versions of what workers' control is and might be that seem to inform much of the radical discussion on this topic. Further, it will go on to suggest that the parameters of this discussion must be recast if the very important issues it involves are not to be lost in what may well be fruitless debate.

Several points, implicit in the preceding analysis, should be made explicit at this time. The first concerns the kinds of relationships that develop between economic and political agents when workers' councils are responsible for microeconomic decision making and a responsive government and/or political party shaped by and committed to an ideology stressing democratic socialism and workers' control of production is in power. These are elements common to all radical proposals for workers' control, regardless of whether they advocate economic planning or use of the market as the main methods of resource allocation. They are also the elements whose interaction causes a politicoeconomic system based on workers' control to experience a continual internal conflict between primary reliance on planning and primary reliance on the market, with all the political and economic consequences such strains involve.

At the heart of the plan-market conflict is a basic tension inherent in any system of workers' control occurring at the level of its prime component, the enterprise workers' council. Here, the central problem in both planned and market systems is that although a workers' council is elected by and represents only the employees of the particular firm it manages, it nonetheless must take other factors and preferences into account each time it makes a decision. Like elected representatives in any political unit, a workers' council leads,

209

makes decisions for, and is accountable to the constituency that elects it; unlike a political entity, however, the unit a workers' council manages (the enterprise) does not produce and supply goods and services to be used primarily by those within it, nor does it acquire most of its necessary inputs (land, capital, raw materials, etc.) from its labor force. While its formal structure as a political body acts to make a workers' council substantially independent of influences from outside its contituency, its practical functions as an economic agent make the council highly dependent on external forces it cannot control. At the same time, if the main managerial personnel of a labor-managed firm are also held accountable to the firm's labor force through periodic elections and other mechanisms, they too will continually confront the same dilemma.

The attempts of workers' councils and elected executives to resolve this tension, when translated and aggregated politically, easily become pressures for restructuring the economy. If the economy is planned, the tension works itself out as conflicts between enterprise elites (workers' councils and management) and the planning bodies to whom they are subordinated (be they higher-level councils elected by production units, as in Gramsci's workers' democracy, or banks, government agencies, and communes, as in Yugoslavia). Approached from a slightly different angle, such conflicts in a planned economy have their roots in a break in the bureaucratic chain of command inherent in workers' control: the lowest unit of the planning hierarchy, the workers' council, derives its authority not from those above it but from its nominal subordinates (the enterprise labor force, its electorate). With a power base independent of planning authorities, the ambitious workers' council and management are in a strategic position to widen a break in the bureaucratic chain of command into a chasm.

Although there are certainly conflicts between enterprise directors and plan authorities in Soviet-type planning systems as well, they are not complicated by the break in the hierarchical command system that arises from electing enterprise decision makers.[2] In the U.S.S.R., management is responsible to state planning bodies; it is appointed, transferred, and removed by them, receives many of its orders from them, acquires its bonuses through them. If a Soviet director wishes to build a base of support to buttress his position in the firm, he will seek it in state bureaucracies and the party *apparat,* not among the labor force of the enterprise he manages. There is rarely any tension between responding to the demands of the labor force and conforming to external authorities; lacking such a tension, there is slight rationale to resolve it by widening the firm's sphere of autonomy. If Soviet management adopts strategies dysfunctional to the planning system as a whole, it is in order to comply with directives, not to resist them.

Nevertheless, if workers' councils in a planned economy are a necessary condition of pressures in favor of increasing enterprise independence, they are not necessary and sufficient to produce an overall change; a receptive government willing to act on these pressures must also be present. Nor does the mere presence of workers' councils at the enterprise level guarantee a responsive government. As the 1956 events in Poland indicate, a government may react to demands voiced by workers' councils for greater plant-level control over microeconomic decisions by ignoring or emasculating the councils that make them.[3] Radical proponents of planning and workers' control, however, do normally postulate that government must be responsive, particularly to the demands of workers' councils.

In Gramsci's outline of workers' democracy, these conditions were met in the requirement that the entire structure of political and economic decision making and execution be elected out of the factory councils themselves. In addition, the single party prescribed by Gramsci was given the specific task of "generalizing" and articulating demands from the "base," while the ideology guiding it posited factory councils as the sine qua non of socialist society and endowed them with political legitimacy as organs of worker representation.

In Yugoslavia in the 1950s, these conditions were satisfied somewhat differently. Workers' councils never acquired the direct political power Gramsci had awarded them, despite the somewhat abortive attempt to establish a chamber of the legislature elected out of the various work communities. However, that workers' councils were initially introduced partly as a means of solidifying domestic opinion behind the regime in the aftermath of the Cominform break suggests that Yugoslav leaders looked to the self-managed firms as a potentially important source of political support. Ideologically, in the 1950s Yugoslav socialism increasingly emphasized self-management along with growing criticism of bureaucratic methods and "deformations." In addition, the importance Yugoslav leaders at all levels of government attached to rapid industrial development placed self-managed enterprises in a strategic position to influence local and national economic policy.

At the local level, where the performance of self-managed firms was a vital part of commune development plans, ties were particularly close between political officials in government and party organizations and enterprise elites in management, workers' councils, and party branches. Certainly, this did not prevent frequent conflicts from erupting between the two groups when enterprises sought to evade government regulations or resist political pressures or when political authorities were unable or unwilling to satisfy enterprise demands. Yet in Yugoslavia, there were, so to speak, two breaks in the bureaucratic chain of command created by the planning system. The first arose out of the establishment of workers' councils and an elected management inside Yugoslav firms, leading to conflicts between political agencies and economic units. The second was within the planning apparatus itself: between local governments, responsible for the development of the territory under their jurisdiction, and the national government, anxious to pursue a development policy that would ensure high growth rates while evening out regional inequalities and economic imbalances. It was the regional competition for politically allocated investment funds which supplied the critical political mechanism pushing local firms and local governments together, allowing the claims of regions and enterprises skeptical of centrally determined investment priorities to be aggregated up to the national level of both the government and the League of Communists. Eventually, Yugoslav leaders, reflecting the conflicting demands of different territorial and economic interests, found themselves at an impasse in which they could no longer agree on plan priorities. The outcome, as we have seen, was the abandonment of planning.

The presence of a responsive government that recognizes the political legitimacy of workers' council demands can also have important effects on how workers' councils seek to resolve the tension between their aspirations for autonomy as a political unit and their functional interdependence as an economic unit. That is, whatever the grass-roots support for enterprise autonomy, it may never materialize past the point of resentment and apathy unless the government is perceived as potentially responsive to such a demand. As we saw in Klek, whatever dissatisfaction there was in the work collective with the cumbersome reorganization mandated by the 1974 Constitution, it did not take the form of overt resistance to what the entire collective saw as an inevitability. At the same time, how the government is perceived is a function partly of its past actions and partly of the ideology it employs to justify those actions. If ideology stresses the role of political leaders and agencies independent of the firm as over and above the firm and the labor force within it, demands to increase the autonomy of the enterprise will be perceived as illegitimate even by those who would normally favor them most.

In contrast, if the government is perceived as potentially receptive and ideology centers on the political and economic importance of workers' councils, enterprise elites will be encouraged to resolve the tensions they face within the firm by pressuring government bodies for changes in the external environment. And, of course, if the government is in fact responsive, the aggregation of these pressures among higher-level political bodies should pro-

duce a major economic restructuring in favor of enlarged enterprise autonomy, one that will necessarily involve giving market forces much greater play
within the economy.

WORKERS' COUNCILS, RESPONSIVE GOVERNMENT, AND THE MARKET

In a market economy, the same tension between formal accountability and
independence on the one hand and the empirical conditions and practical
necessities of decision making on the other reappears at the level of the firm
in altered circumstances. Whereas in a planned economy, this tension becomes most acute in the more efficient and dynamic firms, those who feel
most constrained by the actions of external authorities to restrict or redistribute the benefits of their productivity, in a market economy it becomes
particularly dramatic in firms experiencing difficulties under the pressures of
competition. Again, workers' councils of such firms will seek the aid of
government to stabilize their economic environment and guarantee operating
conditions under which they can make decisions reflecting their constituency's
preferences. Indeed, in Yugoslavia, not only marginal enterprises sought
government protection; some of the most prosperous and profitable firms
also attempted to utilize political connections to ward off the threats of
potential competitors or to ensure their access to capital suppliers.

Furthermore, the development of occupational differentiation and stratification accompanying the growth of a competitive labor market and the need
for firms to make rapid decisions on a technically sophisticated basis may
impair workers' councils' ability to make policy reflective of their constituencies' preferences even in relatively well-off firms. In theory, all employees
of the labor-managed firm are equally represented in decision making and
share equally in responsibility and risk taking; in practice, certain groups and
individuals will turn out to be far more influential than others in deciding the
course of action the enterprise as a whole will pursue. Certainly, the dominant
influence on decision making exerted by managerial personnel in Yugoslav
firms after the 1965 reforms has been well documented in this respect.

At the same time, as occupational strata come to be more sharply defined
by their identifications and attitudes as well as their functions, decisions
taken under the influence of one group may depart sharply from the perceived interests of others. In particular, the economic requirement that the
distribution of personal income and other benefits coincide with marginal
productivity, a requirement that would tend to favor managerial and technical
elites, may result in a highly skewed distribution of wage and nonwage
benefits regardless of the preferences of the majority of the work collective.
As a result, disadvantaged groups, particularly blue-collar workers, may well

capture and politicize workers' councils, engage in strike actions, form or
utilize trade unions, or employ other forms of political association to press
for political measures to modify the workings of the market and provide an
altered economic framework within which their grievances can be righted.
The rash of strikes and work stoppages in Yugoslavia in the 1960s, many of
which were settled by the mediation of government officials, is significant in
this regard. So too are the sharp conflicts over distribution issues which
characterized worker-management relations at Klek.

Certainly, it is a time-honored business tradition in Western capitalist
countries to run to government for protection when the competitive market
appears overly threatening; Yugoslavia hardly invented the protective tariff or
the industry-specific investment credit. Likewise, it is common practice for
trade unions to apply political pressures on governments to provide for social
welfare, full employment, greater income equalization, and the like. Yet in
a capitalist economy, the demands business and labor respectively make on
government and the policy priorities they propose are normally different and
usually in conflict. Thus, although the cumulative outcome of their respective
pressures may be increased government intervention in various and discrete
areas of the economy, their conflicting demands, mutual suspicions, and
potential refusal to cooperate may actually act to deter large-scale and long-
term government coordination of the economy as a whole.

Significantly, in the more recent instances where Western governments have
acted to coordinate and "rescue" single industries, it has usually been in
response to pleas for such actions by both labor and business within the
industry. It is in these limiting cases where business and labor goals coincide
in the capitalist economy that the normal conditions of the labor-managed
market economy are duplicated. In the latter, there is no institutionalized
opposition between organized business and organized labor; economic distinctions and political cleavages take place between firms and industries and
between occupational groups, permitting the pressures of disadvantaged firms
and disadvantaged groups to converge on a much wider range of issues.[4]

The question, of course, is how the government of a labor-managed economy
will react to such pressures. If the presence of labor-managed firms and a competitive market facilitates the emergence of demands aggregating into pressures for political coordination of the economy, they do not guarantee
government action in this direction. Moreover, for such a change to take
place, it is not enough for government to be "responsive" in general; it must
be especially responsive to disadvantaged firms and groups hurt by a competitive economy. Ideology and whom political leaders perceive as their source of
support will be important factors influencing government action here. If

government leaders are committed to nonintervention, regard enterprise autonomy as more important than enterprise control by the workers within it, and do not perceive economic and social equality as concomitants of workers' control, there is little reason for them to respond favorably to the demands of beleaguered firms and low-income wage earners. Similarly, if government leaders do not rely on the support of these elements to stay in power, they can simply ignore or repress such claims. Thus, when the Lip watch factory was occupied in 1973 and the workers appealed for state support, the French government equivocated for months, until the affair had become a cause celebre on the French left and had won the sympathy of even some of the government's own supporters.[5] An analogous case occurred in Canada, when Dunlop Tires announced the closing of its Toronto plant. Workers, through their trade union branch, called on provincial authorities to forestall the closure and facilitate the workers' purchase of the plant. Although they received strong support from the opposition New Democratic party, the Tory provincial government refused to take any action on their behalf.[6]

Similar examples from other non-labor-managed economies abound; the lesson radical proponents of workers' control have derived from these experiences is embodied in their postulate that the establishment of workers' control at the enterprise level would be accompanied by a government that interprets workers' control as a formula for economic democracy and equality as well as for enterprise self-determination and whose prime constituency is the rank-and-file labor force of the self-managed firms. Proudhon presents somewhat of an anomaly here, for he literally provides no government at all in mutualism. Nevertheless, even in Proudhon's prescription, the probability of pronounced economic instability and increasingly sharp conflicts between and within mutualist and federative associations suggests that society and even the more prosperous cooperatives will find the operation of the market an increasingly costly method of economic organization. Furthermore, if Proudhon himself makes no explicit provision for government, he certainly provides the rationale for one in his stress on equality and justice as guiding ideological norms of mutualist society and in his condemnation of the evils of monopoly. Yet if government is introduced in order to stabilize the economy and provide for equality and justice, it will mean that the authoritative decisions of political bodies will begin to reshape and replace the competitive market in the allocation of economic resources.

In Yugoslavia, too, political leaders proved receptive to the pleas of struggling firms and discontented workers; the government's response was finally embodied in the 1974 Constitution and the antitechnocracy campaign. Both came about after a protracted struggle between promarket and antimarket

forces within the government and the League of Communists. While the promarket forces initially emerged victorious in 1965–66, the economic downturn that followed the reform and the liberals' inability to either agree on its
causes or find suitable remedies soon caused the political winds to move in
the direction of their opponents. Critical to this change was an implicit and
often explicit shift in the political position of many of the self-managed
enterprises who, at first so supportive of the reform, increasingly found themselves forced to turn to government bodies to shore up their deteriorating
finances. Industry, which had enjoyed a privileged status prior to the reform,
was particularly hard hit by the new foreign competition and the postreform
monetary contraction; what looked like a flow of money and investment
capital out of industry and into banking and commerce provoked outcries
against "centers of economic power" and demands that authorities take steps
to restrict them.

   At the same time, inequalities and inflation caused blue-collar industrial
workers to become increasingly disenchanted with the reforms as well, resulting in a wave of strikes and work stoppages that could hardly be ignored by a
party that still considered itself fundamentally an organization of the working
class. The consequence was an essentially political alliance within the LCY
on behalf of disadvantaged firms and occupational strata and in favor of
correcting the workings of the market through political means. Ideology provided an important underpinning for the coalition of factions favoring a
greater role for the government in the economy: if the "struggle of ideas"
philosophy allowed antimarket forces to remain in the party and capitalize on
the growing disillusionment with the reforms, "distribution according to
work" and guaranteeing "equal conditions of economic operation" provided
legitimizing slogans for enlarging the scope of government in the economy.
While the new system put into effect by the 1974 Constitution was far from a
return to the old forms of investment planning, it was clearly a step away
from what political leaders disparagingly began to refer to as the "anarchy"
of the market.

   Although the Yugoslav variants on the highly utopian outlines supplied by
Gramsci and Proudhon help to refute arguments that socialism and plant-
level democracy is visionary and impractical,[7] they also confound the claims
of enthusiasts that workers' control is somehow a solution to bureaucracy,
alienation, and economic and political inequalities. While a politicoeconomic
system based on elected workers' councils at the enterprise level and a socialist government responsive to their claims does indeed "work," it works
according to its own dynamics and may very well create many of the problems its proponents argue it would solve. Further, the thrust of this analysis
indicates that such dynamics arise out of the structural conditions contained

in the radical definition of workers' control itself, and not from the particular form the economy takes (plan or market) or from the circumstantial, empirical characteristics of a particular social setting.

YUGOSLAVIA—A SPECIAL CASE?

This brings us to the second point implicit in the earlier analysis which should be made explicit at this time, one that concerns the relevance of the Yugoslav experience for other countries. Here it is worth considering the arguments of a number of advocates of workers' control who are nonetheless critical to greater and lesser degrees of various aspects of Yugoslav self-management. The gist of these arguments runs as follows: judging by its past and current performance, Yugoslav self-management has not been completely successful in realizing the goals of workers' control; nonetheless, these goals can be attained in other countries either because they can avoid the "mistakes" the Yugoslavs have made or because they are not plagued by Yugoslavia's "particular" circumstances.[8]

One variant of this critique attributes Yugoslavia's inability to eliminate state bureaucracy and economic and political inequalities to its one-party system and the nature of the single party that dominates it. These features, the argument continues, have allowed a "new ruling class" to monopolize political life in its own interest and confine workers and workers' councils to the narrow and basically trivial sphere of economic questions. Accordingly, in a country with a more open and pluralistic political system, workers theoretically would have more control over their government, be more successful in eliminating bureaucracy, alienation, and inequality, and have a greater incentive to participate in political and economic decision making.

To the degree that this argument serves to remind us that Yugoslavia has a well-defined political elite, a relatively authoritarian political system, and that the state is far from "withering away," it is certainly correct. So, too, is its contention that there are implicit limits on the range of dissent and opposition tolerated in Yugoslav society, limits felt within the self-managed enterprises as well as outside them. As we saw in the case of Klek, when the party branch was determined to go through with an action, no one was going to distinguish himself by standing in its way, even when the action itself was of dubious legality.

Nevertheless, insofar as the "ruling class" argument goes on to suggest that Yugoslavia's political elite is isolated from currents of opinion and pressures stemming from the base of the political pyramid, that it is unresponsive and has merely allowed cosmetic changes to occur since 1950, and that it has tolerated no significant criticism at all, the argument is open to very serious question. As I have illustrated in detail, Yugoslavia has undergone a series of major structural, economic and political reforms in the postwar period, reforms in some ways more dramatic and far-ranging than any undertaken by Western governments in the same period. Moreover, these reforms affected the structure, composition, and role of the League of Communists as much as they affected other institutions; while Yugoslavia retained its character as a single-party system, the League of Communists in 1969 was a very different organization from the League of Communists of 1952. In addition, the various reforms did not simply spring out of the arbitrary whims of a monolithic leadership determined to maintain a tight grasp on the reins of power; rather, they emerged out of disagreement within the political leadership itself, disagreement that reflected pressures exerted by grass-roots organizations outside the party itself and by labor-managed firms and workers in particular.

Finally, if we look at the deeper problems and strains involved in the plan-market tension, it is difficult to see how the presence of a more pluralistic political system would solve them; on the contrary, it would merely facilitate and perhaps intensify their expression. In short, Yugoslavia's seeming inability to eliminate bureaucracy, alienation, and inequality simultaneously is due less to a lack of workers' control than to its presence; the plan-market conflict operates there despite the presence of a single party, not because of it.

A second variant of this argument also recognizes deficiencies in Yugoslav self-management, but attributes them to Yugoslavia's underdevelopment. According to this explanation, Yugoslavia's relatively late industrialization meant it introduced self-management before a mature working class, capable of running industry and the economy, developed. As a result, bureaucracies in the state or in the enterprises easily usurped the position that by right belonged to workers. Furthermore, the argument goes, the conditions of Yugoslav underdevelopment were and are such that no form of economic organization can achieve the goals of workers' control until a higher standard of living is attained. Accordingly, workers' control and its goals may well be realized when Yugoslavia acquires the status of a "developed" nation; in the meantime, Yugoslavia's difficulties are not particularly relevant for more advanced economies and should not deter other nations from instituting workers' control in a context where such a system and its goals can become a reality.

Certainly, it cannot be doubted that self-management was introduced to Yugoslavia under less than optimal circumstances. It is also true that firms whose labor force is predominantly composed of peasant-workers and recent recruits to industry do seem to show a disproportionate tendency to have autocratic managements and weak organs of worker representation. Moreover, since these are typically firms with high unskilled labor components, low productivity rates, low wage scales, and marginal profitability, they are also firms that have tended to look more to political transfers of resources rather than to their own ability to attract or create capital.

Nevertheless, the behavior patterns observed at Klek, a firm with a well-educated, urbanized, and sophisticated labor force, should caution us against attributing too much to "underdevelopment." Although Klek's management can hardly be described as "autocratic," it certainly dominated decision making, as the workers in the firm were well aware. At the same time, management's near-monopoly of influence in some of the most critical areas of policy formulation was accomplished not by "usurping" the workers' rights, but with their implicit and often explicit agreement. Where disagreement occurred on distribution questions, it did not arise simply from an objectively low standard of living experienced by the production workers, but out of their conviction that they were not receiving what they felt to be the fruits of their labor. In sum, worker dissatisfaction at Klek was grounded on perceptions of *relative* deprivation, a phenomenon as common in advanced industrial societies as in less developed ones.

On a wider scale, it is perhaps significant that "technocracy" in the enterprises was not perceived as a serious problem until the late 1960s, when Yugoslavia was well on the way to becoming a "developed" country. Moreover, the problem was not confined to the more backward regions of Yugoslavia but, on the contrary, was viewed as being most acute in the wealthiest areas and enterprises. Hence, one is forced to conclude that it was primarily the operation of the market and the autonomy granted to the firms that led to managerial domination of Yugoslav firms, not the lack of sophistication of Yugoslav workers. If anything, disgruntlement over a low standard of living led workers to challenge management and force wages above productivity levels rather than stand by and watch their real incomes be eroded by inflation on management's advice.

The Klek example is illustrative in another regard as well. That is, despite the characteristics of the labor force and the fact that on paper the firm showed a profit, the Klek collective did not hesitate to appeal for politically allocated funds to correct a capital shortage partly of its own making. Nor did the collective hesitate to accept a loan from the city reserve fund, despite the restrictive conditions attached to it. In short, the government did not intervene over the protests of the Klek collective but as a solicited response to the desperate appeals of a work collective that could hardly be characterized, even by Western standards, as "immature."

Furthermore, it should be noted that the areas that protested the loudest

against the concentration of capital in banking and commerce that followed
the abandonment of investment planning were Croatia and Slovenia, the
"developed" republics. It was these republics who led the fight to bring the
banks under republic (political) control, which again suggests that the consequences of the market—not underdevelopment in and of itself—were behind
the move back to political coordination of investment.

More profoundly, the major flaw in the "underdevelopment" argument's
underestimation of the relevance of Yugoslav self-management for Western
countries lies in its assumption that "development" and "underdevelopment"
are absolute, static, and qualitatively different states. On the contrary, they
are relative, dynamic, and quantitatively different conditions: one country's
"development" problem is another nation's "growth" problem, and yester-
day's high standard of living is today's poverty line. "Scarcity" is a function
of social and historical needs, not an objective given.

Thus, it is highly questionable that workers' control and a competitive
market will be more successful in achieving the goals of workers' control in
an advanced industrial society than they were in Yugoslavia. It is difficult to
see why the same interindustry and interenterprise differentials and oligopolistic practices that plagued Yugoslavia would not occur at a higher level
of affluence in Western countries; if relative deprivation and nonentrepreneurial
attitudes motivated highly skilled machinists in Zagreb, it is unclear why they
would not possess equal appeal for unskilled automobile workers in Detroit or
Turin; if firms threatened with bankruptcy and unable to meet their payrolls
appealed for government aid in Yugoslavia, it is hard to see why firms faced
with similar problems would not do the same in a Western country—and surely
the argument does not assume that Western affluence guarantees growing
profits for all firms. Moreover, if economic incentives and the inequalities they
generate are necessary for development in a poor country, by the same logic
they would also be necessary for growth (or simply rational resource allocation) in a rich one. Alternatively, they may not be necessary in either, but in
neither case is there a basis for assuming that the problems an underdeveloped
country encounters with equality and inequality will not be as pressing in an
advanced country simply because it is wealthier.

At the other end of the spectrum, if the underdevelopment argument is
taken to mean that workers' control and planning will be more successful in
an advanced country, it is still highly dubious. In the first place, the assumption that affluence in and of itself will magically produce agreement on
planning priorities between industries and regions (and the workers within
them) is highly tenuous. Indeed, because of its complexity and diversity and
because more alternatives are open to it, it may even be more difficult to

arrive at agreements on priorities in an advanced economy. Conceivably, affluence may reduce the stakes of the game somewhat (everyone can get something), but in doing so, it may also dissipate resources to the extent that affluence itself is eventually threatened. Second, it is equally unclear why labor-managed firms in an affluent society would be any less jealous of their autonomy than they appear to be in Yugoslavia. Certainly, a large part of the pressures from rank-and-file workers in Yugoslavia for greater control of enterprise earnings in the late 1950s was caused by their aspirations for higher wages. Even if we optimistically accept the contention that affluent workers will be less concerned with wage benefits, it still does not follow that they will be any less concerned with controlling their individual work places in order to achieve other goals, be they restructuring the work process to make it more interesting or allocating more time for leisure and self-development.

The final variant of the argument that contends that Yugoslavia's difficulties with self-management are unlikely to be repeated elsewhere emphasizes the role of ethnic tensions in the patterns of Yugoslav postwar development. Here, particular stress is placed on regional inequalities and their role first in the breakdown of investment planning and later in the abandonment of the 1965 reforms. The implication is that in countries without a history of nationality conflicts and a heritage of regional disparities, workers' control would function far more smoothly and successfully.

The importance of ethnic tensions and regional rivalries in Yugoslavia cannot be underestimated, and it is not my intention to detract from their central role in Yugoslav development. However, the suggestion that the simple presence of a homogeneous population is sufficient for the smooth and successful operation of workers' control is open to serious challenge, and one must question any assertion that nationality conflict was the sole factor causing the changes or even that it operated independently of self-management.

There are and have been numerous multinational states in the world, and there are or have been numerous nations with pronounced regional inequalities. Nevertheless, one is hard put to find any that restructure their economies every decade and go through three constitutions in less than thirty years under the same government. Clearly, various governments have responded in different ways to ethnic cleavages: some have simply repressed potentially disruptive minority sentiments (Spain, U.S.S.R.); others have conceded a greater or lesser degree of autonomy to militant minorities (Britain, Canada, Switzerland); yet others have allocated special monies to underdeveloped regions (Italy).

None of these alternatives, however, proved satisfactory for Yugoslavia because of self-management and the relationships it caused to spring up be-

tween local firms, local governments, and national political leaders. Without
these relationships, there would surely have been ethnic tensions, but it is
doubtful that they would have assumed the form they finally took. Had there
been Soviet-style central planning along with a Soviet-style government and
party to match it, each republic and autonomous province might well have
insisted on central funds with which to construct its own university, but one
wonders if the complaints of enterprises concentrated in developed regions
over insufficient incentives would ever have been voiced, much less listened
to. Had there been a capitalist market economy and a multiparty system, there
might have been a replay of the cloak-and-dagger politics of the thirties, but
the issues would have been secession versus national unity, not planning versus
the market. Or had capitalism been accompanied by a simple dictatorship in
the recent Spanish tradition, there would have been protests for greater ethnic
freedom of expression and local autonomy, but it is difficult to imagine them
culminating in a demand to divide up the assets of banks among the regions.
In sum, while the desire of Yugoslav political leaders to avoid fanning the
flames of ethnic discontent may have been a critical factor in their responsiveness to demands for economic restructuring, ethnic hostilities and regional
enmities were not the cause of the demands themselves. For this, it appears,
self-management must claim credit.

TOWARDS A REDEFINITION OF THE PROBLEM OF WORKERS' CONTROL

According to the analysis developed here, when a politicoeconomic system
based on workers' control of industry and government embodies elements of
planning and hierarchical coordination of resource allocation, it sets up organizational structures, aligns interests, and creates political pressures that move
it in the direction of utilizing a market mechanism. Yet if changes are made
and reforms enacted to approximate a competitive market more closely, organizational identities are redefined and interests realigned, bringing pressures
in favor of hierarchy into play. If this is an invariable syndrome, workers'
control's most profound sociopolitical output may be little more than continual demands to reorganize workers' control.

Thus, the operation of workers' control in either a planned or a market
economy presents its respective advocates with a problem and a paradox, not
a solution or a formula. The difficulty is not so much that workers' control
does not—and, in light of our theoretical analysis, cannot—provide every single
benefit its advocates claim for it; one can hardly criticize a practical or proposed politicoeconomic system simply because it fails to achieve instant utopia.

However, if the combination of enterprise-level workers' councils and responsive government does not produce instant utopia, then such a system must

make trade-offs between the degrees to which and kinds of goals it should and can orient itself toward achieving. Yet at the same time that workers' control in either planned or market economies necessitates trade-offs, the structural strains to which it gives rise greatly complicate the political process of making them. As noted at the start of this work, tensions between the use of hierarchy and the use of the market and between centralization and decentralization are not new to the world of politics and economics. Nevertheless, labor-managed politicoeconomic systems not only seem to be especially prone to these tensions, but also appear to have particular difficulties in resolving them, for one resolution seems to generate pressures for introducing its opposite.

It is far from my intention to assert a priori that the paradox workers' control presents is irresolvable; on the contrary, I believe it has been buried all too long under plan versus market polemics. Nor should this book be read as implying that Yugoslav self-management has been a failure; rather, it should stand as testimony to the resiliency of self-management and the flexibility of Yugoslav leaders in dealing with its unintended consequences.

The point, however, is that these "unintended consequences" seem to occur with a certain degree of predictability and their underlying causes have been obscured rather than clarified by the plan-market debate. In this regard, rather than continuing to argue the virtues of workers' control and planning against the virtues of workers' control in a market economy, radical concerns must be redirected to analyzing the effects of workers' control in both planned and market economies. Rather than searching endlessly for evidence to support the belief that the difficulties self-management has encountered in Yugoslavia will not occur elsewhere, we should regard the Yugoslav experience as one with wider relevance and study it in the light of the plan-market tension produced by structural conditions implicit in the notion of workers' control itself.

Meanwhile, the problem that remains is designing institutional mechanisms both consistent with the retention of enterprise-level workers' councils and responsive government and capable of making trade-offs between goals, and then adapting allocation methods accordingly. Prescribing what such institutional mechanisms might look like and what possible mixes of hierarchy and the market might result is a task beyond the scope of this inquiry. Yet this task must be approached from a vantage point that regards the goals of workers' control not as givens or standards for judgment, but as alternatives that must be balanced off against each other and against what is realistically feasible in a given social system. Here, it would seem, lie the critical choices workers' control systems must make, not in the realm of deciding on the abstract desirability of planning or the market.

APPENDIXES

APPENDIX A

Content Analysis of Relevant "Discussions" at the 1957 Congress of Workers' Councils

First Commission: The Economic Framework of Producers' Self-Management

Remark	Number of Comments
More independence to firm in disposition of funds; let more funds be kept within it; have fewer regulations; etc.	41
Complaints on effects of current government policies (discriminatory treatment, etc.)	24
Complaints of government interference with rational business conduct (meddling, retroactive laws, etc.)	10
Pleas for more government aid	3
Problems peculiar to industry	15

Second Commission: The Relationship of Workers' Councils to Other Organizations

Remark	Number of Comments
Give more independence to the firm and, within it, more power to the workers' council (change status of firm, change industrial classification, etc.)	37
Have clearer and fewer laws; complaints on discriminatory effects of certain laws and laws causing unnecessary problems	26
Economic associations and chambers should do more and work more directly with the workers' councils; give economic chambers more authority (strengthen the production principle in economic organization)	24
Council of Producers ineffective; it should do more for the enterprises, etc.	12

Competition is too rough   3
Particular problems   13

Third Commission: Economic Conduct of the Workers' Councils

Remarks	Number of Comments
Let firms have authority over larger portions of their funds; less regulation as to the use of funds; lower taxes	34
Need for specialists	20
Complaints on discriminatory effects of laws	21
Make getting credit easier	11
Difficulties owing to inadequate incentives for firms and individual workers	15
Others and particular problems	20

There were six commissions in all; the "discussions" in the other three, however, did not concentrate as much on firm relations with political authorities.

Note that there were no demands for the abandonment of investment planning per se but only recommendations for greater enterprise autonomy, greater control over enterprise funds, and contrasting recommendations for changes in the instruments of planning—suggestions that, when taken as a whole, amounted to undercutting the entire planning apparatus (either by taking its funds away and giving them to the firms or by forbidding it to discriminate among industries in allocating monies).

APPENDIX B

The Self-Management Structure and the Sociopolitical Organizations at Klek

The following is a description of the specific councils and commissions comprising the self-management structure and of the branches of the mass organizations present at Klek.

THE SELF-MANAGEMENT STRUCTURE

Klek's self-management structure was outlined in a 1973 self-management agreement between the newly created BOALs. Like the legislation it was patterned on, the agreement contained numerous ambiguities, making its implementation partly a product of trial and error, and partly a function of whichever groups and bodies were most aggressive about asserting their rights. For these reasons, the precise powers and responsibilities of Klek's self-management bodies were still in a very fluid state even in late 1974.

The Assemblies

The 1972 amendments and the new constitution, stressing the participation of the "direct producers" in decision making, called for increased use of the assemblies. Each BOAL in Klek had its own assembly, which was composed of all those working in the division and which formally constituted the final authority on all matters of enterprise policy.

The size of the assemblies was thus much larger than any of the elected self-management bodies. At Klek, the Service Division assembly convened on its own premises and was not observed during this study. The assemblies of BOAL I and III met together at the main plant, either during the midmorning break or after the first shift. Because of the plant's physical layout, assemblies were held right on the factory floor, the production workers' turf, so to speak. In contrast, meetings of other self-management bodies convened either in an executive's office or in the factory canteen.

The numerical proportions of the various occupational groups were also strikingly different at meetings of elected councils and at assembly gatherings. At the former, even if the elected delegates were predominantly blue-collar workers, meetings were also attended by a large number of supervisory personnel. But if the twenty or so executives who frequently attended sessions of the various elected self-management bodies came to the assemblies, so too did an additional two hundred production workers who would never show up at any other meetings. Hence, the numerical "balance of forces" at assemblies was in sharp contrast to the proportions prevailing at other self-management meetings.

Because of their inclusiveness, assemblies at Klek had the character of mass meetings. They oscillated between complete docility, with little or no participation or involvement of the rank-and-file labor force, and open revolt, with the blue-collar workers forming the main source of contention.

The BOAL Councils

Starting in 1973, each BOAL in Klek had its own council, to which each department (work unit) elected a representative. Although by 1974, the councils had been operating for well over a year, there was still no written document detailing their areas of jurisdiction. The relative novelty of the councils and their lack of precisely defined powers were a source of endless confusion, and what issues a council actually considered were largely a function of common sense (a division council handles problems arising in the division) and the competence and assertiveness of the division directors and council presidents. That enterprise assets were still not distributed among the BOALs created an additional complication, since theoretically no money could be spent by any one division council without the expense being approved by the other and/or the central workers' council.

In such a situation, the division councils differed greatly among themselves in what they saw as their spheres of authority. The Service Division tended to resolve most of its problems independently and rarely requested approval from either the central self-management bodies or the other division councils. Its greater cohesiveness, its geographical separation, and its superior economic performance allowed it to use the new constitutional grant of authority to practically emancipate itself from the surveillance of the other two units. The increased bargaining power it enjoyed because, in effect, it subsidized the other divisions perpetuated the situation and encouraged it to scorn any criticism directed at it from the main plant.

The BOAL I council, on the contrary, would regularly send recommendations and reports to the central workers' council; in fact, a majority of the latter's time was spent considering problems in production, much to the annoyance of the representatives from the Service Division. BOAL III had yet a third pattern of activity. Lacking a director and with a council president who, being a sales representative, was frequently out of the enterprise, the division council initially managed to simply evade a host of issues nominally falling within its competences. Owing to its inactivity, most of these questions were dealt with by other self-management bodies or handled within the organizational structure altogether. A new council was elected in June, and with an aggressive president who had held an executive position at Klek, the

Table B.1. Formal Composition of BOAL Councils, to June 1974

	BOAL I	BOAL II	BOAL III	Total
White-collar workers (total)	4	4	4	12
Blue-collar workers (total)	8	1	2	
Production workers	8	1	0	9
Maintenance workers	0	0	2	2
Total	12	5	6	23

BOAL III council began making decisions with a vengeance, even handling an issue or two that rightfully should have gone to the central workers' council.

Since council members were elected by departments, the size of each council was different. The largest council, with twelve members, was in the Production Division; it was also the council with the largest number of blue-collar workers elected to it (table B.1). Formal composition, however, is not all that significant in explaining the actions the councils took. Decisions were always made by consensus, and votes were never taken; discussion, rather than voting, was the critical source of influence. In this regard, a good number of managerial personnel were always present at meetings as "observers" and in fact participated far more actively in the discussions than did the elected delegates. Moreover, elected members did not always attend council meetings, even when they were held during work hours. Particularly in BOAL I, workers were much more frequently absent than either technicians or non-member managerial personnel, owing to the necessity of meeting their daily production quotas.

Nevertheless, making too sharp a distinction among blue-collar workers, technicians, and supervisors distorts the context in which division council meetings took place. Their atmosphere was one in which all saw themselves as working towards a common goal: a smoothly running enterprise. Discussions were often lively, but disagreements stemmed from differences in opinions among individuals as opposed to conflicts between competing group interests. If the influence and participation of supervisory personnel in decision making was disproportionately high, meetings were small enough so that anyone, regardless of qualification, was able to contribute to the discussions, providing he or she had something to say. In short, division councils at Klek were problem-solving groups rather than bodies designed to reconcile opposing interests.

The Workers' Council

At the center of the self-management process stood the enterprise workers' council, the oldest and perhaps most developed self-management body. The intention of the constitutional changes was to delegate many of the issues it traditionally had handled to the BOAL councils, and at Klek, this was reflected in a drop in the frequency of workers' council meetings: from 1966 to 1973, the workers' council met on average 11.5 times a year (and possibly more often, as minutes of past meetings were missing), while from January to October 1974, it convened only seven times. Yet because no BOAL had funds at its disposal, the actual content of workers' council meetings (the items placed on the agenda) was quite similar before and after 1973.

The main substantive change over time in the items handled by the workers' council was not related to decentralization. That is, the questions dealt with at greatest length were, quite understandably, the "crisis" issues: when things were functioning smoothly, they were left alone or examined in only the most cursory fashion. For example, from 1965 to 1969, Klek was experiencing major difficulties in marketing its machinery. A good deal of the workers' council's time, therefore, was devoted to considering sales reports. Eventually sales picked up, and the periodic reports were dropped from the agenda; only a brief paragraph on sales appeared in the annual financial statement, and it was not discussed even then.

Such a practice had several implications. First, it meant that an authoritarian supervisor who managed to get his and his department's work done rarely found the self-management organs trespassing on his territory. Second, it permitted some units to escape the control of the others; in this sense, the BOAL structure merely facilitated a process in the Service Division which had already been underway for some time. Finally, such a procedure logically implied that when all is going well, there is no need for self-management at all, except perhaps to give routine approval to plans, contracts, and the like.

The composition of the workers' council, in contrast, changed considerably with the introduction of the BOALs. Its total membership dropped from thirty-six to twenty-one, but more important, elections were now conducted on a division basis. The divisions' legal autonomy was further interpreted to mean that each was entitled to an equal number of delegates, even though the Production Division contained twice as many people as did the other two BOALs. Consequently, the proportion of blue-collar workers on the council dropped from its usual two-thirds to less than half of the formal council membership. Moreover, there was an enormous discrepancy of votes between the elected representative with the highest number of votes and the one with the lowest (table B.2).

Clearly, the effect of the new system on formal representation of the "direct producer" in the Klek workers' council was precisely the opposite of its proclaimed intentions. The elections held in June 1974 allowed the same individuals elected to division councils to sit on the workers' council. (In 1973, separate elections were held for the workers' council and the BOAL councils.) Whether this meant that the Production Division would now have twelve delegates as opposed to five and six for Service and Collective Services respectively was unclear, however. Indeed, the only meeting of the postelec-

Table B.2. Election Results of June 1973

	Production Division (BOAL I)	Service Division (BOAL II)	Collective Services Division (BOAL III)
Number of votes for elected delegate with highest total votes	130	69	50
Number of votes for elected delegate with lowest total votes	98	42	29
Average votes per elected delegate	118.1	51.5	40

tion workers' council held before this study concluded was attended by members of both the outgoing and incoming workers' councils, and all were counted as voting members in order to obtain a quorum.

The casualness with which this last meeting was conducted should serve as a caution against overestimating the importance of formal representation in the self-management process at Klek. As in the division councils, the consensus format of workers' council meetings militated against the power of the vote in favor of the power of the voice. Again, this meant that managerial personnel could easily dominate decision making without being voting members of the council. If the minutes are any indication, the dichotomy between extremely high participation on the part of nonmember executive personnel and extremely low participation by elected members was just as pronounced at Klek from 1965 to 1974 as in the meetings observed during this study. Choosing 1966 at random, a content analysis of the minutes reveals that twelve executives spoke a total of 193 times, while nineteen of the thirty members whose comments are recorded spoke 99 times. The ratio of executive to member participation was thus on the order of five to one. Despite its highly educated labor force, Klek's participation patterns do not appear to differ very much quantitatively from the patterns in other Yugoslav firms.

Note, however, that the possibility for participation at meetings by interested observers cuts both ways. If it allows management to exert a strong influence on decision making, it also permits nonelected workers, dissatisfied or mistrustful of their representatives, to come to meetings and present their grievances just as if they were council members. This indeed occurred at Klek in the dispute over overtime rates in September 1974.

Issues treated by the council fell broadly into two categories. The first consisted of questions that had been settled before coming to the council and were presented for formal ratification. Within this category, we can distinguish two subtypes: ratification pure and simple, and ratification with discussion. In either case, such decisions were characterized by the lack of any explicit alternative to the proposal under discussion. Whether there was ratification with or without discussion and, in particular, discussion involving more than just supervisory personnel, depended on whether the proposal related to past work or whether it concerned a future action. Where the item on the agenda was a report on some activity already in progress, such as the quarterly production report or financial statement or the report on a commission's work, acceptance with discussion occurred. The report then became an occasion for commenting on all kinds of difficulties and dissatisfactions that had arisen; all too often, however, the criticisms merely took the form of exhortations that never went beyond the declamatory stage. On the other hand, when the report was a plan for an activity Klek would undertake in the future, such as annual production targets or the investment plans, very little discussion followed, and almost without exception, supervisory personnel were the only participants.

The second broad category of issues that came before the workers' council was composed of conflicts other self-management or technical bodies had been unable to resolve. The issue at hand was usually either an individual appeal, such as apartment or credit allocations, disciplinary sanctions, or points, or a matter where two or more suggested decisions had been proposed, necessitating debate and a choice. For example, when the decline in sales forced a production cutback in 1968, four variants of the production plan came before the workers' council; the variant requiring layoffs was chosen, and a wide-ranging discussion over how to select the superfluous workers followed.

In a sense, the workers' council appears to be quite comparable with many modern legislative bodies; the tendency to have most of its proposals and decisions drawn up for it by other bodies, domination by the executive, and representatives with scant experience in many of the matters they are called on to regulate are all too familiar. At least at Klek, however, there was real representation on the workers' council, and pressure from the base called forth a response. Frequently, however, such pressure was lacking, and this led to the representatives' isolation and their acting as atomized individuals rather than as carriers of a clearly defined collective interest. Moreover, the assemblies provided a much more direct vehicle for expressing pressures from the base than did the enterprise workers' council.

The Managing Board and The Commissions

As described by workers' council minutes and back issues of the factory bulletin, the managing board's heyday at Klek was prior to 1971. At that time, it served both as a tutelary organ to the workers' council, reviewing and commenting on proposals before it, and as its executive committee, with many of the questions too cumbersome for the council to deal with referred to it for final disposition. The managing board's smaller size, more frequent meetings, higher average qualification level, and greater occupational homogeneity all made it well adapted for such a role.

In May 1971, the managing board was dissolved by the workers' council. A business board, composed of Klek executives, took its place until December 1972. When it was reestablished, the managing board never regained its former preeminence. It apparently enjoyed an initial burst of activity at the start of 1973, but once the division councils began functioning, most of the material that had previously passed through the managing board now went to the workers' council via the BOAL councils or directly from the executives and specialists.

The workers' council or the division councils rarely referred anything to the managing board. At the same time, performing the independent functions delegated to it by the 1973 self-managing agreement proved too technical and/or too ambitious for the managing board to undertake. These functions of control, review, and innovation fell to the *kolegija*, the specialist staff, or special commissions appointed by the workers' council. If the managing board's regular weekly meetings were a throwback to its activist days at Klek, the frequency with which these meetings were canceled were symptomatic of its new, very peripheral role. All that remained of its old tasks were arbitration of individual requests and approval of petty expenditures. Even here, the work load was greatly diminished by the division councils, and often it seemed almost arbitrary whether individual appeals would wind up at the managing board or at the division councils.

The standing commissions of the workers' council experienced a similar atrophy after 1972. Here again, to a certain extent, the division councils ended up handling many of the items the commissions had once dealt with, such as equipment purchases, job transfers, scholarships, and so forth. More profoundly, the decline of the commissions' importance is related to the growth of Klek's white-collar specialist staff. In this sense, the commissions' marginality parallels the managing board's experience with the *kolegija*.

For example, proposing and administering an annual plan for training personnel had once been accomplished by a Commission for Personnel Education. Once a personnel department was set up, these functions were assumed by it as part of its regular (paid) tasks, with the plan submitted directly to the workers' council. Similarly, a standing commission on equipment purchases had been very active until 1972-3. In 1974, however, the president of the commission tried to resign, noting that "the most important purchases were decided on outside the commission," and that "it is impossible that [the commission] carry the responsibility for what 'someone' does or for things done in its name." Significantly, the only standing commission still active at Klek was the Commission on Social Standards, responsible for allocating apartments and credit to members of the collective. In contrast to, say, the

Commission on Equipment Purchases, the Social Standards Commission had an essentially nontechnical, distributive task and so understandably had an important function to perform that could not be done within the organizational structure.

The special commissions of the workers' council were only the exception to prove the rule. Special commissions were set up when something urgently had to be done and the task did not fall within an existing job definition (e.g., conducting the analytical job evaluation). Thus, it could not, as with the more technically oriented standing commissions, simply be de facto transferred to the organizational structure. Typically, special commissions met intensively over relatively short periods (two or three times a week for six months to a year) rather than occasionally over a long period as did the standing commissions (maybe once every month or two for a mandate of two years). Further, special commission members received their regular salaries for the time they devoted to meetings, and if meetings were held after work, they were paid overtime. Membership on standing commissions, in contrast, was at least in theory unreimbursed, even if in practice they often met during work hours.

In general, then, as Klek's organizational structure became increasingly articulated and complex and as its technology became more complicated, a tendency for the decisions once made within the self-management structure by elected representatives to be made within the organizational structure by salaried employees was set into motion.

The Kolegija

The *kolegija* included all supervisory personnel above the foreman level as well as the crew of university-trained engineers and economists in the R & D department. It is best described as an institutionalized informal group, meeting once a week but having no legal status. Hence, it formally was not a part of the self-management structure.

The regular format of the meetings was to review one sector or department a week on a rotating basis; in this way, the executives themselves performed many of the functions of coordination and control that were formally the responsibility of the self-management organs. Should an item come up that seemed more urgently in need of discussion than the scheduled one, the standard routine was broken. Such items might include problems falling totally within the organizational structure, such as the perennial difficulties of the supply department in purchasing semifabricated steel, or proposals formulated for eventual submission to the self-management bodies, such as plans. Thus, by the time any major policy proposal came before a self-management body, it had already had an initial screening by the major managerial and technical personnel and had proved itself acceptable to them.

Basically, the *kolegija* accomplished on an informal basis, without worker participation and within the organizational structure, many of the tasks the managing board had once performed in the self-management structure. In fact, under Amendment XV to the 1963 Constitution, the *kolegija*, renamed the business board, formally replaced the managing board altogether in May 1971. The new amendments and the antitechnocracy campaign soon put an end to that, however.

Partly, the active role of the *kolegija* compared to the managing board was owing to its members' higher level of expertise. More important, however, was that the executives were responsible for a smoothly running production process as part of their regular jobs. In contrast, the elected members of the managing board had no individual authority in the organizational structure to carry out whatever decisions they might make as a collective body.

Nevertheless, the influence of the *kolegija* as a body was not felt very much at Klek. Its ability to police the performance of individual sectors was still quite limited, partly because of its informal status and partly because any one executive was reluctant to intervene too aggressively into another's department. Proposals it considered came to the self-management bodies through the individual executive or specialist who had formulated them; once the business board was eliminated, no proposal was ever accompanied by a formal recommendation from the *kolegija* as such, although support for a proposal from several executives was common. Although the influence of management at Klek was pervasive, it was not perceived as a body that met and considered various recommendations once a week, but as the set of individual executives responsible for the business operations of the firm.

BRIDGE ORGANIZATIONS BETWEEN THE ENTERPRISE AND THE COMMUNITY

Enterprise sociopolitical organizations have always been a critical supplement to legislation and the market mechanism in integrating the Yugoslav firm into the fabric of the larger society. Not only do they bring outside influences to bear in internal decision making; they also play an important role in protecting enterprise interests in political bodies external to it. In addition to the voluntary sociopolitical organizations, the 1974 Constitution created two formally elected bodies to tie enterprises more closely to wider political and administrative bodies. These were the delegations, out of which enterprise representatives to the Chamber of Associated Labor were chosen, and the self-management workers' control, a kind of ombudsman linked with the Social Accounting Service.

At Klek, the only sociopolitical organizations of any importance were the League of Communists and the trade union; a youth organization was also present but was by and large inactive. Other firms, however, not only have an active youth organization but also a women's organization as well as branches of other mass organizations.

The League of Communists

Klek's branch organization of the League of Communists had forty-eight members in June 1974, less than ten percent of the labor force. A major aspect of its activity was its role as a pressure group on Klek's behalf with outside political bodies. This activity was extremely important, varying from speeding up routine bureaucratic procedures (e.g., obtaining a building permit) to literally saving the firm's economic life by helping it obtain the price increase and loan of 1972-73.

The party's role as a pressure group on outside political bodies was also a factor conditioning its activities inside of Klek. A key task in this regard was the LCY's superintendence of the formal procedures governing the self-managment structure. It was the party organization which had initiated the establishment of the BOALs following the 1971 amendments; it was the party which had both proposed and put an end to the replacement of the managing board by the business board under Amendment XV.

The role of Klek's LCY organization as a protector of socialist legality in the firm was an important factor in maintaining its political credit with outside bodies. Nor did simple establishment (or disestablishment) of self-management bodies exhaust the party's activity in this area. At Klek, the LCY branch also felt responsible for seeing that the bodies functioned with at least a semblance of efficiency, especially when the outcomes of internal decisions affected external political agencies. For example, when the Social Standards Commission seemed unable to pull itself together to draw up regulations for allocating the apartments Klek had received from the trade union federation's Solidarity Fund, it was on party initiative that a meeting was finally called.

Nonetheless, the LCYs abiding concern with the structures and processes of self-management cannot be equated with intervention in the content of decisions. Here the influence of Klek's party organization was much weaker, for a number of reasons. First of all, the Yugoslav League of Communists has long been committed to an ideology stressing high productivity, industrialization, and "efficient" use of labor and capital. "Efficiency," however, is a product of the firm's organizational structure: how production is organized, what is manufactured, marketing techniques, and so on. Although the self-management bodies formally made the key decisions affecting these areas, at Klek—and at most other firms—management was in fact the critical influence on the decisions taken. At the same time, the party organization itself had no standards of "efficiency" distinct from those of management nor any reason to suspect that management proposals were not, in fact, the best that could be done in a given situation. Hence, at Klek, it would normally either take no position at all or operate simply as a support group for the plans submitted to the self-management bodies and as a mobilizing agent in executing the decisions taken. In such circumstances, the party's influence was necessarily more peripheral than when it initiated a proposal or carried through an action itself.

A noninterventionist stance in matters of business policy was reinforced by the party's need for political credit: it stood to reason that a party organization from a prosperous and expanding firm would be viewed much more benevolently by local officials than one from an enterprise constantly lagging behind in production and floundering about in a financial morass.

This did not mean that the party never voiced opinions or intervened at all in the content of decisions. The Klek party secretary regularly attended meetings of the self-management bodies and often participated in discussions; his suggestions, however, would be accepted or rejected on their merits. Even when his proposals were based on national party policy, (e.g., his nomination of a young machinist for president of a division council in June 1974 stemmed from the Tenth Congress's stress on involving youth and workers in self-management), this by no means guaranteed their adoption. (In this case, the machinist, a party member himself, argued against his own candidacy and voted for his opponent, who was elected.)

This brings us to a second reason for the party's lack of substantive influence: the way in which it made its positions felt. At Klek, this was done either by individual argument, as in the nomination process described above, or by "creating a climate." The latter involved putting up posters in the enterprise, writing articles in the factory bulletin, and calling meetings to explain proposed changes and to discuss their implementation. In such a way, a system of informal cues would be set up whereby everyone understood if not the need for, then the inevitability of, the change. While creating a climate was critical in enabling the Klek party to perform its role as guardian of the self-management structure and allowed it to have some marginal influence in the content of some decisions, it could only be used when the party organization as a whole was united around a certain course of action. Otherwise, only individual arguments by party leaders could be used, arguments presented in self-management bodies and frequently opposed most articulately by the rank-and-file party members themselves.

This is the third, and perhaps most significant, reason why the party's role in Klek was so much a procedural, rather than substantive one: the cleavages occurring within the work collective were simply replicated inside the party organization. Thus, the LC could act as a unified group in representing Klek's interests before external bodies and it could stand firm on internally implementing decisions and laws made by outside bodies, but when an issue polarized the collective, the party also split on it. In short, Klek's party organization often had only a peripheral influence on the actual content of decisions, because it couldn't agree itself on what those decisions should be.

The League of Communists' internal role at Klek was largely formal: it was most effective in setting up structures for self-management decision

making, exerted some pressures in seeing that decisions got made, and played
a marginal role in making and executing them. After the Tenth Congress,
however, signs of a change began to appear, although it is difficult to predict
how permanent they might be. The antitechnocracy campaign meant that,
at least to some degree, enterprise party organizations' political credit depended
on challenging management prerogatives as well as supporting "efficiency"
in the firm. The new lines laid down by Tito's Letter and confirmed at the
Congress encouraged outside bodies to put more pressure on enterprise organizations to bring society's influence into the firm, causing the latter to play
a wider and more independent role in enterprise decision making. Moreover,
the shake-ups in the firms caused by the constitutional reorganizations provided an excellent opportunity to do so. Further, the return to democratic
centralism meant that many of the positions enterprise party branches would
be taking would actually be formulated in forums outside the firm. Hence,
party action in the firms would be less subject to the divisions that occurred
when branch organizations made their own decisions. Finally, there were
hints that enterprise LC branches would be given formal authority in enterprise statutes for certain tasks, diminishing their need to rely on the voluntary
compliance of the work collectives in exerting influence.

   The cumulative effect of these changes was to encourage enterprise party
organizations to act on behalf of outside bodies independently of both
management and the general work force. At Klek, this was manifested in a
slight but perceptible estrangement between the party (especially the party
leadership) and the rest of the collective, including management. At the same
time, the locus of power in the party branch appeared to shift somewhat
from the party organization as a whole to its executive committee, the secretariat, a smaller and more cohesive body. The new role and the collective's
reaction to it were most apparent in the June 1974 elections, held on the initiative of the secretariat and without even the formal approval of some of the
self-management bodies authorized to call them.

The Trade Union

   Klek's trade union branch was largely taken up with social welfare functions
inside the enterprise, while on the outside it supplemented the party organization as a pressure group for Klek in higher political bodies. For most of the
time during which this study was conducted, Klek's trade union was dominated by a single individual, Comrade E, a skilled worker who was its president.
If such a concentration of responsibility made the union somewhat more
active than branches at other enterprises, it was also a sign of and contributing
factor to its fundamental weakness and marginality.

   Comrade E's assumption of personal responsibility for the union did mean
that at least someone was doing something, and the union—at least from
the outside—appeared to be very active. The by-product of E's activism, how-

ever, was that no one else in the firm had a clear idea of what the union was doing. Thus, anything E did not do himself simply did not get done.

E was also very active in touting Klek's cause in outside bodies, and indeed, his own political career prospects were tightly interwoven with the status of the firm. At the same time, E's activity outside the firm and control of the union inside it meant that Klek's union was going to be basically concerned with "safe" problems whose resolution would simultaneously be smiled on by outside agencies while not rocking the boat inside the enterprise. This was one cause for Klek's trade union sticking so closely to social welfare functions rather than breaking new ground in other areas, such as work discipline. Whereas nonperformance of social welfare tasks would jeopardize the standing of Klek's politicoeconomic leadership and of Comrade E himself, performance of Western-type trade union functions might well have had equally compromising effects by providing evidence to outside parties that all was not well in the firm and/or that the union was causing trouble.

The 1974 Constitution specifically assigned enterprise union branches more Western-type revendicatory functions. Not only were the unions to participate in wage determination in the industrywide self-management agreements, but they were also supposed to "present" workers' grievances to third parties to settle work disputes. At Klek, Comrade E had been present for the concluding of the self-management agreement regulating the Zagreb metalworking industry; grievances, however, were much more coherently articulated by the workers themselves than by the union or its president.

The difficulty Klek's union had in assuming such a role appears related to the more general dilemma of Yugoslav trade unions: their need to represent "society" and their membership simultaneously. This is a tension that neither the party nor the self-management bodies share; the party's genuinely voluntary recruitment policy enables it to represent "society," while the self-management bodies, as elected organs, need only be responsible to their consituency. This divided allegiance also explains why trade unions continue to find themselves in a position of high ideological status and low political significance. At the same time, their ideological legitimacy makes them attractive vehicles for those wishing to pursue a political career by doing a little routine work and attending some extra meetings. In short, the very emptiness of their form and their "captive" membership creates a standing invitation for one person or a small group to come in and supply the missing content. In this sense, Klek's one-man union organization was as much a product of the union's rather undefined function in self-managing socialism as it was due to Comrade E's particular personality.

The Political Aktiv

I was not permitted to observe *aktiv* meetings, which suggests that fairly sensitive aspects of Klek's relationship with outside bodies were discussed here

in addition to the ways in which the sociopolitical organizations related to
each other and to the rest of the work collective inside Klek.

Klek's political *aktiv* was an informally organized body to coordinate the
activities of the enterprise sociopolitical organizations. It consisted of the
leaders of both the sociopolitical and the self-management bodies, while the
fact that its meetings were held in the director's office suggests that firm
executives occasionally took part in discussions too. According to workers'
council minutes, the factory bulletin, and notices posted in the enterprise,
the *aktiv*, like the sociopolitical organizations generally, appears to have been
more of a policy-implementing than a policy-making body. It also served as
a coordinating committee to handle Klek's relations with political bodies on
the outside.

The members of the *aktiv* were all party members, and the LC was probably
its dominant element, although undoubtedly the *aktiv* was a body in which
organizational cross influences could be expressed. As Klek's political elite, it
could act quite decisively when its actions depended only on the compliance
of its own members (e.g., putting an item on the workers' council agenda,
sending a delegation to the bank for a short-term loan), but when its decisions
demanded the cooperation of a wider group of people (e.g., speeding up production to get the plan completed), its effectiveness was correspondingly
reduced. In this respect, the *aktiv* appeared no more able to enforce its own
decisions than were any of the other sociopolitical organizations.

The Delegations

The delegate system, introduced by the 1974 Constitution, was designed as
a formal link between Yugoslav work organizations and the state. Previously,
enterprises directly elected representatives to the local legislature. Under
the new system, however, each BOAL elected a delegation based on the size
of its work force; the BOAL delegations, in turn, elected enterprise representatives to the commune Council of Associated Labor.

Thus, a smaller, organized group was placed between the representative
and his larger constituency. Such a group could, theoretically, both exert more
control over the representative and mobilize the constituency around specific
issues. In a sense, the delegations were a workers' council for "sociopolitical"
issues, meeting periodically to consider questions up for debate in the local
assembly.

The Klek delegations were chosen in noncompetitive elections in March
1974. The lack of choice was no small source of complaints when members of
the collective came to cast their ballots. Nevertheless, the delegations at Klek
were quite representative in the sense of being "typical." Although their members were somewhat more active in self-management than the average member
of the work collective, they were by no means highly politicized individuals.

Indeed, the attitudes they held were so typical that the delegates could practically have been chosen at random.

Both the best and worst characteristics of the collective at large—its propensities for pluralism to the point of fragmentation, its lack of a clear sense of what could be expected from the government, its distrust of "politicians" and the low level of political efficacy, its lack of regular leadership—were mirrored in the delegations. At the same time, all shared the prevalent belief that "what's good for Klek is good for us." Significantly, their meetings continually revolved around this question, rather than around how the interests of any particular group within the firm would be affected by local legislation. In larger firms, solidarity in the delegations might well center around the BOAL rather than the enterprise. At Klek, a small firm with functionally interdependent units, this was not the case.

If Klek is typical, the delegations' commitment to the firm could potentially make them into an important source of pressure on the local government on behalf of the firm, given the proper circumstances and leadership. In this sense, the delegate system may prove an important element buttressing the bargaining power of work organizations vis-à-vis the state.

The Workers' Control

The workers' control was set up at Klek in 1973. Part of the changes aimed at strengthening internal and external controls over management, the workers' control was to be both an ombudsman and a policing agent within the firm. Not only was it to investigate complaints, but it was expected to exert an influence on both policy making and execution so that complaints did not arise in the first place. Its power stemmed more from its connection with agencies outside the enterprise, such as the public prosecutor, than from any intraenterprise base. Within the firm, it could only recommend measures to the authorized self-management bodies, but if its proposals were turned down, it could appeal to outside political and administrative bodies.

Klek's workers' control was composed of representatives elected from each BOAL: three production workers, a technician, and a white-collar worker. All were quite articulate, often critical of the way things were done at Klek, and could reasonably be expected to be in touch with dissatisfactions emanating from the rank and file.

Nevertheless, Klek's workers' control never carved out much of a role for itself. Meetings were held irregularly, and individual grievances continued to be handled directly by the division councils, the workers' council, the managing board, or even individual executives. Collective dissatisfactions were expressed either at meetings of other self-management bodies or not at all; in no case did the workers' control act as a body to voice the murmurings heard from below, even though its individual members were often the most articulate spokesmen for these complaints at other meetings.

Nor did the workers' control appear to be having much success exerting control as a representative of "social" bodies outside the firm. Its membership was no less prone than was the general work force and management to keeping problems within the firm and presenting a united front to the outside. In this sense, Klek's workers' control appeared to be a good example of what, in effect, is the practical impossibility of exerting social control on an enterprise through a body set up, elected from, and functioning within the firm.

Notes

INTRODUCTION

1. See Dino Angelo, "Techniciens et ouvriers à l'usine," *Les temps modernes* 29 (September–October 1972): 489–523; Michael Best and William Connolly, *The Politicized Economy* (Boston: D. C. Heath, 1976); Charles Bettelheim and Paul Sweezy, *On the Transition to Socialism* (New York: Monthly Review Press, 1971); Dennis Butt, "Workers' Control," *New Left Review*, no. 10 (July–August 1961): 24–34; Ken Coates and Tony Topham, *The New Unionism* (Middlesex, England: Penguin Books, 1972); André Gorz, *Strategy for Labor*, trans. Martin Nicolaus and Victoria Ortiz (Boston: Beacon Press, 1967); Lars E. Karlsson, "Industrial Democracy in Sweden," in *Workers' Control*, ed. Gerry Hunnius, G. David Garson, and John Case (New York: Random House, 1973), pp, 176–94; Ernest Mandel, "Yugoslav Economic Theory," *Monthly Review* 18 (April 1967): 40–49; M. Marković, "Basic Issues of Self-Management," paper presented at Korčula Summer School, August 1973, mimeographed; Helmut Schauer, "Critique of Co-Determination," in *Workers' Control*, ed. Hunnius et al., pp. 194–210; Albert Meister, *Où va l'autogestion jougoslave?* (Paris: Editions Anthropos, 1970); Paul Sweezy and Leo Huberman, "Peaceful Transition from Socialism to Capitalism?" *Monthly Review* 14 (March 1964): 569–89; Sharon Zukin, *Between Marx and Tito* (New York: Cambridge University Press, 1975).

Not all of these writers treat Yugoslavia specifically, nor are they in agreement on the scope or kind of planning they see as desirable. All, however, see socialism and workers' control as excluding competition, profitmaking, and "commodity" production, while including plant-level workers' councils.

2. See Daniel Bell, "Work, Alienation and Social Control," in *The Radical Papers*, ed. Irving Howe (New York: Doubleday/Anchor, 1963), pp. 89–101; John Case, "Vision of a New Social Order," in *The Nation*, 14 February 1972, pp. 200–206; Roger Garaudy, *The Crisis in Communism*, trans. Peter and Betty Ross (New York: Grove Press, 1970); R. Harrison, "Retreat from Industrial Democracy," *New Left Review*, no. 10 (July–August 1961): 32–38; Branko Horvat, *An Essay on Yugoslav Society* (White Plains, N.Y.: International Arts and Sciences Press, 1969); David Jenkins, *Job Power* (Baltimore: Penguin Books, 1973); R. Selucky, "Marxism and Self-Management," in *Self-Management*, ed. Jaroslav Vanek (Baltimore: Penguin Books, 1975), pp. 47–62; Mario Soares, talk given before the Department of Political Science, Yale University, January 1976; Svetozar Stojanović, *Between Ideals and Reality* (Boston: Beacon Press, 1972); Rudi Supek, "Some Contradictions and Insufficiencies of Self-Managing Socialism," *Praxis* 3/4 (Spring 1971): 375–99; and Jaroslav Vanek, *The Participatory Economy* (Ithaca, N.Y.: Cornell University Press, 1971).

Again, not all of these theorists explicitly treat Yugoslavia, and there is a wide range of opinion as to how "free" a market should be. All, however, stress the autonomy of the individual firm in conducting its own business policy and conceive of socialism and workers' control as compatible with a competitive price mechanism.

3. See Paul Blumberg, *Industrial Democracy* (London: Constable, 1968); M. Barratt Brown, "Yugoslavia Revisited," *New Left Review*, no. 1 (January–February 1960): 39–43; idem, "Workers' Control in a Planned Economy," *New Left Review*, no. 2 (March–April 1960): 28–31; Gerry Hunnius, "Workers' Self-Management in Yugoslavia," in *Workers' Control*, ed. Hunnius et al., pp. 268–325; Carole Pateman, *Participation and Democratic Theory* (Cambridge: Cambridge University Press, 1970); Fred Singleton and Tony Topham, "Yugoslav Workers' Control: The Latest Phase," *New Left Review*, no. 18 (January 1964): 73–86; David Tornquist, *Look East, Look West* (New York: Macmillan, 1966); and Bogdan Denitch, *Legitimation of a Revolution* (New Haven: Yale University Press, 1976).

4. All translations from the original Italian, French, and Serbo-Croatian are my own, except where specifically noted.

CHAPTER 1

1. Antonio Gramsci, "Il Consiglio di fabbrica," in *Scritti politici*, ed. Paolo Spriano (Rome: Editoria Riuniti, 1969), p. 336. (Hereafter cited as *SP*.)

2. "Il programma dell' 'Ordine Nuovo,'" *SP*, p. 355.

3. "Sindacalismo e consigli," *SP*, p. 261.

4. "Sindacati e Consigli," *SP*, p. 340.

5. "L'operaio di fabbrica," *SP*, p. 303.

6. "Il Consiglio di fabbrica," *SP*, p. 336.

7. "Sindacati e Consigli," *SP*, pp. 248–49.

8. "La Conquista dello Stato," *SP*, p. 222.

9. "Sindacati e Consigli," *SP*, p. 340.

10. "La crisi italiana," *SP*, p. 582.

11. "Sindacati e Consigli," *SP*, p. 340.

12. "Sindacati e Consigli," *SP*, p. 250.

13. Ibid., p. 249.

14. "Sindacati e Consigli," *SP*, p. 340.

15. Except, presumably, those who are elderly, incapacitated, below working age, and so forth.

16. "Il programma dell' 'Ordine Nuovo,'" *SP*, p. 354.

17. "Sindacati e Consigli," *SP*, p. 248.

18. "Democrazia operaia," *SP*, p. 208.

19. "Il programma dell' 'Ordine Nuovo,'" *SP*, p. 355.

20. "Socialisti e anarchisti," *SP*, p. 239.

21. "La conquista dello Stato," *SP*, p. 222; "Individualismo e collettivismo," *SP*, p. 110.

22. "L'operaio de fabbrica," *SP*, p. 303. See also John Cammett, *Antonio Gramsci and the Origins of Italian Communism* (Stanford: Stanford University Press, 1967), p. 78.

23. Antonio Gramsci, *The Modern Prince and Other Writings*, ed. and trans.

Louis Marks (New York: International Publishers, 1957), p. 170. On "hegemony," see Luciano Gruppi, "Introduzione," to *Quaderni del carcere*, by Antonio Gramsci, 6 vols. (Rome: Editori Riuniti, 1971), 1:xxix-xxx.

24. Branko Horvat, *An Essay on Yugoslav Society* (White Plains, N.Y.: International Arts and Sciences Press, 1969), pp. 131-32.

25. "Partito di governo e classe di governo," *SP*, p. 310.

26. "Il Consiglio de fabbrica," *SP*, p. 337.

27. "Il problema del potere," *SP*, 277; and "Il Partito e la rivoluzione," *SP*, p. 294.

28. Gramsci, *The Modern Prince*, pp. 178-79. See also Cammett, *Antonio Gramsci*, p. 86.

29. Gramsci, *The Modern Prince*, p. 178.

30. On these problems and others, see Robert Dahl and C. E. Lindblom, *Politics, Economics and Welfare* (New York: Harper and Row, 1953), pp. 372-85.

31. "Sindacati e Consigli," *SP*, p. 340.

CHAPTER 2

1. See Pierre-Joseph Proudhon, *Oeuvres Choisies*, ed. J. Bancal (Paris: Gallimard, 1967), p. 216. (Hereafter cited as *OC*.)

2. See Proudhon, quoted in James Joll, *The Anarchists* (New York: Grosset and Dunlop, 1966), p. 71.

3. Pierre-Joseph Proudhon, *De la capacité politique des classes ouvrières* (Paris: Librairie des Sciences Politiques et Sociales, 1924), pp. 94-95; 187-88. (Hereafter cited as *CP*.)

4. Pierre Joseph Proudhon, *Selected Works*, trans. and ed. S. Edwards (New York: Doubleday/Anchor, 1969), p. 71 and p. 150. (Hereafter cited as *SW*.)

5. *CP*, pp. 121-26 passim; *SW*, pp. 180-81.

6. *OC*, pp. 110-13; *CP*, p. 132.

7. Hence, Proudhon's famous Credit Bank of 1849. See Joll, *The Anarchists*, p. 65.

8. *SW*, p. 97.

9. Ibid., p. 47.

10. Ibid., p. 83.

11. Ibid., p. 180.

12. *OC*, p. 71.

13. *CP*, pp. 122-23.

14. Ibid., pp. 124-25.

15. Ibid., p. 155.

16. Ibid., p. 152.

17. Ibid., p. 155.

18. *OC*, p. 60; *SW*, p. 71.

19. *CP*, p. 121.

20. *OC*, p. 175.

21. *SW*, p. 98.

22. *OC*, pp. 165 and 175.

23. *CP*, p. 125.
24. *OC*, p. 180.
25. *SW*, p. 97.
26. *OC*, p. 176.
27. Ibid., p. 200.
28. Ibid., p. 197.
29. Ibid.
30. *SW*, p. 136.
31. Ibid., p. 127.
32. Ibid., p. 136.
33. Ibid., p. 137.
34. *CP*, p. 124.
35. *SW*, p. 70.
36. *OC*, p. 190.
37. *SW*, p. 133.
38. Ibid., p. 91.
39. Although there is no absolute prohibition on wage labor, for purposes of simplicity, let us assume at the outset that no one in mutualist society works for a wage; all are self-employed, either collectively or individually. To make Proudhon's case stronger, let us also assume that wage labor never becomes a predominant form of employment in mutualist society.

CHAPTER 3

1. A. Ross Johnson, *The Transformation of Communist Ideology* (Cambridge: M.I.T. Press, 1972), p. 161. See also Zagorka Pešić-Golubović, "Socialist Ideals and Reality," *Praxis* 3/4 (Spring 1971): 402; and Sharon Zukin, *Between Marx and Tito* (New York: Cambridge University Press, 1975), p. 21.

2. Edvard Kardelj, quoted in Johnson, *Communist Ideology*, p. 107. See also Josip Broz Tito, "Factories to the Workers," 1950 speech, reprinted in *Socialist Thought and Practice* 15 (June 1975): 13-14; Milovan Djilas, *The Unperfect Society: Beyond the New Class* (New York: Harcourt, Brace and World, 1969), pp. 220-21.

3. Many observers share this evaluation of Yugoslav central planning. See Johnson, *Communist Ideology*, p. 30; Albert Waterston, *Planning in Yugoslavia* (Charlottesville: University of Virginia Press, 1964), p. 16; George Macesich, *Yugoslavia: The Theory and Practice of Development Planning* (Charlottesville: University of Virginia Press, 1964), chapter 5; and Rudolf Bićanić, "Economic Growth under Centralized and Decentralized Planning: Jugoslavia—A Case Study," *Economic Development and Cultural Change* 6 (October 1957): 66.

For more benign views of the First Five Year Plan, see Deborah Milenkovitch, *Plan and Market in Yugoslav Economic Thought* (New Haven: Yale University Press, 1971), pp. 68-77; Thomas Marschak, "Centralized versus Decentralized Resource Allocation: The Yugoslav Laboratory," *Quarterly Journal of Economics* 82 (November 1968): 561-87.

4. Egon Neuberger, "Comment," to R. Bićanić, "Interaction of Macro- and Micro-Economic Decisions in Yugoslavia, 1954-1957," in *Value and Plan*, ed. Gregory Grossman (Berkeley: University of California Press, 1960), p. 358. For a more detailed treatment of specific deductions and controls, see the main article by Bićanić.

5. Ichak Adizes, *Industrial Democracy: Yugoslav Style* (New York: Free Press, 1971), p. 20.

6. For more detailed accounts of Yugoslav planning, see Bićanić, "Macro- and Micro-Economic Decisions," pp. 346-61; Milenkovitch, *Plan and Market*, pp. 77-121; Macesich, *Development Planning*; Waterston, *Planning in Yugoslavia*; Branko Horvat, *Privredni sistem i ekonomskih politika Jugoslavije* (Belgrade: Institut Ekonomskih Nauka, 1970), pp. 9-30; Svetozar Pejovich, *The Market-Planned Economy of Yugoslavia* (Minneapolis: University of Minnesota Press, 1966); and R. Stojanović, ed., *Yugoslav Economists on the Problems of a Planned Economy* (White Plains, N.Y.: International Arts and Sciences Press, 1964). For more political accounts, see Richard Lowenthal, "Development vs. Utopia in Communist Policy," in *Change in Communist Systems* (Palo Alto: Stanford University Press, 1970), pp. 68-85; Michael Barrett Brown, "Yugoslavia Revisited," *New Left Review*, no. 1 (January– February 1960): 39-43; idem, "Workers' Control in a Planned Economy," *New Left Review*, no. 2 (March-April 1960): 28-31; and Dennison Rusinow, *The Yugoslav Experiment* (Berkeley: University of California Press, 1977), pp. 47-70.

7. Milenkovitch, *Plan and Market*, p. 102.

8. Waterston, *Planning in Yugoslavia*, p. 10.

9. Rudolf Bićanić, "The Economics of Socialism in a Developed Country," in *Comparative Economic Systems*, ed. Morris Bornstein (Homewood, Ill.: Richard D. Irwin, 1969), p. 227. See also Horvat, *Privredni sistem*, pp. 83-86.

10. Waterston, *Planning in Yugoslavia*, p. 79.

11. Adizes, *Industrial Democracy*, p. 22.

12. My account of local government under the 1953 Constitution is drawn from the collection of essays in "The Yugoslav Commune," *International Social Science Journal* 63 (1961); Waterston, *Planning in Yugoslavia*; G. Hoffman and F. Neal, *Yugoslavia and the New Communism* (New York: Twentieth Century Fund, 1962); F. W. Neal, *Titoism in Action* (Berkeley: University of California Press, 1956); Albert Meister, *Socialisme et autogestion* (Paris: Editions du Seuil, 1964); Radivoje Marinković, *Ko odlučuje u komuni* (Belgrade: Institut za društvenih nauka, 1971); Brown, "Yugoslavia Revisited," pp. 39– 43; idem, "Workers' Control," pp. 28-31; as well as the worked cited in n. 6.

13. That is, depending on the priorities of the national plan, federal funds were more readily available for some purposes than for others. At the same time, enterprise profits formed the local tax base for commune budgets. See J. Đorđević and N. Pašić, "The Communal Self-Government System in Yugoslavia," *International Social Science Journal*, pp. 389-408. Note that both the allocation of investment and federal funds for commune development were

governed by multiple and qualitatively different criteria, allowing a good deal of space for local political maneuvering and regional pressures.

14. J. Đorđević, *Socijalizam i demokratija* (Belgrade: Savremena administracija, 1962), p. 237.

15. The Council of Producers was elected solely by employees of enterprises and cooperatives. Representation was based on a firm's "contribution to the social product." The system thus worked to overrepresent some groups at the expense of others: the "socialized" sector over private peasants and artisans, industry over agriculture, large industry over small, employed over unemployed. Since the assent of the Council of Producers was required to adopt all "social plans," such staggered representation helped guarantee industry a preeminent position in the macroeconomic allocation of resources, even though a simple majority of the population was engaged in agriculture.

Nevertheless, the Council of Producers never became a very strong chamber of the legislature at any level of government. See Neal, *Titoism*, pp. 97-98; Speeches of Đuro Salaj and Hasan Brkić to the 1957 Workers' Council Congress in *Kongres radničkih saveta Jugoslavije*, ed. A. DeLeon and L. Mijatović (Belgrade: Rad, 1957), pp. 38 and 165-66. Cf. also the study of five Croatian communes summarized in "Zbornik radova Institut za društveno upravljanje u Zagrebu," *Sociologija* 1 (February–March 1959): 150-54.

16. See Đuro Salaj, "Dosadašnja iskustva i dalji razvoj radničkog samoupravljanja u Jugoslaviji," *Kongres radničkih saveta*, ed. De Leon and Mitjatović, p. 51; Juraj Hrženjak, "Neko problemi radičkog samoupravljanja," *Ekonomski pregled* 8, no. 5 (1957): 311-18.

17. A trade union delegate to the Workers' Council Congress observed, "Today it is not so rare to encounter the opinion that every interest of an economic organization is simultaneously the interest of the social community. They are identified in price increases, eliminating competition, and so forth." In *Kongres radničkih saveta*, ed. DeLeon and Mijatović, p. 181.

18. See complaints voiced in *Kongres radničkih saveta*, ed. DeLeon and Mijatović, p. 217; Hrženjak, "Neki problemi," p. 314. Cf. Meister, *Socialisme et autogestion*, p. 67; Lowenthal, "Development vs. Utopia," p. 67.

19. Howard Wachtel, *Workers' Management and Workers' Wages in Yugoslavia* (Ithaca, N.Y.: Cornell University Press, 1973), p. 103.

20. Peter Wiles, *The Political Economy of Communism* (Oxford: Basil Blackwell, 1962), pp. 134-35.

21. Ibid., p. 138.

22. See Meister, *Socialisme et autogestion*, p. 42; Horvat, *Privredni sistem*, p. 93.

23. Paul Shoup, *Communism and the Yugoslav National Question* (New York: Columbia University Press, 1968), p. 242. See also Tito's statement in *Kongres radničkih saveta*, ed. DeLeon and Mijatović, p. 13.

24. Shoup, *National Question*, p. 242.

25. Salaj, "Dosadašnja iskustva," p. 51.

26. See Dušan Đerić, "Delatnost komunista u integrisanim radnim organizacijama," *Socijalizam* 7 (June 1964): 838-49.

27. Lowenthal, "Development vs. Utopia," p. 68.

28. V. Bakarić, quoted in Shoup, *National Question*, p. 244.

29. Antun Vratusa, "Introduction," *International Social Science Journal*, p. 370. See also *Yugoslavia's Way: The Program of the Yugoslav League of Communists*, trans. Branko Pribičević (New York: Simon and Schuster, 1958).

30. Adizes, *Industrial Democracy*, p. 21.

31. Meister, *Socialisme et autogestion*, p. 300.

32. Resolution cited by Johnson, *Communist Ideology*, p. 203. On institutional changes made at the Sixth Congress, see Rusinow, *Yugoslav Experiment*, pp. 74-76; Bogdan Denitch, *Legitimation of a Revolution* (New Haven: Yale University Press, 1976), p. 103.

33. Josip Tito, Speech to the members of the First Proletarian Division, in *Savez komunista u uslovima samoupravljanja*, ed. Miloš Nikolić (Belgrade: Kultura, 1967), p. 21.

34. Waterston, *Planning in Yugoslavia*, p. 84; Meister, *Socialisme et autogestion*, p. 82.

35. Meister, *Socialisme et autogestion*, p. 32.

36. See Johnson, *Communist Ideology*, p. 210; Rusinow, *Yugoslav Experiment*, pp. 95-96.

37. Johnson, *Communist Ideology*, p. 3. See ibid. p. 212 for details on continued use of "the old methods of direct control."

38. Meister, *Socialisme et autogestion*, p. 83.

39. Josip Tito, Speech to the Seventh Congress of the Yugoslav League of Communists, *Savez komunista*, ed. Nikolić, p. 125.

40. See Shoup, *National Question*, p. 189; Rusinow, *Yugoslav Experiment*, p. 162.

41. See Tito, "Factories to the Workers," p. 13; idem, "Statement" in *Kongres radničkih saveta*, ed. DeLeon and Mijatović, p. 13; and Salaj, "Dosadašnja iskustva," *Kongres radničkih saveta*, ed. DeLeon and Mijatović, p. 36.

42. See Ašer DeLeon, *The Yugoslav Worker* (Belgrade: Yugoslav Trade Unions, 1962), p. 18.

43. See V. Hadžištević, H. Kratina, and F. Đžinić, *Tendencije i praksa neposrednog upravljanja radnika u ekonomskim jedinicama* (Belgrade: Institut za društvenih nauka, 1964), p. 93; J. Brekić, "Pokretljivost u organima radničkog samoupravljanja," *Sociologija* 3 (January 1961): 61-70; Benjamin Ward, "Workers' Management in Yugoslavia," *Journal of Political Economy* 65 (October 1957): 373-85; Jiri Kolaja, "A Yugoslav Workers' Council," *Human Organization* 1 (1961): 27-31; idem, *Workers' Councils: The Yugoslav Experience* (London: Tavistock, 1965); Meister, *Socialisme et autogestion*, p. 103.

44. See Nikolić, ed., *Savez komunista*, p. 777.

45. See above and sources cited in n. 34. If party members rarely had a majority on workers' councils, they were nonetheless overrepresented in view of their proportion (10 percent) of the labor force. See also Kolaja, *Workers' Councils*, p. 21.

J. Brekić, in a study of five Croatian firms, concludes, "The frequency of election [to self-management bodies] is proportional with the level of qualifications a self-manager has." Party membership, he found, also correlated positively with election to self-management bodies. Further, he adds, "There is a significant proportion of self-managers who have been elected five, six, and seven times to the workers' council. In the majority of cases these are supervisors." In "Pokretljivost radničkog samoupravljanja," p. 67. Parenthetically, my own field research suggests that these "supervisors" were not high-level executives, but low-level managerial personnel (foremen, department heads) who were in daily contact with the workers they represented.

46. Salaj, "Dosadašnja iskustva," p. 46. See also Kardelj's statement to this effect, quoted in Johnson, *Communist Ideology*, p. 153.

47. Joel Dirlam and James L. Plummer, *An Introduction to the Yugoslav Economy* (Columbus, Ohio: Merrill Publishing, 1973), p. 158. Figures taken from ibid., p. 144 and Macesich, *Development Planning*, p. 21.

48. Data from George Macesich, "Major Trends in the Postwar Economy," in *Contemporary Yugoslavia*, ed. W. Vucinich (Berkeley: University of California Press, 1969), p. 209; and Dirlam and Plummer, *Yugoslav Economy*, pp. 128 and 159.

49. Yet other factors are enumerated by Egon Neuberger in "The Visible Hand: Why Is It No More?" International Development Research Center Working Paper, Indiana University, 1971.

50. See Salaj, "Došadasnja iskustva," p. 36; Tito, "Statement" in *Kongres radničkih saveta*, ed. DeLeon and Mijatović, p. 18; and Vladimir Bakarić, "Prednacrt ustava i raspodjela," *Naše teme* 7 (March 1963): 163–210.

51. DeLeon points out, "The very fact that the handing over of the net income to the working collective for its free disposal has not been unfavourably reflected on the formation of funds, as in 1959 the working collectives handled 780,000 million dinars of the net income, increased their funds by 27% (in relation to the previous year), despite the fact that they could spend the money freely and even allocate the whole amount to personal incomes—is a very significant proof of the consciousness and maturity of the production collectives" (DeLeon, *The Yugoslav Worker*, p. 27).
Unions, 1962], p. 27).

52. Cited by ibid., p. 72.

53. Wachtel, *Workers' Management and Workers' Wages*, p. 130. The data in table 3 supports this statement to some extent.

54. Ibid., p. 132.

55. Neal, *Titoism*, p. 142.

56. Živan Tanić, "Neke tendencije u dosadašnjem radu radničkih saveta," *Sociologija* 2 (February 1961): 101–12.

57. Meister, *Socialisme et autogestion*, p. 89.

58. Tanić, "Neke tendencije radničkih saveta," pp. 108–9. See also Adolf Sturmthal, *Workers' Councils* (Cambridge, Mass.: Harvard University Press, 1964), p. 108; Slavko Luković, "Ekonomsko poslovanje radničkih saveta," in *Kongres radničkih saveta*, ed. DeLeon and Mijatović, pp. 265–66.

59. See D. Mišić, *Ekonomika industrije Jugoslavije* (Belgrade: Savremena administracija, 1962), p. 181; Meister, *Socialisme et autogestion*, pp. 82 and 88. Brekić found labor mobility of workers' council members to be equal or higher than that of nonparticipants ("Pokretljivost radničkog samoupravljanja," pp. 68–69). Cf. Also Kolaja, *Workers' Councils*, p. 63. On court suits, see Zdravko Mlinar, "Društvene vrednosti, razvoj i konflikti," *Sociologija* 13 (March 1971): 379–95.

60. See J. Sinadinowski, "Prvi pokušaji empirijskih istraživanja radničkog samoupravljanje," *Sociologija* 1 (January 1959): 146; Kolaja, *Workers' Councils*, pp. 57–60; Hadžištević et al., *Tendencije i praksa neposrednog upravljanja*, p. 100; DeLeon, *Yugoslav Worker*, p. 45; Ward, "Workers' Management," pp. 377–78; G. Bosanac, M. Poček, and S. Matić, "Informiranost u radnom kolektivu," *Naše teme* 5 (December 1961); and D. Drašković, "Društveno-politički svest radnika," *Sociologija* 4 (March–April 1962): 65.

61. R. Bićanić, "Tipovi mješovite seljačko-radničke obitelji s obzirom na raspodjelu dohotka," *Sociologija* 1 (January 1959): 110–20. Bićanić also supplies data to suggest that there may even have been an incentive for peasant workers to retain their ties to agriculture, despite the inconveniences of commuting and the headaches it produced for the enterprises. That is, as a group, rural households with one or more members employed in industry were able to save far more than were households whose members were employed exclusively in agriculture or industry.

62. C. Kostić, "Peasant Industrial Workers in Yugoslavia," *Man in India* 39 (September 1959): 221–34.

63. "Bureaucratism" covered a variety of phenomena, from delegates distancing themselves from the rank and file to voting themselves special privileges to meeting during work hours. See Salaj, "Došadasnja iskustva," pp. 47–48; DeLeon, *Yugoslav Worker*, p. 19.

64. See Luković, "Ekonomsko poslovanje," p. 263.

65. As late as 1962, only 29.5 percent of enterprise directors had a postsecondary school education, and only 27.3 percent had even completed secondary school. S. J. Rawin, "Social Values and the Managerial Structure: The Case of Yugoslavia and Poland," *Journal of Comparative Administration* 2 (August 1970): 140. See also Slobodan Bosnić, "Profesionalna struktura i pokretljivost," in *Socijalna struktura i pokretljivost radničke klase Jugoslavije*, ed. M. Ilić (Belgrade: Institut za društvenih nauka, 1963), pp. 397–406; Lowenthal, "Development vs. Utopia," p. 72.

66. Sinadinowski cites a survey that stated that 55 percent of the workers interviewed felt that their supervisors "do not tolerate objections and get angry when criticized." See Sinadinowski, "Prvi pokušaji," p. 150. Hadžištević et al. also found that a third of the workers who did not make suggestions at meetings of their economic unit attributed their nonparticipation to fear of their supervisors (*Tendencije i praksa neposrednog upravljanja*, p. 222). On the bypassing of workers' councils, see "Discussion" of the Second Commission in *Kongres radničkih saveta*, ed. DeLeon and Mijatović, pp. 170–251.

67. M. Ilić, "Radnička klasa Jugoslavije i globalno jugoslovensko društvo," in *Socijalna struktura i pokretljivost*, ed. Ilić, p. 100.

68. Meister, *Socialisme et autogestion*, p. 56; Kolaja, "A Yugoslav Workers' Council," p. 29. Kolaja also received a surprisingly high number of positive responses to his query "How many employees feel that the factory is theirs?" Two-thirds of the respondents answered, "All or many," although this figure dropped to one-half among unskilled respondents. This is nonetheless a respectable showing, especially since legally the factory was not theirs at all. See also Sinadinowski, "Prvi pokušaji," p. 150; DeLeon, *Yugoslav Worker*, pp. 60-70; and Ilić, "Radnička klasa," p. 100.

69. Meister, *Socialisme et autogestion*, p. 74.

70. DeLeon, *Yugoslav Worker*, p. 27. See also R. Radosavljević, "Radnici o nekim pitanjima raspodele čistog prihoda i ličnog dohotka," *Sociologija* 3 (January 1961): 70-79.

71. Meister, *Socialisme et autogestion*, p. 99.

72. See Kolaja, "A Yugoslav Workers' Council," pp. 27-31; Hadžištević et al., *Tendencije i praksa neposrednog upravljanja*, pp. 207-69; DeLeon, *Yugoslav Worker*, p. 72; Brown, "Yugoslavia Revisited," pp. 39-45; idem, "Workers' Control in a Planned Economy," pp. 28-31; and N. Loucks, "Workers' Self-Government in Yugoslav Industry," *World Politics* 11 (January 1958): 68-82.

73. Sinadinowski, "Prvi pokušaji," p. 45.

74. Rawin, "Social Values and Managerial Structure," p. 149.

75. Meister, *Socialisme et autogestion*, p. 70; David Tornquist, *Look East, Look West* (New York: Macmillan, 1966), p. 122.

76. Adizes, *Industrial Democracy*, p. 214.

77. See Pejovich, *Market-Planned Economy*, p. 91.

78. Radosavljević's study reveals that both members of workers' councils and nonmembers gave wages a high priority in the allocation of enterprise income, and nonmembers ranked investment almost as high as council members did. Workers' council and managing board members were slightly (but only slightly!) more prone to justify taxes paid to the commune and slightly (again, only slightly) more satisfied with salary scales. When respondents were asked to make up their own wage scales, *all* raised wages for *all* skill categories. The picture one gets is that members of self-managing bodies were subject to the same wage pressures as the mass of nonmembers but were somewhat more willing to be "patient" and "responsible." See Radosavljević, "Radnici o nekim pitanjima," pp. 70-79. On equality, Hadžištević et al. found employees and workers in the highest skill brackets *more* prone to feel that income differentials were too large than were unskilled workers (*Tendencije i praksa neposrednog upravljanja*, p. 204).

79. See table supplied by DeLeon, *Yugoslav Worker*, p. 9

80. Cultural and social services and government administration (including banking and commerce) are considered "noneconomic" activities in Yugoslavia.

81. This demand emerges clearly from the discussion at the 1957 Workers'

Council Congress. See DeLeon and Mijatović, eds., *Kongres radničkih saveta*. The results from a content analysis of some of these discussions is presented in appendix A.

82. When they did confront each other—as at the 1957 Workers' Council Congress—it was clear that there was disagreement aplenty. The many complaints on the "discriminatory" effects of laws, credit policies, and taxation (appendix A) are testimony to this. Newer enterprises complained that the amortization regulations placed an unfair burden on them as opposed to firms with older machinery; plants with unused capacity or seasonal overloads complained that the capital tax discriminated against them (as compared with firms who utilized their capacity); and so on. See DeLeon and Mijatović, eds., *Kongres radničkih saveta*.

83. Boris Krajger, quoted in Milenkovitch, *Plan and Market*, pp. 173-74.

84. In fact, Dennison Rusinow suggests that the support of enterprises in the less developed areas for a price system that did not hold the costs of the raw materials they produced artifically low was a key factor in bringing political leaders in these areas to the side of the 1965 reform (*Yugoslav Experiment*, p. 109).

85. See Đura Šušnjić, "Neki rezultati analize sadržaja dnevnog lista *Borba*," *Sociologija* 3 (January 1961). Rusinow gives a particularly good account of the role of the trade unions in this debate (*Yugoslav Experiment*, pp. 114-17).

86. See appendix A; see also Neuberger, "Visible Hand," pp. 9-10 and 33.

87. See Tito's 1961 speech in Skopje, quoted in Macesich, *Development Planning*, p. 80. See also his various addresses on the occasion of and immediately following the Eighth Congress, in *Savez komunista*, ed. Nikolić, pp. 124-28.

88. See "Discussions" in *Kongres radničkih saveta*, ed. DeLeon and Mijatović. See also appendix A.

89. See Shoup, *National Question*, pp. 228-46; Milenkovitch, *Plan and Market*, pp. 175-78; Rusinow, *Yugoslav Experiment*, pp. 130-37.

90. Milenkovitch, *Plan and Market*, pp. 179-80.

91. See Rawin, "Social Values and Managerial Structure," p. 157; Pejovich, *Market-Planned Economy*, p. 92.

92. Shoup, *National Question*, p. 209.

93. Ibid., p. 244.

94. See Rusinow, *Yugoslav Experiment*, pp. 130-38.

95. See Vladimir Bakarić, "Savez komunista danas," *Naše teme* 8 (August 1966): 1395-1420; Ante Fiamengo, "Savez komunista u preovladavanju birokratizma," *Naše teme* 8 (December 1966): 2054-58.

CHAPTER 4

1. Paul Sweezy, "The Yugoslav Experiment," *Monthly Review* 10 (April 1958): 362-74; and Paul Sweezy and Leo Huberman, "Peaceful Transition from Socialism to Capitalism?" *Monthly Review* 14 (March 1964); 569-89.

2. My account of the 1965 reforms is drawn from Deborah Milenkovitch,

Plan and Market in Yugoslav Economic Thought (New Haven: Yale University Press, 1971), pp. 175–78; Branko Horvat, *An Essay on Yugoslav Society* (White Plains, N.Y.: International Arts and Sciences Press, 1969), pp. 79–122; Rudolf Bićanić, "Economics of Socialism in a Developed Country," in *Comparative Economic Systems*, 2nd ed., ed. M. Bornstein (Homewood, Ill.: Richard D. Irwin, 1969), pp. 222–35; D. Gorupić, "Trends in the Development of Workers' Self-Management in Yugoslavia," *Eastern European Economics* 8 (Winter 1969–70): 101–82; V. Rajković, "An Appraisal of the Economic Reforms and Current Problems," *Eastern European Economics* 8 (Winter 1969–70): 307–56; Ichak Adizes, *Industrial Democracy: Yugoslav Style* (New York: Free Press, 1971), pp. 5–35; Dušan Bilandić, "Nova ekonomska struktura i njene implikacije za prirodu političkih odnosa i procesa u našem društvu," *Naše teme* 9 (August 1966): 1420–60.

3. In practice, it appears that the actual percentage of net income firms paid to the government was somewhat higher after various contributions and the capital tax were deducted. See Joel Dirlam and James Plummer, *An Introduction to the Yugoslav Economy* (Columbus, Ohio: Merrill Publishing, 1973), p. 161.

4. Ivan Maksimović, "The Economic System and Workers' Self-Management," in *Yugoslav Workers' Self-Management*, ed. M. J. Broekmeyer (Dordrecht, Holland: D. Reidel, 1970), p. 140.

5. See Ustav SFRJ (1963), ch. 3, Introduction; Neca Jovanov, "Definition théorique de la notion et l'essence de l'autogestion en Yugoslavie," *First International Conference on Participation and Self-Management*, 6 vols. (Zagreb: Institute for Social Research, 1972–73), 1: 12.

6. See Horvat, *Essay*, p. 100. See also Egon Neuberger and Estelle James, "The Yugoslav Self-Managed Enterprise: A Systemic Approach," in *Plan and Market: Economic Reform in Eastern Europe*, M. Bornstein, ed. (New Haven: Yale University Press, 1973), p. 257.

7. Josip Županov, *Samoupravljanje i društvena moć* (Zagreb: Naše teme, 1969), p. 13. On collective enterpreneurship, see also Horvat, *Essay*, pp. 97–100; D. Pribičević, "Raspodjela, dohodak, i model socijalističke privrede," *Naše teme* 12 (August 1968): 1081–91; V. Bakarić, "Prednacrt ustava i raspodjela," *Naše teme* 7 (March 1963): 209; Mladen Zvonarević, "Socijalna moć, informiranost, i motivacija u procesu samoupravljanja," *Naše teme* 13 (June 1969): 896–921; Neuberger and James, "Yugoslav Enterprise," pp. 259–64.

8. Jože Goričar, "Workers' Self-Management: Ideal Type–Social Reality," *First International Conference on Participation* 1: 18. On solidarity, see Dušan Bilandić, "Naš društveni razvitak i uloga Savez komunista," *Naše teme* 11 (January 1967): 23.

9. See Benjamin Ward, "The Firm in Illyria: Market Syndicalism," *American Economic Review* 48 (September 1958): 566–89; E. Domar, "On Collective Farms and Producer Co-operatives," *American Economic Review* 56 (September 1966): 734–57; *Teoria dell' impresa jugoslava autogestita e implicazioni macroeconomiche*, "Prospettive Economiche" series, vol. 4

(Trieste, Italy: Istituto di Studi e Documentazione sull 'Est Europeo, 1974). In theory, producer coops should have less labor turnover and be more capital intensive than a capitalist equivalent. In the long run, "only the rapid entry of new firms can offset the impediments to efficiency" (Milenkovitch, *Plan and Market*, p. 213).

10. Milenkovitch, *Plan and Market*, p. 177. While banks also had workers' councils, the councils functioned "merely to bargain for workers' interests with management; they [did] not participate to any significant degree in managerial decisions relating to banking matters" (Dirlam and Plummer, *Yugoslav Economy*, p. 179).

11. See Branko Horvat, "Short Run Economic Instability and Long Run Trends in the Yugoslav Economy's Development," *Eastern European Economics* 14 (Fall 1975): 4; Mitija Kamušić, "Economic Efficiency and Workers' Self-Management," in *Yugoslav Self-Management*, ed., Brookmeyer, p. 108.

12. Dirlam and Plummer, *Yugoslav Economy*, p. 167.

13. See Dragomir Vojnić, "Three Aspects of Development Policy in the Social Plan for 1971–1975," *Eastern European Economics* 10 (Summer 1972): 417–44.

14. Marko Kranjec, "An Analysis of the Effects of Yugoslav Fiscal Policy in the Light of Some Newer Theoretical Concepts," *Eastern European Economics* 14 (Fall 1975): 42.

15. My sources for piecing the picture together are Dirlam and Plummer, *Yugoslav Economy*, pp. 165–99; Marko Kranjec, "Planning and Fiscal Policy," *Eastern European Economics* 12 (Summer 1974): 64–84; idem, "Effects of Fiscal Policy," pp. 32–62; B. Gluščević, H. Hadžiomerić, B. Horvat, N. Kljušer, B. Soškić, and D. Vojnić, "Economic Functions of the Federation," *Eastern European Economics* 11 (Winter 1972–73): 12–42; M. Hanžeković, "The Economic System Since 1965," in R. Bićanić, *Economic Policy for Socialist Yugoslavia* (Cambridge: Cambridge University Press, 1973), pp. 211–39; Horvat, "Short-Run Instability," pp. 3–32; idem, "An Institutional Model of a Self-Managed Socialist Economy," *Eastern European Economics* 10 (Summer 1972): 369–92; and Pero Jurković, "Sistem društvenog finansiranja," *Ekonomski pregled* 28, no. 3–4 (1977): 121–51.

16. Kranjec, "Effects of Fiscal Policy," p. 35.

17. Ibid., p. 42.

18. See below, "The Role of the State: Local Government," pp. 89–93.

19. Kranjec notes the "increasing regressiveness" of the tax structure throughout the postreform years. From 1966 to 1972, revenues from direct taxes (mainly personal income taxes) fell from 37 to 29.1 percent of all gross revenues of budgets. Meanwhile, revenues at all levels of government derived from turnover/sales taxes rose from 41 to 46.6 percent of total budgetary receipts. The portion of the federal budget coming from tariffs similarly rose from 10 to 19.5 percent. See Kranjec, "Effects of Fiscal Policy," p. 36.

20. See Gluščević et al., "Economic Functions of the Federation," p. 23.

21. Ivan Ribnikar, "Monetary Planning," *Eastern European Economics* 12

(Summer 1974): 92.

22. Ibid., pp. 87-88.

23. Laura Tyson, "Liquidity Crises in the Yugoslav Economy: An Alternative to Bankruptcy?" *Soviet Studies* 29 (April 1977): 286.

24. Eirik Furbotn and Svetozar Pejovich, "Property Rights, Economic Decentralization, and the Evolution of the Yugoslav Firm, 1965-1972," unpublished manuscript, 1972, p. 5 (mimeographed). On "privatization" of accumulation, see also Josip Županov, "Samoupravljanje i reforma" *Naše Teme* 12 (May 1968): 673-88.

25. Furbotn and Pejovich, "Property Rights," p. 5.

26. Horvat, "Short-Run Instability," p. 15.

27. Dirlam and Plummer, *Yugoslav Economy*, pp. 183-84.

28. See World Bank, *Yugoslavia: Development with Decentralization* (Baltimore: Johns Hopkins Press, 1975), pp. 14-15.

29. Svetozar Pejovich, "The Banking System and the Investment Behavior of the Yugoslav Firm," in *Plan and Market: Economic Reform in Eastern Europe*, M. Bornstein, ed. (New Haven: Yale University Press, 1973), p. 307.

30. "From a total of 567 in 1960, the number of banks (other than cooperative savings) had shrunk to 74, with 465 offices, by December 31, 1968, and to 29 on March 31, 1971" (Dirlam and Plummer, *Yugoslav Economy*, p. 178).

31. See Edvard Kardelj, *Osnovni uzroci i pravci ustavnih promena* (Belgrade: Komunist, 1973), p. 16.

32. World Bank, *Development with Decentralization*, p. 123.

33. See "Appendix" in Barišića, "Tipovi integracije u nas," *Moderna organizacija*, no. 2 (1971) for a comparison of the largest Yugoslav industrial and commercial enterprises. Cf. also David Granick, *Enterprise Guidance in Eastern Europe* (Princeton: Princeton University Press, 1975), pp. 418-20.

34. World Bank, *Development with Decentralization*, pp. 282-83.

35. Stephen Sacks, *Entry of New Competitors in Yugoslav Market Socialism* (Berkeley: University of California, Institute of International Studies, Research Series, no. 19), pp. 59-60.

36. See D. Atlagić and V. Milanović, eds., *Kritika socijalnih razlika* (Belgrade: Komunist, 1972); Rudi Supek, "Some Contradictions and Insufficiencies of Self-Managing Socialism," *Praxis* 3/4 (Spring 1971): 375-99; Albert Meister, *Où va l'autogestion jougoslave?* (Paris: Editions anthropos, 1970), pp. 319–41.

37. Gluščević et al., "Economic Functions of the Federation," p. 18. Italics added.

38. For a comparison of economic performance in 1955-64 and 1964-72, see table in Horvat, "Short-Run Instability," p. 4.

39. Meister, *Autogestion jougoslave*, p. 285.

40. See Adizes, *Industrial Democracy*, p. 23; Josip Županov, *Samoupravljanje i društvena moć*, pp. 121-44.

41. See Meister, *Autogestion jougoslave*, p. 288 circa; *Statistički godišnjak SFRJ* (Belgrade: Savezni zavod za statistiku, 1971), tables 104-18, "Prestanci radnih odnosa," p. 97.

42. Dirlam and Plummer, *Yugoslav Economy*, pp. 53 and 19-105, passim.

43. Horvat, "Short-Run Instability," p. 11.

44. See Sacks, *Entry of New Competitors*, p. 70 on the "fine art" of lobbying for funds.

45. Evidence on interregional capital mobility is mixed. For alternative viewpoints on the investment/nationality question, see V. Veselica, "Nesporazumi oko investicije," *Naše teme* 11 (December 1967):2134-54; Stipe Šuvar, "Da li je Hrvatska eksploatirana?" *Naše teme* 13 (December 1969): 2018-62. See also Jack Fisher, "The Emergence of Regional Spatial Planning: The Slovenian Experience," in *Eastern Europe: Essays in Geographical Problems*, ed. G. Hoffman (London: Methuen, 1971), pp. 301-26.

46. Veljko Cvjetičanin, "Charactèristiques et dilemmes du socialisme autogestif jougoslave," *Praxis* 3/4 (Spring 1971): 512.

47. See Fisher, "Regional Spatial Planning," p. 306; Veljko Rus, "Nacija kao faktor koćenja društvenog razvoja," *Naše teme* 14 (August 1970): 1379.

48. Meister, *Autogestion jougoslave*, pp. 26-28.

49. Ustav SFRJ (1963), ch. 5, art. 96.

50. Sacks, *Entry of New Competitors*, table 4.2, pp. 82-83. Sacks gives data on the number of new entrants for the period 1961-68. Breaking down his data into two periods (1961-64 and 1965-68), one finds that the ratio of new enterprises to new plants was approximately 1:2 in the first period and dropped dramatically to less than 1:8 from 1965-1968. Note, however, that this is only a rough index of direct commune participation. Not all new enterprises were founded by communes in either period, and some communes may have participated—overtly or covertly—in the financing of new plants. Moreover, commune officials frequently have been instrumental in pressuring local banks to extend credit to existing firms seeking to found new plants. See also Granick, *Enterprise Guidance*, pp. 410-20.

51. Figures interpolated from Dirlam and Plummer, *Yugoslav Economy*, p. 195.

52. See Eugen Pusić and Ann-Marie Hauck-Walsh, *Urban Government for Zagreb, Yugoslavia* (New York: Praeger, 1968), pp. 64-86.

53. See J. Fisher, "The Yugoslav Commune," *World Politics* 3 (April 1964): 418-41; R. Marinković, *Ko Odlučuje u komuni* (Belgrage: Institut za društvenih nauka, 1971), pp. 147-67.

54. Bićanić, "Economics of Socialism". p. 231n.

55. Eugen Pusić, *Social Welfare and Development* (Paris: Mouton, 1972), p. 162.

56. Pusić and Hauck-Walsh, *Urban Government*, p. 45. The authors also point out that increased financial independence of communes "contrasts directly with trends in other nations, where the role of central government in urban programs is generally growing" (p. 45).

57. Pusić, *Social Welfare*, p. 161.

58. Data on such inequalities appear in World Bank, *Development with Decentralization*, pp. 191 and 468, and V. Obradović, "Expenditure on Medical Care and Public Health, 1966-1972," *Yugoslav Survey* 5 (November 1974): 104.

59. See above, pp. 77–80.

60. See M. Skrbić, "Specificnost ekonomskih odnosa u zdravstvu," *Naše*

260 NOTES TO PAGES 92-96

teme 14 (January 1970); M. Skrbić and B. Popović, "Socijalne nejednakosti na području zaštite zdravlja," *Naše teme* 17 (March 1973): 572-89.

61. See N. Filipović and S. Sokol, "Aktuelni problemi odnosa izbornog i političkih sistema," *Naše teme* 12 (June 1968); N. Pašić, "Self-Management as an Integral Political System," in *Yugoslav Self-Management*, ed. Broekmeyer, pp. 1-37.

62. There were also, of course, many informal ways in which service institutions could make their influence felt in local assemblies. See, for example, William Burger, "Public Decision-Making and Self-Management in an Industrializing Rural Commune," *First International Conference on Participation* 6: 43.

63. See Pusić, *Social Welfare*, p. 174; Burger, "Public Decision-Making," p. 39; Marinković, *Ko odlučuje*, pp. 167-89; J. Jerovšek, "Struktura uticaja u opštini," *Sociologija* 11 (February 1969). Marinković, however, suggests that the occupational chambers were more successful in having an impact on local policy making and budgets than was the chamber based on geographical representation. Presumably this was because of the greater cohesiveness of their interests and greater expertise in the matters concerning them.

64. Dirlam and Plummer, *Yugoslav Economy*, p. 192. See also R. Lukić, "Društeveno raslojevanje kao uzrok društvenih sukoba u Jugoslaviji," *Sociologija* 13 (March 1971): 340-55.

65. Kranjec, "Planning and Fiscal Policy," p. 66. Additional funds existed at republic and federal levels.

66. Milka Šeat-Lašić, "Nove dimenzije političke participacije u uvjetima samoupravljanja," *Zbornik Radova, 1960-1970* (Zagreb: Institut za društvena upravljanja, 1970), p. 600.

67. See Granick, *Enterprise Guidance*, pp. 395-413.

68. See Eugan Pusić, *Samoupravljanje* (Zagreb: Nardone novine, 1968), chap. V-B; Pavel Novosel, "Politička kultura u SR Hrvatskoj," Zagreb, Fakultet političkih nauka, 1969 (mimeographed); M. Zvonarević, *Javno mnijenje građana SR Hrvatskoj o samoupravljanju* (Zagreb: Institut za društvena istraživanja, 1967); Krsto Kilibarda, *Samoupravljanje i Savez komunista* (Belgrade: Sociološki institut, 1966); Sharon Zukin, *Between Marx and Tito* (New York: Cambridge University Press, 1975).

69. Pusić, *Social Welfare*, p. 174.

CHAPTER 5

1. World Bank, *Yugoslavia: Development with Decentralization* (Baltimore: Johns Hopkins Press, 1975), p. 105.

2. Ibid., table 6.2, p. 155; table 1.17, p. 382; and table 2.8, p. 392; Albert Meister, *Où va l'autogestion jougoslave?* (Paris: Editions anthropos, 1970), p. 135; and Joel Dirlam and James Plummer, *An Introduction to the Yugoslav Economy* (Columbus, Ohio: Merrill Publishing, 1973), p. 121n.

3. See "Note" to table 10, below.

4. See *Statistički godišnjak SFRJ* (Belgrade: Savezni zavod za statistiku, 1973), table 104-4, "Zaposleno osoblje prema školskoj spremi i granama delatnosti," p. 99.

5. Deborah Milenkovitch, *Plan and Market in Yugoslav Economic Thought* (New Haven: Yale University Press, 1971), p. 260.

6. Josip Županov, "Egalitarizam i industrijalizam," *Naše teme* 14 (February 1970): 269. Županov also cites a Zagreb survey of League of Communist members that found that fully one-third of those who believed "exploitation exists in Yugoslavia" attributed it to private entrepreneurs (p. 270).

7. See M. Kranjec, "An Analysis of the Effects of Yugoslav Fiscal Policy in the Light of Some Newer Theoretical Concepts," *Eastern European Economics* 14 (Fall 1975): 37. Again, it is not clear how much of this tax evasion was real or imagined. Conversations with Triestine bank workers, however, attest to a growing number of savings accounts held in Italian banks by Yugoslavs, employed largely as small entrepreneurs or private professionals.

8. Strictly speaking, only Slovenia, Croatia, Serbia, Macedonia, Montenegro, and Bosnia-Herzegovina have "republic" status. Vojvodina and Kosovo-Metohija are "autonomous provinces" within the republic of Serbia. For stylistic reasons, I treat them as republics, for they have many of the rights associated with republic status. Slovenia, Croatia, Vojvodina, and Serbia proper are generally considered "developed" areas; Macedonia, Kosovo, and Montenegro are "underdeveloped" areas, with Bosnia-Herzegovina somewhere in between, usually landing with the underdeveloped areas.

9. Forty-three percent as compared with 49 percent in the developed areas (World Bank, *Development with Decentralization*, p. 195).

10. Ibid., pp. 191 and 498.

11. See Dirlam and Plummer, *Yugoslav Economy*, p. 121n.

12. See Stephen Sacks, *Entry of New Competitors in Yugoslav Market Socialism* (Berkeley: University of California, Institute of International Studies, 1973), Research Series, no. 19, pp. 72–73. According to Sacks' data, with the exception of Energoinvest (Bosnian), the firms participating in joint ventures with foreign firms were all from Slovenia, Croatia, and Serbia proper. As for Yugoslav firms and their reluctance to expand into the underdeveloped areas, see Tito's comments before the Ninth Congress in "Ninth Congress of the Yugoslav League of Communists," selected documents, *Socialist Thought and Practice*, special issue, 1969, p. 19 circa.

13. See S. Šuvar, "Da li je Hrvatska eksploatirana?" *Naše teme* 13 (December 1969): 1970.

14. Howard Wachtel, *Workers' Management and Workers' Wages in Yugoslavia* (Ithaca, N.Y.: Cornell University Press, 1973), p. 134.

15. The data on which this section is based are taken from *Statistički godišnjak SFRJ* (Belgrade: Savezni zavod za statistiku, 1971–72), table 122-5, "Prosečna neto lična primanja i indeksi nominalnih i realnih primanja po granama delatnosti."

16. See Wachtel, *Workers' Management and Workers' Wages*, table 6.8 and *Statistički godišnjak* (1971), table 122-5. Wachtel's data apply to manufacturing and mining only. Popov finds a similar pattern when nonindustrial sectors are included, although her analysis is based on a comparison of the five highest and five lowest wage industries only. Table 7 (above) suggests that Popov should not have found increasing interindustry differentials in the

social sector as a whole; nonetheless the differentials that did exist are undoubtedly owing to the causes she gives. See S. Popov, "Intersectoral Relations
of Personal Incomes," *Yugoslav Survey* 13 (May 1972): 66-80.

17. Wachtel, *Workers' Management and Workers' Wages*, pp. 118-19;
Vladimir Bakarić, "Prednacrt ustava i respodjela," *Nase teme* 7 (March 1963):
165.

18. Popov, "Intersectoral Relations," p. 77. See also R. Bićanić, *Turning
Points in Economic Development* (Paris: Mouton, 1971), p. 260.

19. See Sacks, *Entry of New Competitors*, p. 101; David Granick, *Enterprise Guidance in Eastern Europe* (Princeton: Princeton University Press,
1975), pp. 401-8. However, Granick notes a fairly vigorous merger movement
in 1969-70, primarily affecting firms with less than 250 employees. Moreover, a recent issue of *Ekonomska politika* (special September 1977 issue,
"100 najvećih") suggests that in 1970-72, the share of the 100 largest enterprises' revenues in the total revenues of the manufacturing and mining sector
went from 40.7 percent to 49.6 percent; their share of total industrial employment also increased from 29.8 percent to 34 percent in these years.
Nevertheless, insofar as these figures may only represent existing firms
branching out into new areas of activity, they need not imply decreased com-
petiveness in any particular industry, although they do suggest a trend toward
"bigness" picked up steam at the turn of the decade. Note also that various
organizations and trade associations can be utilized to foster collusive practices
without requiring firms to merge with one another. See Joel Dirlam,
"Problems of Market Power and Public Policy in Yugoslavia," in *Comparative
Economic Systems*, 2nd ed., ed. M. Bornstein (Homewood, Ill.: Richard D.
Irwin, 1969), pp. 236-53.

20. See Sacks, *Entry of New Competitors*, pp. 112-13. According to
Sacks's data, concentration ratios in production (the output of the four
largest firms as a percentage of domestic production) of industries such as
coal and coke, ferrous metallurgy, metal products, electrical products,
chemicals, and rubber drop 10 percent or more when adjusted for imports
and exports (i.e., the output of the four largest firms as a percentage of domestic consumption).

21. See Granick, *Enterprise Guidance*, p. 418.

22. The main examples here appear to be petroleum, shipbuilding, and
electrical energy, all with high concentraion ratios for domestic production
and sales. The exceptions are printing/publishing and perhaps film and construction design (no concentration ratios are available), where the skill
structures of the industry account for the high wage pattern. High-wage
branches of nonindustrial sectors also are widely recognized in the Yugoslav
literature (and confirmed by my own observations) as monopolistic or oligopolistic, although I can find no concentration ratios for them. These are:
air transport, sea transport, foreign trade firms, business associations, economic chambers, and social insurance institutes.

23. Popov, "Intersectoral Relations," p. 80. Popov, however, uses supply
concentration (Sacks' percent of domestic production) as an index of monop-

opy. Had she used share of domestic sales, she presumably could have accounted for yet more of the interindustry variation.

24. See D. Atlagić and V. Milanović, eds., *Kritika socijalnih razlika* (Belgrade: Komunist, 1972); Lazo Antić, "Neopravdane socijalnih razlike u oblasti stanovanja i stambene izgradnje," *Naše teme* 18 (March 1973): 556-72; and Zdenko Has, "O nekim izvorima društveno neprihvatljivih društvene nejednakosti," *Naše teme* 18 (March 1973): 511-44.

25. Neca Jovanov found low personal income to be the immediate cause of 26.6 percent of strikes, and late pay to have caused another 14.9 percent. See Neca Jovanov, "Le rapport entre la grève comme conflit social et l'autogestion comme système total," *First International Conference on Participation and Self-Management*, 6 vols. (Zagreb: Institute for Social Research, 1972-73), 1:89-90; idem, "Prilog razmatranju pojave štrajka u našem društvu," *Naše teme* 15 (February 1970): 309-20; Ichak Adizes, *Industrial Democracy: Yugoslav Style* (New York: Free Press, 1971), pp. 177-87.

26. A similar phenomenon occurs in comparing average wages in manufacturing and mining with average wages in "noneconomic" activities (social services and government administration). The ratio between the extremes within manufacturing and within the "noneconomic" activities sectors increased after the reform, although the difference in average wages between them decreased. Hence, the difference between average wages of, say, workers in oil refining and banks remained fairly stable, that between workers in oil refining and school teachers increased to the detriment of teachers, and that between workers in the low-wage textile industry and in banks widened in favor of bank workers. See *Statistički godišnjak* (1972), table 122-5.

27. See V. Milanović, "Socijalno-ekonomska diferencijacija i kriza društvenih odnosa," in *Kritika socijalnih razlika*, ed., Atlagić and Milanović, p. 42.

28. Tito straddled these issues admirably at the Ninth Congress. With a little imagination, his statements there could be construed as endorsing practically any measure a local or republic government chose to take. See "Ninth Congress," pp. 12-16.

Regarding the growth of factions, see Dennison Rusinow, *The Yugoslav Experiment, 1948-1976* (Berkeley: University of California Press, 1977), pp. 214-73. On clique struggles in communes, see J. Županov, "Samoupravljanje i društvena moć u radnoj organizaciji," *Moderna organizacija*, no. 6-7 (1971): 460; F. Bučar, "The Participation of the State and Political Organizations in the Decisions of the Working Organization," *First International Conference on Participation*, 1:41-61. See also chapter 6, "Ideology and the Political Climate."

29. See Dirlam and Plummer, *Yugoslav Economy*, p. 46; Granick, *Enterprise Guidance*, p. 425; Josip Županov, "Samoupravljanje i reforma," *Naše teme* 12 (May 1968): 685, and other cited works of this author. Fear of ad hoc intervention helps to explain why not only wages and productivity but also employment rose most rapidly in Yugoslavia's high-wage industries after the reform.

30. See Sacks, *Entry of New Competitors*, pp. 58-59.

264											NOTES TO PAGES 107–109

31. Ibid.; R. M. B. Flaes, "Yugoslavia: An Experience of Workers' Self-Management," *First International Conference on Participation* 6: 119.

32. Aleksander Bajt argues that such a "wage chase" syndrome was a prime cause of the postreform inflation. See *L'economia jugoslava alla fine del 1970* (Trieste: I.S.D.E.E. prospettive economiche, 1971), pp. 64–69.

33. On enterprise-state relationships, see J. Jerovšek, "Self-Management System in Yugoslav Enterprises," *First International Conference on Participation* 1: 121; F. Bučar, M. Kamušić, V. Rus, and J. Županov, "Osnovne dileme daljeg razvoja samoupravljanje," *Moderna organizacija*, no. 1 (1968): 3–14; Pavel Novosel, "Reforma, samoupravljanje i socijalna psihologija preindustrijskog mentaliteta," *Naše teme* 12 (December 1967): 2160; Đ. Pribičević, "Raspodjela, dohodak, i model socijalističke privrede," *Naše teme* 12 (August 1968): 1085 circa; S. Vukmanović, "O prilivanje viška rada i ujednačavanju uslova privređivanja," *Naše teme* 12 (June 1968): 686–706; Dirlam and Plummer, *Yugoslav Economy*; J. Županov, *Samoupravljanje i društvena moć* (Zagreb: Naše teme, 1968); idem, "Egalitarizam i industrijalizam," p. 255; and Granick, *Enterprise Guidance*, pp. 407–8.

34. See Jerovšek, "Self-management System," pp. 120–21; V. Arzenšek, "Socijalne vrednosti radnika zaposlenih u jugoslovenskoj industriji," *Moderna organizacija*, no. 9–10 (1970): 623–30.

35. See V. Arzenšek, "Socijalne vrednosti," pp. 623–30. idem, "Stavovi zaposlenih u jugoslovenskoj industriji o riziku preduzeća," *Moderna organizacija*, no. 3–4 (1971): 268–75; J. Županov, *Samoupravljanje i društvena moć*, part I; M. George Zaninovich, "Elites and Citizenry in Yugoslav Society: A Study of Value Differentiation," in *Comparative Communist Political Leadership*, ed. C. Beck et al. (New York: McKay, 1973); Silvano Bolčić, "The Value System of a Participatory Economy," *First International Conference on Participation*, 1: 97–113.

36. Research on which this section is based by and large relates only to "economic" work organizations.

37. See B. Pribičević, "Prilaz ispitivanju socijalnih razlika u Jugoslaviji," in *Kritika socijalnih razlika*, ed. Atlagić and Milanović, p. 18; Edvard Kardelj, *Osnovi uzroci i pravci ustavnih promena* (Belgrade: Komunist, 1973), p. 45.

38. See World Bank, *Development with Decentralization*, p. 109.

39. See B. Horvat, "Short-Run Instability and Long-Run Trends in the Yugoslav Economy's Development," *Eastern European Economics* 14 (Fall 1975): 13–15; M. Kranjec, "Planning and Fiscal Policy," *Eastern European Economics* 12 (Summer 1974): 76.

40. Rudolf Bićanić, *Turning Points in Economic Development*, p. 261.

41. Ibid., p. 261. See also Tito, "Ninth Congress," p. 14.

42. The record on strikes is again illuminating. Asked what the "real" (as opposed to immediate) internal causes of strikes were, 26.8 percent of the respondents gave "absolutely low personal incomes" as the reason, while 36.4 percent cited unfair *distribution* of income within the firm. Again, "objective" wage differentials seem below what their subjective impact on blue-collar workers was. See Jovanov, "Le rapport entre la grève," p. 90.

43. V. Milanović, "Socijalno-Ekonomska Diferencijacija," p. 45.

44. See World Bank, *Development with Decentralization*, p. 103.

45. Ibid., p. 104.

46. See Meister, *Autogestion jougoslave*, p. 222; Branko Horvat, "O socijal-noj diferencijaciji u našoj zemlji," in *Kritika socijalnih razlika*, ed. Atlagić and Milanović, p. 58. As late as 1974, a rather high tuition was charged by the Workers' University (college-level night school) in Zagreb, while those who attended the regular faculties as full-time students paid only a nominal amount in fees.

47. Among the numerous studies that found oligarchic power structures in Yugoslav enterprises are: V. Arzenšek, "Participacija zaposlenih u jugo-slovenskoj industriji," *Moderna organizacija*, no. 1–2 (1971): 134–43; idem, "Analiza ankete u kadrovskoj politici," *Moderna organizacija*, no. 7 (1968): 553–61; O. Bajić, "Proces samoupravnog odlučivanja posmatran u pojedinim fazama i celini," (Master's thesis, University of Zagreb, 1973); Silvano Bolčić, "Value System," pp. 103–16; Zlatko Jeličić, "Distribucija utjecaja nekih odluka u radnoj organizaciji," *Moderna organizacija*, no. 5–6 (1970); idem, "Analiza problema participacija radnika u samoupravnom odlučivanju na nivou radničkog savjeta," *Moderna organizacija*, no. 10 (1971): 807–21; J. Golčić, *Analiza strukture uticaja u samoupravnom odlučivanju u brodogradi-lištu "3 maj" Rijeka* (Zagreb: Institut za društvena istraživanja, 1970); M. Kamušić, "Economic Efficiency and Workers' Self-Management," in *Yugoslav Workers' Self-Management*, Broekmeyer, ed. (Dordrecht, Holland: D. Reidel, 1970), pp. 80–108; idem, "Predlozi za razmišljavanje," *Moderna organizacija*, no. 6–7 (1971); Josip Obradović, "Distribucija participacija u procesu dono-šenja odluka," *Revija za Sociologiju*, no. 1 (1972): 15–48; J. Obradović, W. Rodgers, J. French, "Workers' Councils in Yugoslavia," *Human Relations* 23 (October 1970): 459–71; N. Pastuović, Distribucija utjecaja u privrednim organizacijama," *Moderna organizacija*, no. 5 (1968); V. Rus, "Influence Structure in Yugoslav Enterprises," *Human Relations* (February 1970): 149–60; idem, "Status stručnog i rukovodećeg kadra s obzirom na komuniciranje, moć, i odgovornost," *Moderna organizacija*, no. 5 (1968): 386–96; Tito Favoretto, "Sviluppo economico e autogestione operaia," *Economia e lavoro* 5 (November–December 1971): 819–36; Josip Županov and Arnold Tannen-baum, "Control in Some Yugoslav Industrial Organizations," in *Control in Organizations*, ed. A. Tannenbaum (New York: McGraw-Hill, 1968), pp. 91–112.

48. See V. Rus, "The Limits of Organized Participation," *First Interna-tional Conference on Participation* 2: 171.

49. Kardelj, *Osnovni uzroci*, p. 13. See also B. Kavčić, "Techničko–techno-loška organizacija i samoupravljanje," *Moderna organizacija*, no. 3–4 (1971): 295.

50. See Županov, "Samoupravljanje i društvena moć u radnoj organizaciji," pp. 466–67; Adizes, *Industrial Democracy*, chap. 7.

51. See researches cited in n. 47. Županov cites a Zagreb survey of League of Communist members that asked, "Does your basic organization [enterprise party cell] take positions and initiate actions independently of what individ-ual executives think, or does it only help management?" Of over 3,000

respondents, 43.2 percent saw the party cell as autonomous, while 49.4 percent felt it merely helped the management (7.4 percent gave no answer). See J. Zupanov, "Samoupravljanje i društvena moć u radnoj organizaciji," p. 460n.

52. See Adizes, *Industrial Democracy*, pp. 281-322; A. Meister, *Autogestion jougoslave*, pp. 161-99.

53. Mladen Zvonarević, "Socijalna moć, informiranost i motivacija u procesu samoupravljanja," *Naše teme* 13 (June 1969): 910.

54. See Arzenšek, "Participacija zaposlenih," pp. 134-43; Rus, "Influence Structure," pp. 149-60; Jeličić, "Analiza," pp. 807-21.

55. On manipulation, see Zupanov, "Samoupravljanje i društvena moć u radnoj organizaciji," pp. 459-66; Bučar, "The Participation of the State," pp. 41-61; Joze Goričar, "Workers' Self-Management: Ideal Type–Social Reality," *First International Conference on Participation*, pp. 18-33. On "reliable" people, see Goričar, "Workers' Self-Management," pp. 18-33. On harassment, see Favoretto, "Sviluppo economico," p. 830.

56. See Adizes, *Industrial Democracy*, pp. 200-250; Emerik Blum, "The Director and Workers' Self-Management," in *Workers' Self-Management*, ed. Broekmeyer, pp. 170-200; Pavel Novosel, "Self-Management, Participation and the Great China Wall of Communication," *First International Conference on Participation*, 6: 279-83. David Granick cites examples of executives simply withholding information from workers' councils (*Enterprise Guidance*, p. 370).

57. Obradović et al., "Workers' Councils," p. 470.

58. See Josip Zupanov, "Da li se rukovođenje poduzećem 'profesionalizira?'" *Moderna organizacija*, no. 10 (1968): 806-20; idem, *Samoupravljanje i društvena moć*, part I; idem, "Egalitarizam i industrijalizam," pp. 250-95; "Anketa o ličnim dohocima među učesnika simpozijuma na Bledu," *Moderna organizacija*, no. 6 (1968); S. Micki, "Socijalna diferencijacija–diferencijacija stavova," *Sociologija* 14 (March 1972): 320-31.

59. See Zupanov, *Samoupravljanje i društvena moć*, part I; S. Možina, "Interesi samoupravljača za odlučivanje," *Moderna organizacija*, no. 9 (1968): 611-17; V. Arzenšek, "Stavovi zaposlenih o riziku preduzeća," pp. 268-75.

60. Zupanov, *Samoupravljanje i društvena moć*, part I; idem, "U čemu se sastoji ekonomska funkcija proizvođača u samoupravnoj radnoj organizaciji?" *Moderna organizacija*, no. 6 (1969): 406-12.

61. Zupanov, "Da li se rukovođenje 'profesionalizira?'" pp. 806-20; Možina, "Interesi samoupravljača," pp. 611-17; Jeličić, "Distribucija utjecaja"; idem, "Analiza problema," pp. 807-21; Arzenšek, "Analiza ankete u kadrovskoj politici," pp. 553-61. Cf. also S. Možina, "Izvori konflikti u radnim organizacijama," *Sociologija* 13 (March 1971): 416-29; J. Zupanov, "Upravljanje industrijskom konfliktom u samoupravnom sistemu," *Sociologija* 13 (March 1971): 430-43.

62. Cited in Z. Mlinar, "Društvene vrijednosti, razvoj i konflikti," *Sociologija* 13 (March 1971): 379-95.

63. See R. Lukić, "Društveno raslojevanje kao uzrok društvenih sukoba u Jugoslaviji," *Sociologija* 13 (March 1971): 340-55; V. Rus, "Klike u radnim

organizacijama," *Gledišta*, no. 8-9 (1966); idem, "Influence Structure," pp. 149-60.

64. See Jovanov, "Le rapport entre la grève," pp. 62-97; idem, "Prilog razmatranja štrajka," pp. 308-20; idem, "Protest Work Stoppages," *Socialist Thought and Practice* 27 (July-September 1967): 68-82; D. Tornquist, "Strikes in Yugoslavia," *Working Papers for a New Society* 3 (Spring 1975): 51-62.

65. See Možina, "Izvori konflikti," pp. 416-29; Jovanov, "Le rapport entre la grève," pp. 62-97.

66. Meister, *Autogestion jougoslave*, pp. 171-77.

67. See Bučar et al., "Osnovne dileme razvoja samoupravljanja," esp. p. 10.

68. Možina, "Interesi samoupravljača," pp. 611-17.

69. Lukić, "Društveno raslojevanje," pp. 340-55.

70. See Kardelj, *Osnovni Uzroci*, p. 25.

71. Data on representation of blue-collar workers in self-management and political bodies is given in Jovanov, "Le rapport entre la grève," pp. 67-69.

72. See Bogdan Denitch, *Legitimation of a Revolution* (New Haven: Yale University Press, 1976), p. 94.

CHAPTER 6

1. Dennison Rusinow, "Marxism Belgrade Style," *Antioch Review* (Winter 1967-68): 481.

2. On the party reforms of the Eighth Congress, see Rusinow, "Marxism Belgrade Style," pp. 477-90; M. Nikolić, ed., *Savez komunista u uslovima samoupravljanja* (Belgrade: Kultura, 1967); Branko Horvat, *An Essay on Yugoslav Society* (White Plains, N.Y.: International Arts and Sciences Press, 1969), pp. 187-235; Savez komunista Jugoslavije, *Osmi kongres* (Belgrade: Kultura, 1964); Dušan Bilandić, "Naš društveni razvitak i uloga Savez komunista," *Naše teme* 11 (Jarnuary 1967): 2-38; V. Bakarić, "Trideset godine komunističke partije Hrvatske," *Naše teme* 11 (November 1967): 1973-1984; G. Ionescu, *The Politics of the East European Communist States* (New York: Praeger, 1971), pp. 240-48; Albert Meister, *Où va l'autogestion jougoslave?* (Paris: Editions anthropos, 1970).

3. Josip Tito, "Report," in "Ninth Congress of the League of Communists of Yugoslavia," selected documents, *Socialist Thought and Practice*, special issue (1969): 3-69; S. Šuvar, "Ne odgadati otvorenu i odlučnu bitku za samoupravljanje," *Naše teme* 12 (May 1968): 758-858; A. Dragičević, "Ekonomika i politika u sistemu samoupravljanja," *Naše teme* 12 (May 1968): 691-708.

4. Cf. issues of *Naše teme* and *Gledišta* from 1965 to 1970 for examples of the criticisms younger activists leveled at the party. *Praxis*, which began to appear in 1967 and received a certain amount of notoriety in the West by billing itself as a journal of dissent and publishing an international edition, appears a voice of moderation in comparison with some of these critiques.

5. Tito, cited by the Commission for the Preparation of the Report for the Tenth Congress of the LCY, "Draft Report on the Activities of the League of Communists and Presidency of the LCY Between the Ninth and Tenth

Congresses," pp. 15-16. Press release, May 1974, courtesy of the Yugoslav Information Service, New York (Multilith).

6. See Dennison Rusinow's wonderful descriptions of the free-for-all elections in 1969 and their predecessor in 1967. In *The Yugoslav Experiment 1948-1974* (Berkeley: University of California Press, 1977), pp. 261-64 and 222-24.

7. See Tito, "Introductory Address," in "Ninth Congress," p. 75; idem, "Report," p. 31; Edvard Kardelj, "Introductory Address," in *The Second Congress of Self-Managers of Yugoslavia*, ed. S. Starčević, D. Radovanović, S. Vučković, Zoran Zlatanović, and Sava Mijalković (Belgrade: Međunarodna politika, 1972), p. 43; and Rusinow, *Yugoslav Experiment*, pp. 192-308.

8. See Josip Tito, "The Struggle for the Further Development of Socialist Self-Management in Our Country and the Role of the LCY," speech before the Tenth Congress of the Yugoslav League of Communists. Press release, May 1974, courtesy of the Yugoslav Information Service, New York (Multilith). On general patterns of consensus and conflict among Yugoslav political elites, see P. Jambrek, *Development and Social Change in Yugoslavia* (Lexington, Mass.: D. C. Heath, 1975); A. Barton, B. Denitch, and C. Kadushin, *Opinion-Making Elites in Yugoslavia* (New York: Praeger, 1973); and Kardelj, "Introductory Address," p. 34.

9. Marko Nikežić, statement in *Vjesnik* 2 August, 1969. Cited by Dunja Rihtman-Auguštin, "Samoupravljanje kao kulturno-antropološki fenomen," *Naše teme* 14 (January 1970): 48.

10. See Paul Shoup, *Communism and the Yugoslav National Question* (New York: Columbia University Press, 1968), p. 210; Rusinow, *Yugoslav Experiment*, pp. 163-202.

11. George Schopflin, "The Ideology of Croatian Nationalism," *Survey* 19 (Winter 1973): 126. On the development of ethnic tensions after the reform, see also Paul Shoup, "The National Question in Yugoslavia," *Problems of Communism* 21 (January-February 1972): 18-29; Gary Bertsch, "The Revival of Nationalism," *Problems of Communism* 22 (November-December 1973): 1-15; S. Šuvar, "Marginal Notes on the Nationality Question," *International Journal of Politics* 2 (Spring 1972): 44-77; Kardelj, "Introductory Address," pp. 31-33; and Rusinow, *Yugoslav Experiment*, pp. 250-260.

12. For example, B. Gluščević, H. Hadžiomerić, B. Horvat, N. Kljušer, B. Šoškić, and D. Vojnić, "Economic Functions of the Federation," *Eastern European Economics* 11 (Winter 1972-73): 12-42.

13. See Schopflin, "Croatian Nationalism," p. 131; V. Rus, "Nacija kao faktor kočenja društvenog razvoja," *Naše teme* 14 (August 1970): 1375-82; I. Kuvačić, "O karakteru sukoba u našem društvu," *Naše teme* 14 (August 1970): 1371.

14. K. Džeba, in radio discussion published in *Naše teme* 12 (May 1968): 836. See also Meister, *Autogestion juogoslave*, pp. 319-37.

15. See Jambrek, *Development and Social Change*, chap. 4; Barton et al., *Opinion-Making Elites*, chaps. 6-8; M. George Zaninovich, "Elites and Citizenry in Yugoslav Society," in *Comparative Communist Political Leadership*, ed. C. Beck, F. Fleron, M. Lodge, D. Waller, W. Walsh, and G. Zaninovich (New York: McKay, 1973), pp. 226-98.

16. See Edvard Kardelj, *Osnovni uzroci i pravci ustavnih promena* (Belgrade: Komunist, 1973), p. 16.

17. Veljko Cvjetičanin, "Pretpostavke i perspektive samoupravljana," *Naše teme* 14 (February 1970): 501.

18. Commission for the Report to the Tenth Congress, "Draft Report," pp. 6-7.

19. See Kardelj, *Osnovni uzroci*, p. 16; Starčević et al., eds., *Second Congress*, pp. 87-91.

20. See J. Županov, "Egalitarizam i industrijalizam," *Naše teme* 14 (February 1970): 250-95; idem, "Smanjivanje socijalnih razlika—kampanja ili politika?" *Naše teme* 17 (March 1973): 590-604.

21. See chapter 5, "Interskill Differentials and Inequalities within the Firm."

22. Robert Dahl and C. E. Lindblom, *Politics, Economics and Welfare* (New York: Harper and Row, 1953), p. 473.

23. See Kardelj, *Osnovni uzroci*, p. 34; Rikard Lang, "Ustav i razvitak privrednog sistema," *Ekonomski pregled* 25, no. 5-7 (1974): 257-69; V. Rajković, "Sistem samoupravnog planiranja," *Ekonomist pregled* 25, no. 5-7 (1974): 321-333.

24. See Branko Horvat, "Društveno vlasništvo," *Ekonomist* 30, no. 3 (1976): 389.

25. See Mirjana Pavlović, "Samoupravno planiranje i organizacija rada," *Socijalizam* 20 (February 1977): 244-53.

26. See *Quarterly Economic Review of Yugoslavia*, no. 1 (1975): 3.

27. This tax, the analogue of a corporate income tax, was in addition to the "contributions" firms paid based on the portion of enterprise income allocated to consumption. The latter were now to be used exclusively for financing social services and other specific special funds. See Pero Jurković, "Sistem društvenog finansiranja," *Ekonomski pregled* 28, no. 3-4 (1977): 121-51.

28. See Laura Tyson, "The Yugoslav Economy in the 1970's: A Survey of Recent Developments and Future Prospects," in U.S., Congress, Joint Economic Committee, *East European Economies Post-Helsinki* (Washington, D.C.: Government Printing Office, 1977), pp. 953-54; and idem, "Recent Developments and Problems in the Yugoslav Experiment with Market Socialism and Workers' Self-Management," paper presented at a conference on "Yugoslavia: Accomplishments and Problems," Washington, D.C.: 16 October 1977, p. 4 (mimeographed). Cf. *The Journal of Commerce*, 6 March 1978, p. 8 for details on social compacts in chemicals and communications and transport.

29. See Dragutin Marsenić, "Institucionalni oblici raspodele dohotka u našem privrednim sistemu," *Socijalizam* 20 (January 1977): 85-87.

30. Zoran Jašić, "Yugoslavia's Federal System and Coordination of Economic Policy," *Eastern European Economics* 13 (Fall 1974): 65.

31. Ibid., p. 69. In fact, provisions of a 1976 social compact on unemployment concluded by the Federal Executive Council, the economic chambers' association, and the trade unions included subsidies to keep underemployed workers at their jobs. See *Quarterly Economic Review of Yugoslavia*, no. 2 (1976): 2.

32. See E. Furbotn and S. Pejovich, "Property Rights, Economic Decentralization and the Evolution of the Yugoslav Firm, 1965–1972," unpublished manuscript, 1972 (mimeographed).

33. See Tyson, "The Yugoslav Economy," p. 979; Marsenić, "Institucionalni oblici," pp. 97–105.

34. Deborah Milenkovitch, "Plan and Market: The Case of Yugoslavia," paper presented at the annual meeting of the American Economic Association, Atlantic City, New Jersey, 17 September 1976, p. 8 (mimeographed).

35. For the rights and responsibilities of BOALs, see Ustav SFRJ (1974), art. 10–40, and Zakon o Udruženom Radu, part II, chap. I–II.

36. Edvard Kardelj, "The Integration of Labor and Social Capital under Workers' Control," in *Self-Management: New Dimensions to Industrial Democracy*, ed. I Adizes and E. Borgese (Santa Barbara: Center for the Study of Democratic Institutions, 1975), p. 47n. See also Ustav SFRJ (1974), art. 36.

37. See Starčević et al., eds., *Second Congress*, p. 68; Zakon o Udruženom Radu, art. 62. Cf. Aleksander Bajt, "Struktura tržiśte i kriteriji politike cena," *Ekonomist* 29, no. 1 (1976): 45–50.

38. See statement of Duško Vojvodić, cited by Egon Neuberger and Estelle James, "The Yugoslav Self-Managed Enterprise: A Systemic Approach," in *Plan and Market: Economic Reform in Eastern Europe*, ed. M. Bornstein (New Haven: Yale University Press, 1973), p. 260n.

39. Hence, firms/BOALs would "share in risk," as opposed to "creditor-debtor relations," in which a flat interest charge was paid on borrowed capital.

40. This was the essence of the Law on Associated Labor's prescription that the social services acquire income through a "free exchange of labor." See also Branko Horvat, "An Institutional Model of a Self-Managed Economy," *Eastern European Economics* 10 (Summer 1972): 385.

41. For a detailed description of the actions undertaken by each republic party from 1972 to 1974, see Commission for the Report to the Tenth Congress, "Draft Report," pp. 30–42, and Rusinow, *Yugoslav Experiment*, pp. 308–43.

42. Kardelj, *Osnovni uzroci*, p. 25.

43. Tito, "The Struggle for Further Development," pp. 64–65.

44. Dennison Rusinow, "Yugoslav's Return to Leninism," *American Universities Field Staff Reports*, SE Europe Series 21 (1974): 2.

45. This section represents an abridged version of the author's article, "Yugoslavia in the 1970's: Self-Management and Bargaining," *Journal of Comparative Economics* (forthcoming).

46. High inflation rates, booming unemployment, and record balance-of-payments deficits are symptomatic. The causes seem to be low labor productivity, poor use of capacities and personnel, barriers to capital mobility, excessive borrowing, low enterprise savings, and overly rapid growth of government and social service expenditures. See Pero Jurković, "Aktuelni problemi privrednih kretanja i ekonomske politike Jugoslavije," *Ekonomist* 30, no. 4 (1977): 505–15.

47. See Tyson, "Recent Developments," pp. 33–42.

48. Ibid., p. 4.

49. See Marsenić, "Institucionalni oblici," pp. 90–92; Pavle Gligorić, "Neki aktuelni aspekti izdvajanja dela dohotka OUR-a za opšte i zajedničke društvene potrebe," *Ekonomist* 30, no. 3 (1977): 359–83.

50. See *Ekonomska politika*, 18 April 1977, pp. 11 and 18–20. I am grateful to Peter Cory for sharing his research notes with me for this and future references to *Ekonomska politika*.

51. See *Ekonomska politika*, 13 December 1976, p. 12 and *Ekonomska politika*, 14 May 1977, p. 19; Pavlović, "Samoupravno planiranje," p. 250.

52. See Jurković, "Aktuelni problemi," pp. 505–15; Dragomir Vojnić, "O nekim globalnim aspektima privrednih kretanja," *Ekonomist* 30, no. 4 (1977): 465–79.

53. Drago Gorupić, cited by Jurković, "Aktuelni problemi," p. 509.

54. On the problem of enforcement, see Jože Goričar, "Sankcije u našem samoupravnom pravu," *Socijalizam* 21 (January 1978): 1–30 circa.

55. See Branko Horvat, "Institucionalna osnova predloženog sistema cena," *Ekonomist* 29, no. 1 (1976): 103–7.

56. Mijat Šuković, "Dva teorijska i praktična pitanja unapređivanja delegatskog skupštinskog sistema," *Socijalizam* 21 (April 1978): 36–49; Mirjana Pavlović, "Funkcionisanje delegatskog sistema u samoupravnim interesnim zajednicama," *Socijalizam* 21 (April 1978): 128–31.

57. See Paul Shoup, "Problems Facing the Party," paper presented at a conference on "Yugoslavia: Accomplishments and Problems," Washington, D.C., October 1977 (Xeroxed).

58. See *Basic Theses For the Formulation of Policies and Documents of the Eleventh Congress of the League of Communists of Yugoslavia* (Belgrade: Socialist Thought and Practice, 1978).

PART III: INTRODUCTION

1. In fact, nowadays it may even differ from BOAL to BOAL. See chapter 7.

2. Indeed, insofar as quite a number of these individuals either were or recently had been elected by substantial margins to self-management bodies in competitive elections, their attitudes and values may well have been quite representative in the best sense of the term.

CHAPTER 7

1. The name of the firm has been changed to protect its anonymity. For the same reason, I have altered the industry for which it produced machinery to a different primary sector industry.

2. High enough to provoke complaints at the municipal trade union councils from enterprises that had lost workers and specialists to Klek. Several technicians and specialists told me that they had received a 30–50 percent salary increase when they came to Klek.

3. Note that such an allocation of labor may not have been inefficient. Conversations with personnel directors in some Connecticut machine-tool

plants revealed that the ratio of white-collar to blue-collar workers was about the same in the United States. In fact, one director noted that Pratt-Whitney had a 3:1 ratio of white-collar to blue-collar workers owing to its heavy research commitments.

4. Many in these groups actually had qualifications as skilled workers, however.

5. E.g., Zvonko graduates from technical college and appeals to his division council for a raise because of his higher qualification.

6. See Ustav SFRJ (1974), pt. II, chap. I, art. 29.

7. A detailed account of the bodies comprising the self-management structure and of the sociopolitical organizations is contained in appendix B.

8. Note, however, that political authorities can and do intervene in enterprise organizational structures as well. The problem of commune "meddling" discussed in chapter 3 is one example, as is the 1974 Constitution. By establishing BOALs, the constitution sought to alter both enterprise self-management and organizational structures.

9. This does not exclude the possibility of indirect material consequences, be they negative (unreimbursed time spent at meetings) or positive (using one's influence to have decisions made in one's favor).

10. A description of Klek's sociopolitical organizations and their functions in the enterprise appears in appendix B.

11. Note, however, that individuals can and do refuse to join trade union branches without suffering any consequences. Nonetheless, at Klek there was 100 percent membership in the trade union branch, despite a good deal of dissatisfaction with its activities.

12. See chapter 3, "Self-Management in Operation," pp. 54-64; and chapter 5, "Inequalities Within the Firm," pp. 108-15.

13. See below, pp. 156-58.

14. This section is based on workers' council minutes, factory bulletins, and accounts of older workers and employees in the Klek collective.

15. The figures up to 1970 in table 15 only describe job qualifications and not employee qualifications. Note that the figures for 1968, 1969, and 1970 are planned figures (which, parenthetically, were apparently not achieved, judging by the 1972 figures); they make it clear that at least the intention of the modernization program was to cut down the production force and enlarge the white-collar, highly educated sectors.

16. Unfortunately, it is impossible to supply precise figures, for Klek never calculated such averages. The conclusions noted above are based on the point scale the firm used and the data on the labor force shown in table 15. Note that these conclusions regarding average blue/white-collar earnings are valid even if the increase in unskilled workers in excluded from the calculation. Most of these unskilled workers were involved in janitorial work, construction and maintenance, and in the warehouse rather than in direct production.

17. According to a specialist in the personnel department.

18. According to accounts of older Klek employees and workers.

19. Interview with personnel director. No rate was specified. During the seven months of this study, two of the twenty members of the *kolegija* left the firm.

20. Staff specialist, personnel department. Note that this statement should be interpreted as a *perceived* increase in labor mobility. *Statistički godišnjak* reports that labor turnover in Yugoslavia declined after 1963, although it is possible that Klek or the machine-tool industry in Zagreb is an exception.

21. From conversations with workers and employees who came to the main plant for meetings and with individuals who had recently been transferred to BOAL I or III from the Service Division.

22. "Ideology," as I use the term here, refers to the set of attitudes and values stemming from the individual's membership in a definite social group which individuals use to judge events, attitudes, and values. Ideology "tends to specify a set of values that are more or less coherent and . . . seeks to link given patterns of action to the achievement or maintenance of a future, or existing, state of affairs" (Joseph Lapalombara, "Decline of Ideology: A Dissent and an Interpretation," in *Comparative Politics: Notes and Readings*, 4th ed., ed. R. Macridis and B. Brown [Homewood, Ill.: Richard D. Irwin, 1972], p. 264). At the same time, ideologies attempt "to render . . . social situations meaningful, to so construe them so as to make it possible to act purposefully within them" (Clifford Geertz, "Ideology as a Cultural System," in *Ideology and Discontent*, ed. David Apter [New York: Free Press, 1964], p. 64).

23. A city fund set up to ease the credit shortage plaguing Zagreb at the time. I will deal with what the firm went through to get this loan in chapter 9.

24. BOAL II, meeting in its own assembly, also agreed to work Saturdays.

25. At the time, workers were receiving time-and-a-third for overtime work, again to take into account piece-rate incentives.

26. BOAL II, however, was somewhat less enthusiastic. For the sequel, see chapter 9, pp. 202–03.

27. If Klek is typical, such a practice would raise some doubt as to the applicability of Ward's model of the labor-managed firm to Yugoslav enterprises. See B. Ward, "The Firm in Illyria: Market Syndicalism," *American Economic Review* 48 (September 1958): 566–89.

The kind of noneconomic considerations that entered into decisions to open a new job at Klek (such as the need to maintain the status quo in the distribution of work given disagreement on how to alter it, the fact that the dynamics of self-management made it psychologically cheaper to hire an extra worker or employee rather than override possibly intense objections of individuals to altering their job definitions, etc.), plus the fact that every observer of Yugoslav firms I know of has concluded that they overemploy labor, lead me to believe that Klek is not an isolated case. Cf. World Bank, *Yugoslavia: Development with Decentralization* (Baltimore: Johns Hopkins Press, 1974), p. 150.

At the same time, if economizing on labor costs was not a consideration in individual hiring decisions at Klek, the long-term plans of the firm certainly favored capital intensity as a means of raising productivity and personal incomes. There were both economic (underpriced capital) and political (authorities' and workers' preferences for "modern" factories) reasons for this, and the result may well have been simply that Klek overemployed both labor and capital; in other words, it was operating below capacity.

28. For example, while Klek did not seem to be having any difficulty attracting white-collar help with adequate qualifications, it was unable to recruit the experienced production workers it required. The obvious solution, raising wages, was never suggested, undoubtedly because it would have necessitated an across-the-board wage increase for everyone in the firm; since all salaries were pegged in one way or another to the starting salary of a skilled worker, raising the number of points for jobs at that level would have opened the hornet's nest of adjusting the point allocations for all the others as well.

CHAPTER 8

1. See chapter 5, "Interskill Differentials and Inequalities Within the Firm," pp. 108–15.

2. See above, chapter 7, "BOAL II and Gramsci," pp. 156–58.

3. In fact, the informality present in day-to-day worker-management relations probably contributed to the workers' ability to "tell management off." Certainly, day-to-day labor relations between workers and executives were far more comradely and egalitarian than labor-management relations in the United States, despite the numerous worker complaints over managerial arbitrariness.

4. Although the blue-collar production workers formed the largest group of manual laborers at Klek's main plant, quite a few unskilled manual laborers also worked in janitorial and maintenance capacities. While they were less articulate than the production workers in public meetings, private conversations with them indicated a basic similarity in values and attitudes—including support for precise measurement of actual work performed (piece rates or some such system). This similarity may well be because of the atypical position of the skilled workers at Klek. That is, whereas in many industries, skilled workers constitute a small and often privileged elite among the blue-collar labor force, at Klek they were rank-and-file workers. As a consequence, they may well have been more egalitarian than skilled workers in other industries.

5. This belief was shared by workers throughout Zagreb at the time of this study. Almost without exception, I did not meet a blue-collar worker in any industry who was not convinced that the executives of his enterprise were embezzling. In fact, the "Self-Management Workers' Control" (appendix B) was introduced to Yugoslav enterprises partially in response to these suspicions.

6. For a similar analysis, see J. Obradović, W. Rodgers, and J. French, "Workers' Councils in Yugoslavia," *Human Relations* 23 (October 1970): 459–71.

7. Note that in BOAL II the problem was solved differently. There the executives simply assumed through informal means the formal authority they lacked. The stress on "collective entrepreneurship" and "collective responsibility" was correspondingly less than in BOALs I and III. On collective entrepreneurship and the postreform model of the firm, see chapter 4, "Redefining the Rights to Social Property: The Enterprise as a Collective Entrepreneur," pp. 73–75.

8. This should hardly be surprising in view of the often nonexistent material incentives for highly trained individuals to take on the burden of managerial responsibilities. See Josip Županov, "Da li se rukovođenje poduzećem 'profesionalizira?'" *Moderna organizacija*, no. 10 (1968): 806–20.

9. The workers' council minutes record that in 1972, disciplinary proceedings were recommended by the council for an executive who approved the purchase of a machine for which funds had not yet been formally allocated. The minutes do not record, however, whether or not the proceedings ever took place.

10. Ironically, one effect of the antitechnocracy campaign at Klek was seen in the party's request for the executives to become more active in political affairs. At the April meeting, the party secretariat suggested that executives both begin attending seminars run by the city trade union federation on implementing the 1974 Constitution and start showing more interest and better attendance at enterprise party meetings. Clearly, the intention here was to politicize (and thereby protect) the executives; the probably effect of greater political activity on management's part, however, would simply be to technocratize the party of the working class itself.

11. A role they conformed to admirably, regardless of level of education or expertise. One of the more amazing sessions of the BOAL III council I observed concerned hiring a lawyer for Klek, whose task would be to prosecute (preferably, threaten with prosecution) firms that owed Klek money. Three people applied for the job; one was female. Although she was the preferred candidate of the finance director, who would be her immediate supervisor, the newly elected president of the BOAL III council, himself a former executive, authoritatively argued that the job required an extremely aggressive individual and was therefore (!) a "man's job." Not only did the two women elected to the council nod their full agreement, but the candidate herself, when told by the council president that her job prospects at Klek looked dim because "as we see it, this is a man's job," responded with a sympathetic "I understand."

12. Note that such acceptance is not typical of all Yugoslav enterprises. At Klek, the close relationship between management and experts appears to have been a product of the firm's small size and perhaps of the rebelliousness of the blue-collar production workers. Since the firm was small, there were simply not very many university-trained experts around in addition to the executives themselves, and so those who did not hold supervisory positions found management to be very accessible. This does not appear to be the case in large enterprises, where the supervisory/nonsupervisory distinction is much sharper, for administrative reasons among others. In larger firms, experts are often alienated from management and often perceive themselves as quite uninfluential. See V. Arzenšek, "Participacija zaposlenih u jugoslovenskoj industriji," *Moderna organizacija*, no. 1 (1971): 134–43.

That Klek's management found itself constantly called on to justify the employ of highly paid specialists before worker criticism facilitated close relationships between executives and specialists. At Klek, the main difference between the behavior of executives and specialists appeared to be that the latter took a much less active role in the self-management process.

CHAPTER 9

1. After 1973, earnings were calculated by BOAL and divided on the basis of the needs of the enterprise as a whole. That BOAL III was not a contributor to earnings did not prevent it from getting a share of wages and investment.

2. Letter from director to City Reserve Fund, factory bulletin, December 1973.

3. Director, article in factory bulletin, September 1970.

4. Engineer, article in factory bulletin, December 1967.

5. Party secretary, article in factory bulletin (special issue), May 1972.

6. Director, article in factory bulletin, December 1969.

7. Article in factory bulletin, June 1972.

8. The illegality of the elections first came to light in a meeting of the BOAL I council. The council members were rather disturbed at this sudden and rather arbitrary termination of their mandate; nearly all of them walked out of the meeting, several announcing as they left that they were not going "to be part of this business." In the end, a rump group of three council members made the decision to call the election.

9. For example, when there was a tie vote between a major party figure and the candidate opposing him, the ballots were "recounted" to insure the former's victory. I found out about this purely by accident. Fortunately for the enterprise party organization, no one in the work collective knew of these well-hidden irregularities. Note, however, that well over 70 percent of the delegates elected were not party members anyway.

10. In fact, it may draw workers and executives together. At the BOAL I council meeting called for setting the date of elections, the division director was as disgusted with the party leadership for "dictating" as the council members were.

11. Significantly, the Klek party organization resorted to stacking the electoral commissions largely in response to the uproar over the lack of choice on the ballot when the delegations to elect commune representatives had been elected in March. Although the June elections may have been illegal, every candidate but one (not himself a party member) ran opposed, an indication that the party at least still had pretensions toward being responsive.

12. Despite the secretariat's show of force in June, there was little follow-up to its electoral effort. In October, the enterprise statutes were as far from completion as they had been prior to the election.

CHAPTER 10

1. Concerns voiced in journals like *Working Papers for a New Society* (Cambridge, Mass.), *Radical America* (Cambridge, Mass.), *Socialist Revolution* (San Francisco), *Monthly Review* (New York), *The New Left Review*

(London), *Les temps modernes* (Paris), *Tempi moderni* (Milan), and the now defunct *Praxis* (Zagreb) among others. Other leftist analyses of the possibilities of workers' control are contained in Ken Coates and Tony Topham, eds., *Workers' Control* (London: Panther Modern Society, 1970); idem, *The New Unionism* (Middlesex, England: Penguin Books, 1972); Andre Gorz, *Strategy for Labor* (Boston: Beacon Press, 1967); Root and Branch, eds., *Root and Branch* (Greenwich, Conn.: Fawcett-Crest, 1975); Garry Hunnius, G. David Garson, and John Case, eds., *Workers' Control* (New York: Random House, 1973); Paul Blumberg, *Industrial Democracy* (London: Constable, 1968); C. George Benello and Dimitrios Roussopoulos, eds., *The Case for Participatory Democracy* (New York: Grossman Publishers, 1971); Michael Best and William Connolly, *The Politicized Economy* (Lexington: D. C. Heath, 1976); Jaroslav Vanek, ed., *Self-Management* (Baltimore: Penguin Books, 1975).

2. See Joseph Berliner, "Managerial Incentives and Decision-Making: A Comparison of the United States and the Soviet Union," in *Comparative Economic Systems*, 3rd ed., ed. M. Bornstein (Homewood, Ill.: Irwin, 1974), pp. 396-427; Hedrick Smith, *The Russians* (New York: Ballantine Books, 1976); Jeremy Azrael, *Managerial Power and Soviet Politics* (Cambridge, Mass.: Harvard University Press, 1966); and Jerry Hough, *The Soviet Prefects* (Cambridge, Mass.: Harvard University Press, 1969).

3. See Adolf Sturmthal, *Workers' Councils* (Cambridge, Mass.: Harvard University Press, 1964).

4. See Josip Županov's research on the favorable attitudes of workers and executives in solvent firms toward government aid to enterprises on the verge of bankruptcy. Josip Županov, *Samoupravljanje i društvena moć* (Zagreb: Naše teme, 1969), part I.

5. See Cahiers de Mai, "The Lip Watch Strike," trans. Arlene Pressman, *Radical America* 7 (November-December 1973): 1-19.

6. See Coates and Topham, *The New Unionism*, pp. 101-3.

7. For variations of such arguments, see Hugh Clegg, *A New Approach to Industrial Democracy* (Oxford: Basil Blackwell, 1960); Joseph Schumpeter, *Capitalism, Socialism and Democracy* (New York: Harper and Row, 1942), pp. 200-19; Giovanni Sartori, *Democratic Theory* (New York: Praeger, 1965), pp. 384-416; Ludwig Von Mises, "Economic Calculation in Socialism," in *Comparative Economic Systems*, 3rd ed., ed. M. Bornstein, pp. 120-27; F. A. Hayek, "Socialist Calculation: The Competitive Solution," in *Comparative Economic Systems*, 3rd ed., M. Bornstein, pp. 140-60; N. Glazer, *Remembering the Answers* (New York: Basic Books, 1970).

8. Although I shall deal with three analytically distinct variants of this argument in the text, it is the rare author who espouses only one of them. Authors stressing the "particular" characteristics of Yugoslavia as key explanatory variables of self-management's results include both critics and advocates of the Yugoslav system. Generally, critics of the system tend to concentrate on the "new ruling class" explanation; proponents stress the underdeveopment of Yugoslavia and the early stage of self-management there, often suggesting that at some future time, Yugoslav self-management will

overcome its present "imperfections" and "realize" the goals its advocates have set for it. See Milovan Djilas, *The Imperfect Society: Beyond the New Class* (New York: Harcourt, Brace and World, 1969); Carole Pateman, *Participation and Democratic Theory* (Cambridge: Cambridge University Press, 1970); David Jenkins, *Job Power* (Baltimore: Penguin Books, 1973); Robert Dahl, *After the Revolution?* (New Haven: Yale University Press, 1970); Branko Horvat, *An Essay on Yugoslav Society* (White Plains, N.Y.: International Arts and Sciences Press, 1969); I. Adizes and E. Borgese, eds., *Self-Management: New Dimensions to Democracy* (Santa Barbara, Calif.: Center for the Study of Democratic Institutions, The Fund for the Republic, 1975); Coates and Topham, *The New Unionism*, pp. 236–45; Garry Hunnius, "Workers' Self-Management in Yugoslavia," in *Workers' Control*, Hunnius et al., eds., pp. 268–325; Svetozar Stojanović, *Between Ideals and Reality*, trans. G. Scher (Boston: Beacon Press, 1972); M. Barratt Brown, "Yugoslavia Revisited," *New Left Review*, no. 1 (January–February 1960): 39–43; idem, "Workers' Control in a Planned Economy," *New Left Review*, no. 2 (March–April 1960): 28–31; Sharon Zukin, *Between Marx and Tito* (New York: Cambridge University Press, 1975); and the articles in *Praxis*, 3/4 (Spring 1971).

The Marxist bent of much of this writing leads most of these analyses to view nationality conflicts primarily as "epiphenomena." To give teeth to the final variant of this argument, which certainly has a good deal of plausibility to it (in my opinion, more than the first two), I am taking the liberty of drawing the implications of Paul Shoup's analysis in *Communism and the Yugoslav National Question* (New York: Columbia University Press, 1968) and Deborah Milenkovitch's account in *Plan and Market in Yugoslav Economic Thought* (New Haven: Yale University Press, 1973). Neither Milenkovitch nor Shoup themselves argue that nationality conflicts alone brought about the various reforms in Yugoslavia, nor are they explicit advocates of workers' control in other countries.

Index

absenteeism, 61, 144, 159
accounting regulations, 44
agriculture, 61, 95-96
aktiv, 241-42
alienation, 10
apathy, 198-200
assemblies, 229-30
authority: Gramsci, 10-11; Proudhon, 25-28, 34-35; workers' councils, 55

Bakarić, Vladimir, 50, 120
balance of payments, 40, 70, 104. *See also* foreign trade
banking system: capital allotments, 45; commune and, 93; Constitution of *1974*, 129; decentralization of, 69; decision making, 89; enterprise autonomy, 74-75; monetary policy, 82-83; postreform, 122
bargaining: BOALs, 128; Constitution of *1974*, 124; coordination, 130; planning, 125; self-management, 132-36
benefits, worker, 172. *See also* social services
blue-collar workers. *See* labor
Blum, E., 87
BOAL(s), 133, 134; apathy, 200; consensus, 189, 190; Constitution of *1974*, 128-29, 130; employee values, 174, 184, 186; at Klek, 144-45, 146, 150, 156-65, 167, 201-06, 229-32, 242
budgets, 77-80
bureaucracy and bureaucratization: Gramsci, 20; ideology, 51, 54; Proudhon, 28; workers, 43, 63
business cycle, 30-31, 32, 33, 37-38, 80. *See also* market forces
business failures, 87

Canada, 215
capital accumulation, 58, 84-85
capital allocation: enterprise autonomy, 73, 74, 75; inequalities in, 94, 103; market controls, 44-45; postreform, 83, 88;

Proudhon, 30, 31, 35; regional differences, 69. *See also* investment
capitalism, 11, 28, 37, 43. *See also* market forces
capital-labor ratios, 32
centralization, 69
Chamber of Associated Labor, 130
Chamber of Nationalities, 119
Chile, 141
civil suits, 61, 62
class, 74
class antagonisms, 11
class loyalties, 29. *See also* solidarity
collective entrepreneurship, 73-74
Cominform, 41, 42, 211
command economy, 42
commissions, Klek, 234-36
communes: amalgamation of, 90; autonomy of, 46-47; political party and, 52-53; resource allocation, 50; role of, 75, 89, 91, 93; territoriality and, 47, 49, 50, 70; workers' councils and, 48
communism, 28
competition: monopoly/oligopoly, 83; Proudhon, 23, 25, 29, 31, 32
Congress of Workers' Councils, 227-28
consensus, 188-91
constitutional amendments: *1968-1969*, 88, 119; *1971*, 139, 174, 199-200
Constitution of *1953*, 43, 46
Constitution of *1963*, 68, 75, 92, 124; decision making, 110; fiscal policy, 79, 80
Constitution of *1974*, 124-30, 139, 215, 216; apathy, 199-200; firm reorganization, 134, 135; Klek and, 200-06, 212; worker values, 174
consumption: foreign trade, 85; inflation, 135; market economy, 73; taxation, 77; wage differentials, 105
contract obligations, 30
Councils of Producers, 40, 47, 92, 250n15
credit, 24, 44
Croatia, 119, 131
Czechoslovakia, 195

279

YALE STUDIES IN POLITICAL SCIENCE